Reassessing the Social Studies Curriculum

Reassessing the Social Studies Curriculum

Promoting Critical Civic Engagement in a Politically Polarized, Post-9/11 World

Edited by Wayne Journell

ROWMAN & LITTLEFIELD
Lanham • Boulder • New York • London

Published by Rowman & Littlefield
A wholly owned subsidiary of The Rowman & Littlefield Publishing Group, Inc.
4501 Forbes Boulevard, Suite 200, Lanham, Maryland 20706
www.rowman.com

Unit A, Whitacre Mews, 26-34 Stannary Street, London SE11 4AB

Copyright © 2016 by Wayne Journell

All rights reserved. No part of this book may be reproduced in any form or by any electronic or mechanical means, including information storage and retrieval systems, without written permission from the publisher, except by a reviewer who may quote passages in a review.

British Library Cataloguing in Publication Information Available

Library of Congress Cataloging-in-Publication Data

Names: Journell, Wayne, editor of compilation.
Title: Reassessing the social studies curriculum : promoting critical civic engagement in a politically polarized, post-9/11 world / edited by Wayne Journell.
Description: Lanham, Maryland : Rowman & Littlefield, 2016. | Includes bibliographical references.
Identifiers: LCCN 2016004230 (print) | LCCN 2016004724 (ebook) | ISBN 9781475818116 (cloth : alk. paper) | ISBN 9781475818123 (pbk. : alk. paper) | ISBN 9781475818130 (Electronic)
Subjects: LCSH: History--Study and teaching. | Civics--Study and teaching.
Classification: LCC D16.2 .R395 2016 (print) | LCC D16.2 (ebook) | DDC 300.71--dc23
LC record available at http://lccn.loc.gov/2016004230

∞ ™ The paper used in this publication meets the minimum requirements of American National Standard for Information Sciences Permanence of Paper for Printed Library Materials, ANSI/NISO Z39.48-1992.

Printed in the United States of America

Contents

Acknowledgments		vii
Foreword *Margaret Smith Crocco*		ix
Preface *Michael J. Berson and Ilene R. Berson*		xiii
Introduction: September 11, 2001: The Day that Changed the World . . . But Not the Curriculum *Wayne Journell*		xix
1	International Conflict and National Destiny: World War I and History Teaching *Keith C. Barton*	1
2	9/11 and the War on Terror in American Secondary Curriculum, Fifteen Years Later *Jeremy Stoddard and Diana Hess*	15
3	Including 9/11 in the Elementary Grades: State Standards, Digital Resources, and Children's Books *Elizabeth Bellows*	29
4	How Patriotism Matters in U.S. Social Studies Classrooms, Fifteen Years After 9/11 *Mark T. Kissling*	41
5	National Identity and Citizenship in a Pluralistic Society: Educators' Messages Following 9/11 and *Charlie Hebdo* *Lisa Gilbert*	55
6	The Courage of Hopelessness: Creative Disruption of Everyday Life in the Classroom *E. Wayne Ross*	69
7	Civil Liberties, Media Literacy, and Civic Education in the Post-9/11 Era: Helping Students Think Conceptually in Order to Act Civically *Stephen S. Masyada and Elizabeth Yeager Washington*	83
8	Role-Playing and Role-Dropping: Political Simulations as Portals to Pluralism in a Contentious Era *Jane C. Lo and Walter C. Parker*	95

9 The Psychology of Controversial Issues' Discussions: Challenges and Opportunities in a Polarized, Post-9/11 Society   109
Christopher H. Clark and Patricia G. Avery

Afterword: Living in a Post-9/11 World   121
Ronald W. Evans

About the Contributors   125

Acknowledgments

One of my favorite quotations, one that I have tried to adhere to throughout my professional career, is "surround yourself with people smarter than you." Although an Internet query failed to produce a definitive source on who first uttered those words, the premise behind them has benefited many people throughout history, and I am no exception. I am forever indebted to the wonderful authors, many of whom I consider "academic heroes," who lent their expertise to this book. It was such a rewarding experience working with these individuals, and I believe their efforts have led to a book that is both timely and important. I am certainly better off for having surrounded myself with them.

I also want to thank the editorial staff at Rowman & Littlefield, particularly Tom Koerner, who agreed to this project without hesitation. This is my second collaboration with Rowman & Littlefield, and I have found them to be utmost professionals—responsive, efficient, and transparent—in all aspects of the publication process. I look forward to future collaborations!

I would also like to thank the following scholars who provided critical reviews of the chapters included in this book:

Sohyun An	Kennesaw State University
Michelle Bauml	Texas Christian University
Brooke Blevins	Baylor University
Kristy Brugar	University of Oklahoma
Steven Camicia	Utah State University
Carole Hahn	Emory University
Mark Helmsing	University of Wyoming
Benjamin Jacobs	George Washington University
Jada Kohlmeier	Auburn University
Brett Levy	State University of New York, Albany
John Myers	Florida State University
Kathryn Obenchain	Purdue University
Judith Pace	University of San Francisco
Sarah Shear	Pennsylvania State University, Altoona

Beth Sondel	North Carolina State University
Katy Swalwell	Iowa State University
Christine Woyshner	Temple University
Cory Wright-Maley	St. Mary's University

I know I speak on behalf of each of the authors in saying that the final product is stronger due to each one's diligent reading and constructive feedback.

Finally, I would be remiss not to acknowledge the support of both my professional and personal networks. My colleagues at the University of North Carolina at Greensboro are always supportive of my work and give me the space and flexibility to engage in these types of projects. My family, especially my parents, Allen and Brenda, and my wife, Kitrina, provide emotional support for all of my professional endeavors, and I am always grateful for their love and encouragement. Last, but certainly not least, I am always indebted to my daughter Hadleigh for her constant reminders not to take work too seriously and to stay focused on what is truly important in life. This book, as is the case with all of my scholarly endeavors, has been completed in the hopes that, in my own small way, I can make a difference in the instruction that Hadleigh will receive in her K–12 educational experience.

Foreword

Margaret Smith Crocco

The morning of September 11, 2011, began beautifully in New York City, with crystal clear blue skies and a hint of autumn's chill in the air. Early that day, I made my way across the George Washington Bridge from my home in New Jersey to my office at Teachers College, Columbia University on 120th Street. The view from the bridge never failed to remind me of the singular quality of the Manhattan skyline as it rose above the Hudson River separating New Jersey from New York.

I arrived at my desk before 8:00 a.m. to prepare for a 10:00 a.m. meeting that never happened. Before long, I shifted my attention to the online *New York Times* to take a quick look at the day's headlines when a "breaking news story" appeared about a plane hitting the north tower of the World Trade Center. Presuming this incident to involve a small passenger aircraft that had somehow lost its way, I switched to CNN's website for more information. All too soon, I learned about the terrifying events that had occurred downtown and elsewhere, including the second plane's strike on the south tower, the attack on the Pentagon, and the plane crash in a field in Shanksville, Pennsylvania.

My first thoughts went to my husband, who worked in midtown Manhattan; to a sister who lived near Gramercy Park; and to another sister who was having a business breakfast that morning at a hotel near the World Trade Center. It was impossible to get in touch with any of them because phone circuits were jammed. Next, I thought about our social studies student teachers, who had just begun their placements at Stuyvesant High School and other schools downtown. One by one, I recollected all those we knew who worked in the Twin Towers. As the morning wore on, the scene at Teachers College unfolded as it did elsewhere—confusion, fear, and uncertainty about what was going on, what it all meant, and where we would go from here.

Later that day, my husband joined the hundreds of individuals walking uptown because trains and subways had suspended service. After being shut off to all except emergency vehicles, the West Side Highway and the George Washington Bridge finally reopened to other vehicular traffic. That night, I learned that my sisters were safe. We reflected upon how lucky we were given the number of friends and neighbors who had lost loved ones.

In the ensuing weeks, we coped with the challenges that confronted a now transformed city and nation. At Teachers College, many master's and doctoral students decided that New York City was an unsafe place and left their programs to head home. As elsewhere across the country, visiting scholars couldn't get visas and canceled their trips to campus. Our Muslim students reported that they were now being treated with suspicion and even hostility because they wore headscarves or were known to have family in Pakistan or Afghanistan.

Besides countless public memorials over the next year, many New York City educational organizations sponsored events aimed at trying to make sense of what had occurred, even if real understanding seemed elusive. At Teachers College, these included a teach-in featuring educators from Sun Yat Sen Middle School 131 in Chinatown who shared their gut-wrenching stories about addressing the needs of young students whose parents worked at the Twin Towers but never made it home on the night of 9/11.

Columbia University's Oral History Research Office launched a project to collect testimonies from first responders in the police and fire departments, teachers, taxi drivers, and medical personnel, among others. Faculty from Columbia's law school to the schools of social work, public health, international and public affairs, and journalism used the tools of their trade to respond to the tragedy. At Teachers College, we began to discuss with colleagues in the History Department how the event would be written about in textbooks and taught in schools and colleges.

Since then, the questions concerning recollection and memorialization of this trauma have been widely debated. One early assessment within social studies came in a chapter called, "Citizenship Education and Social Studies Curriculum Change after 9/11" (Thornton, 2004), which forecast several of the topics that would emerge as contentious: wars, homeland security, civil liberties, Islam, globalization, and terrorism. A decade's worth of debates about these matters culminated in the 2011 opening of the National September 11 Memorial Museum at the site of the former World Trade Center (Trofanenko, 2015). Today, the controversies within social education continue, as the chapters in this book make clear.

Much has changed for our nation since the brilliant and beautiful morning of 9/11 was shattered by destruction and terror. One journalist suggests that these changes can be summarized as follows (Green, 2015):

- Increases in defense spending and military deployments overseas as part of a "War on Terror"
- Establishment of the Department of Homeland Security in 2002, which doubled the number of deportations
- Creation of the Transportation Security Administration in 2007, which dramatically changed air travel
- A marked increase in government surveillance efforts, unleashing a backlash concerning threats to Americans' civil liberties

I would add one element to this list: The nation has seen what the Pluralism Project at Harvard University (2015) calls an alarming rise in "Islamophobia," which has been fueled by mainstream and social media as well as recent events worldwide.

Widespread stereotyping of Muslims as terrorists began in the United States in 1993 after the first attack on the World Trade Center. Even in the 1990s, young Muslim students in American schools reported that they felt ashamed of revealing their family's national origins and religion (Crocco, 2005). Even more so today, since 9/11 and the Boston Marathon tragedy, the rise of Islamic State of Iraq and al-Sham/Islamic State of Iraq and the Levant (ISIS/ISIL), the *Charlie Hebdo* shootings in France, the massacres by Boko Haram in Nigeria, and the 2015 Paris attacks, increased media attention to "homegrown terrorists" has pushed stereotyping and profiling of Muslims to an even higher level (Fasciano, 2015).

As educators reflecting on the legacy of 9/11, we might engage our students in deliberating the questions posed after another twenty-first-century American tragedy—Hurricane Katrina—and consider: "What kind of country are we? What kind of country do we want to be?" (Crocco, 2008).

REFERENCES

Crocco, M. S. (2005). Teaching *Shabanu*: The challenges of using world literature in the social studies classroom. *Journal of Curriculum Studies, 37*, 561–82.
Crocco, M. S. (2008). *Teaching* The Levees: *A curriculum for democratic dialogue and civic engagement.* New York: Teachers College Press.
Fasciano, M. (2015). Extreme prejudice. *Teaching Tolerance, 51*, 26–28.
Green, M. (2015, September 10). How 9/11 changed America: Four major lasting impacts. *KQED Public Media for Northern California.* Retrieved from http://ww2.kqed.org/lowdown/2014/09/10/13-years-later-four-major-lasting-impacts-of-911/.
Harvard University. (2015). *Pluralism project.* Retrieved from http://www.pluralism.org/religion/islam/issues/stereotypes.
Thornton, S. J. (2004). Citizenship education and social studies curriculum change after 9/11. In C. Woyshner, J. Watras, & M. S. Crocco (Eds.), *Social education in the twentieth century: Curriculum and context for citizenship* (pp. 210–21). New York: Peter Lang.
Trofanenko, B. (2015). *Seeking a burden of pedagogical responsibility: Comments on the limits of remembering.* Paper presented at the annual meeting of the American Educational Research Association, Chicago, IL.

Preface

Michael J. Berson and Ilene R. Berson

Preparing to drop our children off at their elementary school and drive over to the university was a typical start to the day on September 11, 2001. Reflecting on family and work responsibilities, including meetings, courses, and research projects, left little time to truly notice another beautiful Florida day. Ironically, the president of the United States, George W. Bush, had a similar beginning, just about one hour south of us where he was visiting Sandra Kay Daniel's second-grade class at the Emma E. Booker Elementary School in Sarasota, Florida.

President Bush had stopped by to congratulate the young students on their progress in reading and participate in a read-aloud of the book *The Pet Goat.* At 9:02 a.m., the mundane events of the day transformed into the unimaginable. Our nation's illusion of safety and security was shattered by the menace of terrorism, which left an endurable scar on our collective memory and demarcated the birth of an iconic event in American history.

As Michael sat in his office preparing for the day, a doctoral student came running by asking for assistance with getting a live television feed into his classroom. As the graduate teaching assistant for a science methods course, the doctoral student's instincts had kicked into overdrive when he was confronted with students who came late to class and shared the horrifying news. He wanted to make sure that his undergraduate students could see for themselves what was happening and give them time to talk, ask questions, and express their concerns.

It was around 9:15 a.m., and Michael had no prior knowledge about the events taking place, having arrived on campus early in the morning. He helped get the television feed connected and turned on one of the news channels. Images of a tall building with fire and smoke pouring out filled the screen. At the time, it appeared surreal; several students commented that the sights depicted on television mirrored images they had only previously witnessed in movies. The details of the attacks continued to reverberate throughout the College of Education as other faculty and students dropped in to hear updates.

News commentators narrated the hijacking of the four U.S. planes filled with passengers. As the first jetliners crashed into the upper floors of the North and South towers of the World Trade Center, they toppled the buildings. Subsequently, another plane punctured a hole in the Pentagon. On the fourth flight, the passengers of Flight 93 overtook the hijackers, and the plane crashed in a field in rural Pennsylvania, never reaching its intended target in Washington, D.C. The attacks killed nearly 3,000 people.

Meanwhile, on the other side of campus, Ilene was in her office when the phone rang. It was her mother who lived in upstate New York, about a sixty-minute drive from Manhattan.

Her mother's voice was trembling and asked if Ilene had heard the devastating news of the plane crash in New York. Both Michael and Ilene had been traveling extensively for their work, and Ilene's mother had panicked when she couldn't remember whether they were home or away at a conference.

After assuring her mother that they were safely at work, Ilene tried to return to her mundane, everyday activities. Nonetheless, as she proceeded down the hallway to a meeting, she was met with teary-eyed stares from each person that she encountered. Every office had a broadcast of the news streaming online. Shock, horror, confusion, and fear were evident, and the meeting was quickly canceled as the numbness began to subside and the harsh reality of the events took hold.

As death-related thoughts invaded many people's consciousness, there was an innate need to eliminate or reduce the existential terror that ensued. Like many others who reached out to loved ones, Ilene called Michael. They decided that she should leave work and head to the elementary school where she could provide assistance to the administrators and teachers in responding to the event while maintaining closer proximity to their children in case the events escalated.

The scene at the school was organized chaos. The profound effect of the events on educators, students, and families was evident but not universal. Some families rushed to the school and flooded into the office to sign out their children. While these parents waited for their children to appear among the parade of students, they nervously tapped numbers into their cell phones, making frantic calls to friends and relatives they feared may have been in the vicinity of the attack sites. Some individuals snapped at the staff in their panic and rush to get their children home. The echoes of the horror reverberated throughout the school. Hallways were dotted with teachers who stepped out to compose themselves, tears streaming down their cheeks.

Our children, in kindergarten and third grade, remained in their classrooms, unaware of what was going on but wondering why, one by one, their friends were called to join the mass exodus of children heading to the office for early dismissal. As adults in the school struggled to come to grips with the news, the principal had to make quick decisions about what was in the best interests of the students. The school district had already decided to keep the buildings open, partly out of concern for the Herculean task of coordinating early dismissal and also out of concern that the children needed the schools as a reassuring structure of stability in the aftermath of the destruction.

School leaders agonized over each decision, considering questions such as: What if children returned to an empty home and watched the disaster unfold on television? What if families could not be contacted or were unavailable to race to the school? What if a child lost a parent or relative in the attacks? Extracurricular activities were suspended. Dealing with the children in schools on a day of profound loss proved challenging.

After walking into a fifth-grade classroom of sobbing children and a stunned teacher watching an endless news loop with wrenching images of planes slicing through skyscrapers, the administration ordered all televisions turned off. Offering no explanations, the teachers attempted to continue with the day's lessons while students exchanged puzzled glances each time the classroom phone rang, summoning another child to the office. Quelling rumors became nearly impossible as more seats in the classrooms emptied.

Although many of the elementary students were too young to realize the severity of the situation, they were old enough to detect the distress among the adults around them. As one group of students approached the office, it was clear that the devastating news had trickled into their classroom. Several children in the group had family members who worked at Mac-

Dill Air Force Base with U.S. Central Command, and the students could be overheard speculating, "They're gonna hit Tampa next!"

Recognizing that the decision to maintain silence about the attacks left some students scared and confused, the principal wanted to provide families with guidance on how to talk with their children and help them express feelings and concerns. Familiar with Ilene's work as a nationally certified school psychologist and her expertise on interventions for children who have experienced trauma, she requested Ilene's help in drafting a letter to be disseminated to families and teachers of the school. Responding to the emotional needs of staff members, families, and students was a perfect diversion for Ilene to turn her attention away from the news coverage and distract her from her own reactions of disbelief and shock.

In the rush to provide guidance, Ilene drew from her knowledge of childhood victimization and crisis management, but she recognized that the collective reaction was already far more widespread and had only transitory parallels to previous disasters. Oftentimes she had looked at tragic events from a remote academic perspective, but this time it was personal. The menace of terrorism had shattered our fundamental assumptions about security and invulnerability, and the proliferation of representations that flooded public spaces would continue to escalate the scale of impact. We needed to constructively deal with the horror of the event while managing our own fear, anger, and confusion.

Upon arriving at home that night, Michael and Ilene continued to try to make sense of this tragedy. The National Council for the Social Studies Publications Office contacted us to inquire if we would write a piece to guide social studies educators on how to respond (Berson & Berson, 2001a). More calls came in from other education outlets looking for pieces offering strategies to help teachers deal with the tragedy (M. J. Berson, 2002; Berson & Berson, 2001b, 2002), and we debated the issues that needed to be addressed as we considered each audience (Berson & Baggerly, 2009; Berson & Berson, 2005).

Although our responses and writing were intended to disseminate research-informed guidance on how to support children in a time of crisis, it was difficult not to be influenced by the cultural context in which we were operating. With the extensive representation in newspapers and continuous coverage on television, we had a constructed representation of the event that mirrored the images overshadowing everyone's consciousness. As we were repeatedly bombarded by evocative, memorable, and tragic images, we all bore witness to the events, watching the Twin Towers crumble again and again as the events played out in a loop for days, weeks, and months.

Our initial writing promoted anxiety-buffering and self-esteem–bolstering strategies. We applied wide-ranging generalizations on the basis of anecdotal evidence. In an otherwise uncertain and dangerous world, people sought actions that could reinforce their cultural values and assert that their national identity was intact and indestructible. Classrooms co-opted the media narrative and turned the tragedy into lessons on heroes and citizenship. Flags adorned school lawns and posters were hung, emblazoned with the words "God Bless America." We had an absence of introspective critiques.

As social studies educators, we viewed the events of September 11 through the lens of civic engagement and citizenship. The threatening events of 9/11 elevated the prominence of American symbolism, including reverence for culturally sacred objects, such as flags, and facilitated a current of patriotism. This was codified by the press, government rhetoric, and subsequent texts that reinforced dominant conceptions of national identity and resilience in the face of trauma.

Our advice drew heavily on the long-standing scripts of honoring heroic figures and promoting efforts to give back and help the community. Many of our recommendations for educators reaffirmed the integrity and validity of an American worldview in which civic engagement is represented by noble and constructive behaviors (i.e., charity work, candlelight vigils). Pyszczynski, Solomon, and Greenberg (2003) also noted common reactions among Americans in responding to 9/11, including:

- An increase in searching for meaning and value in life (e.g., praying, going to memorial services)
- An upsurge in nationalistic attitudes (e.g., wearing symbols that reaffirm faith in the American way of life, listening to more traditional patriotic songs)
- Less tolerance and greater hostility toward divergent cultural values and views, greater prejudice or stereotyping or bigotry
- Counter-bigotry activism (e.g., calling for tolerance and understanding)
- Increased altruistic or prosocial behaviors (e.g., seeking and sharing information; spending time talking, empathizing with, or comforting others; donating money or resources)
- Greater appreciation of heroes associated with 9/11 (e.g., respect for rescue workers)

Schools embodied many of these responses, playing a crucial role in helping restabilize children by expressing calm and confidence in the safety and control of their environments.

Although schools soon returned to a new normal, the events of September 11 had lasting effects. Educators were teaching urgent lessons about acts of terror and hatred. Patriotic and nationalistic attitudes and reactions became more prevalent as part of an effort to preserve the "American way of life," which they believed had been under attack (Pyszczynski et al., 2003). Schools also encountered an aftermath in the classroom, including retaliation against children who did not fit the American ideal. Stigmatized by the terrorist attacks, many Muslim and Arab American students felt a continuing obligation to be ambassadors for their faith and their culture.

As time has passed, we are no longer caught in the daze of the events. As closer examination and scrutiny have occurred, we have moved from the reactionary protective stance that mobilized the nation to a more critical eye on the 9/11 events. We often reflect on how our personal reactions were influenced by the media spectacle of terror in which we were immersed.

From the moment that the fatal event occurred, it occupied a disproportionate part of our lived experience, achieved a unique significance that reinforced its historical exceptionality, and situated the event as a dominant part of our national identity. The events of 9/11 monopolized television twenty-four hours a day, marking the event with importance. It was easy to get caught up in the tidal wave of patriotism and pro-America sentiment that bolstered belief in our resilience and strength as a nation.

These responses have become appropriated as part of the educational curriculum. Schools host 9/11 commemoration events each year. These representations of September 11 often draw from simplified, mythical concepts of patriotism, heroism, and evil that were later transplanted into our textbooks and became solidified in the discourse of our classroom instruction.

The collective memory of teachers who watched the horror of an event with such extraordinary significance also perpetuates certain attributed symbolic meaning. For those individuals who were old enough to remember their experiences on September 11, 2001, the date has become immortalized and has assumed a sentimental perspective without space for discourse that resists or reflects on the dominant narrative of national and personal strength to counter the paralyzing inaction or fear that the terrorist acts hoped to elicit.

The events have also become commodified, showcased in films and books. These retellings have often reinforced symbolic representations of courage and guided the moral tales that are central to our idea of being citizens of our nation. As we look back on these events, we wonder how did these early insights get interpreted into the classroom? How have their representations been sustained or reimagined over time? What has become omitted in our collective memory or distorted? Has a resistant or critical discourse on 9/11 emerged?

With the passage of years, our initial representation and reactions have shifted from a purely emotional response, framed primarily as a necessity for protection of our children and youth, to representations that have been altered through political appropriation and commercial adaptation. As our collective memory ages and transforms, historical inquiry and research into the events encounter new dilemmas that mark 9/11 not as a singular experience but more as a turning point that is intertwined with the nation's identity formation and diverse perceptions of the past.

As global contexts continue to shift, the events of 9/11 become critical to how the country has renegotiated its identity. The day's events had a profound impact on the United States, demarcating our commitment to the War on Terror and instigating heightened domestic security measures. What is less obvious is how September 11 has filtered into American curricula. Disconnect between the cultural memory and historical records confounds how the event is rendered in studies within the classroom.

The provocative memories of 9/11 have offered contemporary social studies education the opportunity to address some of its most trenchant issues. This book stands at the threshold of reflecting on the past, while simultaneously ushering in new ways to think about and enact social studies education that draw from the traditions of the field while bringing fresh perspectives that ultimately extend our understanding of the event as well as the social and historical context in which the events occurred. Our once singular portrayal embodied in the solitary images that replayed on the news has been eclipsed by a more complicated conceptualization that has benefited from explication and often reinterpretation.

This reflection is indispensable to the evolution of our thinking about this iconic event and ultimately allows us to act afresh with new perspectives that evoke important questions about citizenship, patriotism, pedagogy, and delivery of social studies education. This book provides important insights into how the metanarrative of the event has converged and diverged from the community of memory as social studies educators grapple with how to represent and study the event. Reflections on 9/11 may become an important focal point for complex questions pertaining to national identity, images of citizenship, and multiple perspectives that rupture through the dominant memories of the past.

REFERENCES

Berson, I. R., & Baggerly, J. (2009). Building resilience to trauma: Creating a safe and supportive early childhood classroom. *Childhood Education, 85*, 375–379.

Berson, I. R., & Berson, M. J. (2001a). The trauma of terrorism: Helping children cope. *Social Education, 65*, 341–343, 385–387.

Berson, I. R., & Berson, M. J. (2001b). Growing up in the aftermath of terrorism. *Social Studies & the Young Learner, 14*(2), 6–9.

Berson, M. J. (2002). A counter-response to terrorism: The hope and promise of our nation's youth. *Theory & Research in Social Education, 30*, 142–144.

Berson, M. J., & Berson, I. R. (2002). September 11: Children's responses to trauma. *Kappa Delta Pi Record, 38*, 73–76.

Berson, M. J., & Berson, I. R. (2005). Children's exposure to trauma and violence in the media: Evolving literacy skills to counter hype and foster hope. In M. S. Crocco (Ed.), *Social studies and the press: Keeping the beast at bay?* (pp. 159–169). Greenwich, CT: Information Age.

Pyszczynski, T., Solomon, S., & Greenberg, J. (2003). *In the wake of 9/11: The psychology of terror.* Washington, DC: American Psychological Association.

Introduction

September 11, 2001: The Day that Changed the World . . . But Not the Curriculum

Wayne Journell

As the narratives that precede this chapter attest, most people of a certain age have a vivid recollection about where they were when they first heard about the 9/11 attacks. My story, although not particularly unique, is apropos to the topic of this book. I was a senior in college, and I happened to be waiting to enter my social studies methods course when I first heard buzzing over early reports of a plane hitting the World Trade Center.

As class started and the events of that morning quickly began to unfold, I remember my professor trying to balance the shock and emotion of the moment with the need to contextualize what the attacks meant for us as future social studies educators. I do not recall her exact words, but the overarching message was that everything we had learned up to that point about social studies was now antiquated. The 9/11 attacks were going to transform a largely fact-based social studies curriculum into a more vibrant discipline that would allow students to make sense of such a horrible event.

That message was reinforced later that afternoon. Something that usually gets a reaction from my preservice teachers is when I reveal to them that 9/11 was my first day of practicum at a local high school. After methods class had ended, I went back to my apartment and watched the live footage of the attacks on television and debated whether I should go to my practicum site. Being the rule-follower that I am, I ultimately decided to go. When I arrived I found anything but a typical classroom setting.

My cooperating teacher had decided to let his ninth-grade students watch the events unfold on television. As they watched, some students appeared shaken, others appeared disinterested, and most appeared confused. Most could not identify where the Middle East was, had never heard of groups like al Qaeda, and could not understand why such people would want to harm us. It seemed clear that my methods professor was correct; 9/11 had magnified the need to overhaul the social studies curriculum and the way in which we shape our students' understanding of the world in which they live. It seemed inevitable.

Fifteen years later, I look back on that experience and realize that little has changed within K–12 education. In the days, weeks, and months following the attacks, educators both within and outside social studies called for significant changes to the existing curriculum (e.g., Apple,

2002; Cary, 2003; Diem, 2002; Pace, 2002). Among these calls were critical discussions of citizenship, a more diligent focus on diversity, a better understanding of the "other," and a greater awareness of current events and historical narratives beyond our own borders.

A common theme that ran across these recommendations was the notion that students should be thinking critically about American society and our place in the world. As Nel Noddings stated less than a month after the attacks, educators needed to help students "realize that they can raise critical questions about the most central and sacred things and they should not then be accused of being disloyal or un-Christian" (cited in Pace, 2002, p. 37). Instead, public education quickly became engulfed in the "either you are with us or you are with the terrorists" (Bush, 2001) rhetoric that swept across the nation in the wake of the attacks.

Ben-Porath (2011) has termed this support for public unity and patriotism in times of war and national crisis "belligerent citizenship." Although patriotism and attempts at unity are always part of our national discourse, the belligerent citizenship that occurs in the aftermath of crisis extols these dispositions at the expense of political tolerance, affirmation of diversity, and public deliberation. Given the unprecedented nature of the 9/11 attacks and the pervasive sentiment of belligerent citizenship across the nation that occurred soon thereafter, it is not particularly surprising that public education followed suit.

Even as the immediate crisis of 9/11 begins to fade into Americans' collective memory, the effects of belligerent citizenship remain. Although fanaticism, terrorism, and political polarization existed before 9/11, the attacks appear to be a watershed moment from which we can draw a direct line to the social and political divides currently present throughout the world. For example, the rise of the Islamic State of Iraq and al-Sham (ISIS), which has conducted multiple acts of terror and rejuvenated fears of radical Islam throughout the Western world over the past several years, is largely a product of American military policy following the 9/11 attacks.

It is also not a coincidence that this period in American history has coincided with the rise of social media and partisan cable news networks. People of likeminded opinions are connected with greater ease than in any other time in history, which has both increased polarization and encouraged greater activism for one's beliefs. In some cases (e.g., the Arab Spring) this greater connectivity has contributed to positive change; however, constant reinforcement of one's beliefs decreases tolerance of other opinions and often leads to increased, often inflammatory, political action (Mutz, 2006).

Two events that occurred within a week of each other in 2015 illustrate the way in which polarization and fanaticism often have a reciprocal relationship. On November 27, three people were killed at a Colorado Planned Parenthood clinic that appeared motivated by the shooter's beliefs on abortion. Although it is unclear what prompted the shooter to act in such a violent fashion, it is likely not a coincidence that this attack occurred in the wake of Republican presidential candidates linking Planned Parenthood to videos of still-living, aborted fetuses being sold for their organs and the subsequent social media firestorm (Barkan, 2015).[1]

Then, on December 2, fourteen people were killed in a San Bernardino, California, shooting. What first appeared as a possible workplace dispute was eventually determined to be an act of terrorism. The married couple responsible for the attack, Syed Farook and Tashfeen Malik, although not known to be officially associated with ISIS, appeared to have become radicalized in the years leading up to the attacks, and it is likely that ISIS's social media presence may have played a part in this transformation. Malik even pledged allegiance to ISIS in a Facebook post shortly before the shootings.

How should social studies teachers respond to the world in which we now live? As Mutz (2006) notes, the only way to combat polarization is with increased communication and discussion of divergent views. Yet, there are still school districts that discourage teaching about 9/11 and subsequent American policies for fear of inciting controversy.[2] Many social studies textbooks published since 9/11 also portray a noncritical, Eurocentric lens to their depiction of the attacks, the subsequent wars on terror, and overarching concepts such as terrorism (Hess & Stoddard, 2007; Romanowski, 2009; Saleem & Thomas, 2011).

Another illustrative example of the whitewashing of the social studies curriculum can be found in the recent debate over the revised advanced placement U.S. history curriculum. Critics have argued that the curriculum presents a version of history that challenges the idea of American exceptionalism and emphasizes negative aspects of our nation's history. Advocates for the curriculum counter that the curriculum encourages students to think critically about our history and contemporary American society (Lerner, 2015). Ultimately, the college board acquiesced to the protests of conservative groups and revised the curriculum (Massey, 2015).

PURPOSE OF THE BOOK

Fifteen years after the attacks, it seems odd to discuss preparing students for a post-9/11 world. After all, today's students only know of life after 9/11. Yet, the social studies curriculum remains stuck within a pre-9/11 mindset. Given the politically polarized climate in the United States since 9/11, it may even be more challenging for social studies teachers to enact progressive instruction in their classrooms than it had been before the attacks.

The purpose of this book, then, is to revisit the question of what social studies education should look like in a post-9/11 world. What separates this book from the recommendations made in the aftermath of the attacks is the hindsight of knowing how both the world and American society have changed over the past fifteen years. For example, critical thinking remains paramount to progressive social studies instruction, but how critical can teachers reasonably expect to be in this current era of political polarization?

Similarly, critical discussions of patriotism and civic dispositions are still needed, but what should these discussions look like when American foreign policy is likely to be defined by threats of terrorism and armed conflicts abroad for the foreseeable future? The chapters that follow explore these questions and other issues related to the current state of the social studies curriculum, as well as offer recommendations to practicing and preservice social studies teachers for how to encourage their students to think more critically about the post-9/11 world in which they live.

STRUCTURE OF THE BOOK

The first part of this book focuses on the legacy of 9/11 as part of the formal curriculum. In the first chapter, Keith Barton provides a historical context for this discussion by using lessons from educators both during and after U.S. involvement in World War I as a guide for delineating between the kneejerk reactions that occur directly following a national crisis and the more gradual long-term effects of that crisis on society. As Barton notes, it seems clear that the prevailing nationalistic ideology that defined American society after the war had a lasting impact on the history curriculum.

Barton's description of educators' calls for curricular change following the war offers an interesting comparison with that which occurred after 9/11 and can be used to contextualize the next two chapters on the teaching of 9/11 in K–12 schools. In their chapter, Jeremy Stoddard and Diana Hess first reflect on a prior study on how 9/11 was represented in high school textbooks and supplemental curricula within the first decade after the attacks. Then they expand upon this work by presenting the results of an analysis of how states, nearly all of which had updated social studies curricula since 2001, represented 9/11 in their curriculum standards.

Elizabeth Bellows builds on this discussion by exploring how 9/11 is represented in state curriculum standards at the elementary level. She argues that most states are either abandoning their responsibility to address the attacks at the elementary level or doing so in extremely narrow, noncritical ways. Bellows concludes her chapter by offering several recommendations and relevant resources for elementary teachers who choose to broach 9/11 in their classrooms.

The next three chapters offer critical discussions of patriotism, nationalism, and American democracy. Mark Kissling starts this conversation by making the distinction between patriotism and nationalism and arguing that a critical, place-based conception of patriotism is most appropriate for American public education. Lisa Gilbert expands upon Kissling's argument by comparing the reaction of American educators following 9/11 and French educators following the *Charlie Hebdo* terrorist attacks. Gilbert argues that schools have a responsibility to offer aspirational definitions of national identity while simultaneously acknowledging dissenting viewpoints.

E. Wayne Ross offers one such viewpoint. He argues that the ethos of democracy, freedom, and equality articulated by the United States and other Western democracies is no longer accurate. Ross, however, argues that social studies educators should not submit to the hopelessness of the times in which we live; rather, he contends that it is the responsibility of educators to engage in aspects of "dangerous" citizenship in which students are confronted with the various contradictions to democracy, freedom, and equality that are present within society yet encouraged to take steps to reach these aspirational ideals in spite of systemic obstacles.

The final three chapters provide practical approaches to several of the challenges that have arisen in enacting progressive social studies education since 9/11. Stephen Masyada and Elizabeth Yeager Washington argue for conceptual thinking as an ideal approach to the critical dispositions students need to better understand the post-9/11 world in which they live. They then provide examples of how a conceptual approach could be used to encourage students to think critically about relevant topics such as civil liberties and media literacy.

Jane Lo and Walter Parker adhere to the notion that the best way for educators to confront the polarized nature of post-9/11 American society is for teachers to promote a pluralistic conception of democracy in their classrooms. In their chapter, they offer guidelines for how teachers can implement political simulations that serve as portals for pluralistic thought. These simulations force students to engage with multiple viewpoints on any given civic issue and, thus, better prepare them to be more tolerant of different conceptions of the good life.

The final chapter by Christopher Clark and Patricia Avery also addresses polarization but focuses on classroom discussions of controversial issues. Although much has been written on the challenges teachers face in implementing successful controversial issue discussions with students, Clark and Avery offer a unique perspective by looking at the psychology surrounding the beliefs that people hold. This information can better help teachers understand the barriers that too often limit students' ability to engage in thoughtful, tolerant discussions of political issues, particularly in an era that has been defined by political polarization.

The authors in this volume offer a variety of perspectives on the nature of social studies education and how best to educate students about critical issues that have arisen since 9/11. Collectively, they raise questions about the viability of the contemporary social studies curriculum to prepare students to be active and engaged citizens in a polarized and often contentious world.

It is my hope that the arguments made in these chapters will generate the types of conversations and reforms within the field and among educators and policymakers that were needed fifteen years ago. As with most attempts at progressive approaches to curricula, change often occurs slower than what is needed at the time. In this case, however, it is better for change to occur late than never at all.

NOTES

1. As of this writing, it is unclear whether the videos were, in fact, shot within Planned Parenthood facilities.
2. In the years following 9/11, some districts even dismissed teachers who expressed anti-war sentiments or encouraged critical discussions of American foreign policies in their classes (Egelko, 2007; Westheimer, 2006).

REFERENCES

Apple, M. W. (2002). Patriotism, pedagogy, and freedom: On the educational meanings of September 11th. *Teachers College Record, 104*, 1760–1772.
Barkan, R. (2015, November 30). NYC mayor decries "toxic rhetoric" after Planned Parenthood shooting. *Observer*. Retrieved from http://observer.com/2015/11/nyc-mayor-decries-toxic-rhetoric-after-planned-parenthood-shooting/.
Ben-Porath, S. (2011). Wartime citizenship: An argument for shared fate. *Ethnicities, 11*, 313–325.
Bush, G. W. (2001). Address to the nation: September 20, 2001. *Washington Post*. Retrieved from http://www.washingtonpost.com/wp-srv/nation/specials/attacked/transcripts/bushaddress_092001.html.
Cary, L. J. (2003). In-between curriculum spaces: The effects of power in a post-9/11 world. *Journal of Curriculum Theorizing, 19*, 85–95.
Diem, R. A. (2002). Some reflections on social studies and one high school: Post-September 11th. *Theory & Research in Social Education, 30*, 145–147.
Egelko, B. (2007, May 14). "Honk for peace" case tests limits on free speech. *SFGate*. Retrieved from http://www.sfgate.com/news/article/Honk-for-peace-case-tests-limits-on-free-speech-2594488.php.
Hess, D., & Stoddard, J. (2007). 9/11 and terrorism: "The ultimate teachable moment" in textbooks and supplemental curricula. *Social Education, 71*, 231–236.
Lerner, A. B. (2015, February 21). AP U.S. history controversy becomes a debate on America. *Politico*. Retrieved from http://www.politico.com/story/2015/02/ap-us-history-controversy-becomes-a-debate-on-america-115381.html.
Massey, W. (2015, July 31). New AP U.S. History teaching framework released after controversy. *CNN.com*. Retrieved from http://www.cnn.com/2015/07/31/living/ap-history-united-states-curriculum-change/.
Mutz, D. C. (2006). *Hearing the other side: Deliberative versus participatory democracy*. Cambridge, England: Cambridge University Press.
Pace, J. L. (2002). Education scholars' reflections on the implications of September 11th for curriculum. *Educational Foundations, 16*, 33–42.
Romanowski, M. H. (2009). Excluding ethical issues from U.S. history textbooks: 911 and the war on terror. *American Secondary Education, 37*(2), 26–48.
Saleem, M. M., & Thomas, M. K. (2011). The reporting of the September 11th terrorist attacks in American social studies textbooks: A Muslim perspective. *High School Journal, 95*, 15–33.
Westheimer, J. (2006). Politics and patriotism in education. *Phi Delta Kappan, 87*, 608–620.

Chapter One

International Conflict and National Destiny

World War I and History Teaching

Keith C. Barton

September 11, 2001, is not the first time that Americans have faced a challenge of global proportions, one that led to new patterns of international involvement and tested assumptions about the country's role in the world. One hundred years ago the First World War, known at the time as the Great War, played a similar role in national life. U.S. involvement was brief—lasting only from entry in April 1917 to war's end in November 1918—and memory of the war in the public imagination may cast it as little more than a precursor to World War II.

In reassessing the war's impact on national life, historians have pointed to significant, long-term changes that originated with the war. Although its impact on the history curriculum has received little attention, the war may have established patterns that endure to this day, including an emphasis on the nation as the basis for historical study and a characterization of the United States as having a uniquely democratic mission. Educators who hope to influence curriculum in the wake of September 11 would benefit from considering how World War I served as a catalyst for these developments, so that contemporary efforts are grounded in a more complete understanding of the relationship between international conflict and curriculum change.

THE GREAT WAR AND PUBLIC OPINION

The First World War was a watershed event in U.S. history, one that led not only to a vastly expanded role for the federal government but also to new and unfamiliar patterns of international involvement. Domestically, the war was accompanied by widespread military training, heightened federal taxation, and increased government regulation of business, industry, and labor.

In mobilizing for war, the government created an array of new agencies and bureaus and, according to Ziegler (2000), "intruded into virtually every area of private life" (p. 57). This expansion of government regulation of both public and private affairs constituted a victory for those progressive reformers who sought to use public planning to bring greater order to public life. Just as dramatic as the expanded role of government was the country's heightened involvement in international affairs, a trend that stood in contrast to traditional U.S. isolationism.

President Woodrow Wilson's delay in entering the war was due, in part, to his concern for laying the groundwork of public opinion. Before entry, support for the war and sympathy for the Allies was mixed. Americans had long held themselves to be superior to Europeans, with their authoritarian governments, imperial ambitions, and convoluted diplomatic entanglements.

The United States and Britain had only in recent decades resolved earlier diplomatic disputes, and Britain's policies during the war—including their blockade of Germany, blacklisting of U.S. firms, and response to the Easter Rising in Ireland—led to renewed resentment and a wariness of becoming wartime partners. Nor was it obvious why the United States should be allied with Russia, which at the beginning of the war was considered the preeminent oppressor of Jewish people. Even after U.S. entry, many people remained confused about reasons for the country's participation (Kennedy, 2004; Ziegler, 2000).

The federal government, then, found it necessary to engage in extensive public relations efforts to develop support for the war, as well as to suppress dissent. Such efforts, however, could not be couched in terms of national self-interest because it was precisely the tradition of rivalry, imperialism, and self-aggrandizement that the U.S. public considered to be the war's chief cause.

U.S. isolationism was rooted not only in Americans' long-standing aversion to becoming entangled in European intrigues, but also in their belief that it was not in the country's character to pursue its own interests at the expense of others. Given the remoteness of the war and its limited effects on U.S. citizens and business, even defensive arguments phrased in terms of national self-interest would have been less than compelling. To create support for the war, Americans had to be mobilized to think of their efforts not in terms of national interests, but of national ideals.

President Wilson (1917) made these ideals clear in his speech advising Congress to declare war on Germany. He proclaimed, "We have no selfish ends to serve. We desire no conquest, no dominion" (para. 15). Rather, the United States was entering the war for more noble reasons: "The world must be made safe for democracy. Its peace must be planted upon the tested foundations of political liberty" (para. 15). The United States, he vowed, would

> fight for the things which we have always carried nearest our hearts—for democracy, for the right of those who submit to authority to have a voice in their own Governments, for the rights and liberties of small nations, for a universal dominion of right . . . as shall bring peace and safety to all nations and make the world itself at last free. (para. 20)

From the jaded perspective of the 21st century, this pronouncement may seem little more than thinly disguised imperial ambition. Wilson's rhetoric certainly obscured his disdain for colonized people around the world, his desire to counteract the threat he perceived from Asia, and his active racism at home. In 1917, however, this appeal to U.S. ideals was both novel and inspiring, and whatever motivations it may have served to mask, it was nonetheless rooted in Wilson's sense of the country's millennial destiny.

If the idea of becoming involved in a European war to support idealistic aims was novel, the government's means of promoting this effort was not. The use of publicity—in the form of broad educational efforts that appealed to people's enlightened selves—was a mainstay of progressive reform and was easily adapted to develop support for the war. This effort was bolstered by the support of liberal intellectuals who backed the war either because they believed that victory would usher in a new era of international peace, democracy, and self-determination, or because they hoped that collective pursuit of idealistic purposes would become the new norm for social action.

Political commentator Walter Lippmann, for example, argued that "we shall stand committed as never before to the realization of democracy in America" (cited in Kennedy, 2004, p. 39), and historian Arthur M. Schlesinger Sr. wrote, "The times call imperiously for the marshaling of the liberals of the country for the purpose of making the war an instrument for the promotion of social justice and public ownership" (cited in Kennedy, 2004, p. 40). Even pacifists such as John Dewey argued that peace could only be achieved through victory over German militarism.

The chief federal agency for developing support for the war was the Committee on Public Information, whose purpose was to make the country's ideals and war aims clear both at home and abroad—to "mantle the war with a transcendent ideological significance" (Kennedy, 2004, p. 41). Led by George Creel, a muckraking journalist, editor, and longtime Wilson supporter, the organization commissioned historians to write pamphlets on topics related to the war, promoted a series of four-minute public addresses (by "Four Minute Men") that justified the country's role in the war, and produced a range of materials for teachers:

- pamphlets on the war and on citizenship
- articles in professional education journals
- a biweekly magazine for elementary and secondary teachers (*National School Service*)
- course syllabi, most notably historian Samuel B. Harding's *Study of the Great War*, originally prepared for military recruits but later distributed to high schools.

Although the primary purpose of the committee was to unify public opinion among adults, schools were regarded as a convenient means for disseminating messages that would make their way to parents (Blakey, 1970). Creel later referred to this barrage of educational efforts as "the world's greatest adventure in advertising" (cited in Todd, 1945, p. 19).

At the same time that public support for the war was being created through propaganda and publicity, the government and private organizations pursued a vigorous campaign to suppress dissent. These propaganda strategies included new federal laws against espionage and sedition, postal restrictions on dissenting publications, legal prosecution of those who voiced antiwar views, and organized vigilante surveillance and violence.

In schools, this propaganda took the form of prohibiting German language courses, censoring textbooks that suggested positive features of German civilization, and questioning the loyalty of teachers with suspect sympathies (Capozzola, 2008; Kennedy, 2004). In *Are American Teachers Free?*, Howard Beale (1936) documented dozens of cases of teachers being fired or facing community pressure during the war for suspected pro-German sentiments—or sometimes simply for a lack of patriotic enthusiasm.

EDUCATIONAL HISTORY AND THE PERIOD OF THE GREAT WAR

A number of historians have investigated how World War I affected schools' attempts to influence students' understanding of the nation and national identity. This work has illuminated short term effects of the war—including censorship (Beale, 1936); restrictions on foreign language instruction (Kibler, 2008); promotion of health campaigns, conservation efforts, manual training, and collection drives (Todd, 1945); and involvement of historians in developing materials for schools (Blakey, 1970)—as well as its impact on longer-term processes such as the assimilation of immigrants (Mirel, 2010). We know little, however, about the war's effect on history teaching.

Reports of censorship and retaliation often do not identify teachers' subject areas, and when they do, it is more often English than history. Analysis of the efforts of the Committee on Public Information and other agencies, meanwhile, has attended to the production and distribution of history materials for schools, but this tells us little about how these materials were received, interpreted, or used. History teachers certainly found themselves the object of a great deal of attention, and they undoubtedly experienced a climate favorable to war and dismissive of dissent. But how did this affect the content of their courses or their methods of instruction?

Although historians of social studies education have devoted considerable attention to the period of the Great War, they have largely ignored the war itself. Most have concentrated instead on the work of the Commission on the Reorganization of Secondary Education, whose 1916 report on social studies has been credited with creating the field as we now know it (e.g., Saxe, 1991).

Scholars have disagreed over the source of the ideas in that report and over the extent of its continuity with previous reports; however, they generally have agreed on its significance and have ignored the role of the war as a possible influence on history education. More recent scholarship (e.g., Barton, 2009) calls into question the impact of the 1916 report, but this work has not attended to the war as an alternative influence on curriculum.

Although historical patterns of enacted curricula are notoriously difficult to uncover, one way of getting closer to classroom practice is by examining teaching journals—the publications that represented practical advice and professional reflection for classroom teachers. Authors of articles in these journals clearly were aware that the war had implications for their subject, and they discussed those implications extensively.

As Burkholder (2012) notes, such sources cannot capture the full complexity of teachers' thought and practice, but they do provide insight into the kinds of discourses that teachers encountered. Teaching journals may also provide a more diverse range of perspectives than those found in journals that circulated among academics and administrators or in the concentrated and short-term publications of government agencies. For the period just before, during, and immediately after the war, such publications included:

- *The History Teacher's Magazine* (renamed *Historical Outlook* in 1918 and later, *The Social Studies*)
- *Popular Educator: A Magazine for Grammar Grade Teachers*
- *The Ohio History Teachers' Journal*
- *Michigan History Magazine*
- *The Texas History Teachers' Bulletin*

Each of these was devoted in whole or in part to articles written for an audience of history teachers; authors included historians, teachers, district administrators, and other educational professionals.

Although *The History Teacher's Magazine* included numerous articles that served as conduits for work commissioned by the Committee on Public Information (Blakey, 1970), the variety of perspectives in those articles, and the inclusion of authors outside the organization (including several whose suggestions were narrow or idiosyncratic), indicates the lack of a single, tightly controlled message. State journals, meanwhile, were even less likely to represent any single perspective. Examining this body of professional literature, and including works published not only during U.S. involvement but also in the years before and after, provides insight into how the war influenced ideas about history teaching.

FROM CURRENT EVENT TO NATIONAL DESTINY

These periodicals reflected important shifts in how educators talked about the war and its connection to history teaching before, during, and after U.S. involvement. Before U.S. entry, the war was simply a "current event" and inspired no single pattern of response: Some schools engaged the topic, while others avoided it; some authors suggested promoting pacifism and internationalism, while others adhered to more traditional academic goals; and even those who suggested studying the war to increase motivation disagreed over whether the war was worthy of study in its own right or whether it was simply an opportunity to spur interest in the existing curriculum.

Once the United States entered the war, opinion narrowed considerably, with most authors arguing that students must be taught to understand the nation's long-standing democratic ideals and their roots in British institutions (as well as their differences from German ideals). This focus on democracy and national destiny coalesced even further after the war, as authors argued that isolationism was no longer possible and that the country must embrace its role as the world's guardian of democracy.

Before the War: Avoidance, Neutrality, Internationalism, and Engagement

Before U.S. entry, articles addressing the relationship between history teaching and the war were scarce, and they did not reflect support for any of the warring sides. School superintendent Cassius Lyman (1914) noted that "as many of our pupils or their parents came from the countries which are at war, we must guard against any controversy about the causes of the war and who is right or wrong in this conflict. We must not stir up race prejudice" (p. 66).

G. Stanley Hall (1915) also found that 22 of the 109 superintendents he surveyed reported their schools avoided discussing the war, sometimes because of this fear of offending students' families; in at least one district, teaching modern European history had been prohibited altogether (Gutsch, 1915). On the other hand, Hall noted that in cities that did teach the war, "We can hear both sides warmly defended by those whose hearts and family traditions are with the side they defend." He proudly declared that children

> whose parents came from lands where for many generations traditional hate, each of the other, was cultivated, here bring into the school each the cold facts, so far as they can be ascertained, about their own sides, compare the reports that emanate from the different capitals, each defend the fatherland . . . while each learns to agree to differ with his mate and to tolerate if not have some respect for the other side. (pp. 67–68)

Some authors suggested that the war be used to promote pacifist or internationalist values. Rather than focusing on who was right or wrong, teachers in Lyman's (1915) district, he explained, used stories about the destruction of the war "to foster a sentiment in favor of arbitration and against unnecessary war"; he went on to note that while stories of the worst atrocities may be exaggerated, "there is truth enough to make us disgusted with war" (p. 66).

Similarly, Carl Eckhardt (1917) argued that "never before has there been such a sentiment for peace" (p. 44). For history teachers, he continued, "the only thing to do is confidently to teach that in the light of history war is not necessarily here to stay, and that the world will get permanent peace when it is sufficiently educated morally to see that other nations have rights, and that world peace cannot exist until there is a world state" (p. 46).

For others, the war was an important object of study not because it led to any particular beliefs, but because it was so obviously a matter of public concern. D. Shaw Duncan (1917), for example, noted that students must understand "what men are struggling for" and that by studying the war, the student "is studying things of present day value; he is tough with life; he is talking the same thing the man on the street is talking; he can talk intelligently with his parents on the vital subjects of the day; he is a citizen of the world" (p. 160).

Some of the superintendents surveyed by Hall (1915) also suggested that "historic tendencies from many centuries are focusing to and will diverge from this momentous epoch, in which history is made day by day more rapidly than ever before." Others, however, indicated that teaching about the war "gives a large surface of contact between the school and life, which tend so strongly to be isolated from each other" (p. 67)

For many, however, addressing the war was not an end in itself but a "vitalizer" of school subjects, as Hall (1915) put it: a means of developing interest in the distant regions and periods found in established curricula. Robert McElroy (1916), for example, argued that current events could not be objects of historical study, because events do not become historical until historians have interpreted them.

McElroy went on to argue, however, that teachers "can and must use current events to give interest and value to history," because contemporary affairs stimulate students' interest in "those epochs of history when ambition for world empire has dominated. . . . In the light of a thrilling current topic, those great efforts at a world domination assume a reality which they could not have if presented merely as the embalmed records of a dead past" (pp. 86–87). Similarly, W. C. Harris (1916), L. A. Chase (1916), and others stressed the pedagogical usefulness of the war rather than any particular perspectives on the war that teachers should encourage.

During the War: Historical Judgment, National Obligation, and Democratic Ideals

Once the United States entered the war, discussion of its curricular implications became more frequent and pointed. Authors continued to exhibit significant diversity of reasoning, although any references to pacifism or the legitimacy of alternative perspectives on the war's cause disappeared. Some authors continued to discuss opportunities for particular teaching methods, such as using maps, photographs, and periodicals; having students create notebooks of newspaper articles; and calling attention to historical analogies to the war (e.g., Paxson, 1918).

A series of survey responses published in *The Texas History Teachers' Bulletin* throughout 1918 suggests that many teachers, in that state at least, used some or all of these methods. Other authors emphasized the need to address geographical and long-term historical factors influencing the war (e.g., Coulomb, 1919; Harding, 1918), and still others hoped the war would counteract what they portrayed as a recent overemphasis on social and material aspects of history (Knowlton, 1918; Violette, 1917).

Many of these authors emphasized well-accepted goals for historical study, such as evaluating evidence and promoting "historical mindedness," but within the context of the war. Howard C. Hill (1918), for example, argued that history teaching should focus on the process of history rather than a body of factual knowledge: "In my judgment, the history teacher who nowadays does not teach his pupils to discern between fact and opinion, between inference and conjecture, between truth and falsehood, is recreant to his trust" (p. 11).

Theodore Clark Smith (1918) also argued that it was the "duty of the history teacher" to counter rash, biased, or unsubstantiated judgments in the media or popular opinion:

> The attitude of the American toward Germany is liable to be marked by more sentiment than reason, simply because of the limitless flood of articles, stories, write-ups and editorials about them with which he has been engulfed. Some of the sentiment takes the childish form of abusing

"the Hun" as a fiend and monster, of hating all Germans, of demanding the extirpation of the whole race. (p. 379)

To counter this, Smith argued, "It is the duty of all those who are trained in historical judgment to use every particle of influence they can exert to steady the minds of those with whom they come into contact" (p. 379).

Most articles, however, suggested more partisan uses of history (sometimes alongside traditional academic purposes). A few suggested that students should simply be taught to support the war, and that they do so because it was being fought for unselfish reasons. Herman V. Ames (1917), for example, unabashedly argued, "It is the duty of the teacher of history and civics to seize the wonderful opportunity afforded by the war to aid in promoting an intelligent and patriotic public opinion in support of the government in these critical times" (p. 191).

Similarly, Homer C. Hockett (1917) maintained that it was the duty of history teachers to dispel "the wide-spread error that we are fighting to defend a mere property right" (p. 156); they should instead engage students in the study of Wilson's speech, so that they would understand that the real purpose of the war was to make the world safe for democracy. And Hill (1918), in addition to emphasizing the need to focus on the process of history, maintained that teachers must counter the perception that the war "was instigated by predatory capitalists." Like Hockett, he urged teachers to publicize the democratic purpose of the war. He prophesied,

> It will prove to be the most holy and the most unselfish war we ever waged. And it is up to us, the teachers of history, to do our part in holding public opinion true to the President's ideal.... As one hundred and forty years ago our ancestors won the independence we now enjoy; as our fathers fought to preserve the Union in which we live; so now men die in France to preserve for them, for us, for coming generations, a heritage of liberty, justice, humanity, democracy. It is a solemn thing nowadays to teach history to the young. (p. 11)

Although the language of obligation was a key feature of public discourse in these years (Capozzola, 2008), few articles so explicitly spoke about "duty" or presented national ideals in such simplistic or ahistorical terms. Some articles, instead, emphasized that students should come to understand the evolution of long-standing democratic traditions in the United States. The most common suggestion for connecting history teaching to the war involved encouraging teachers to emphasize the fundamental similarity of British and U.S institutions, particularly the English roots of U.S. democratic structures.

A number of authors argued that schools had neglected this task and instead had promoted enmity toward the British. This was the theme of Charles Altschul's (1915) book, *The American Revolution in Our School Text-Books*, and it was a position repeated frequently in magazines for history teachers. Frederic Duncalf (1918), for example, called attention to the "unfriendly attitude toward England" (p. 150) in textbooks, and Lucius B. Swift (1918) claimed, "For more than a century we have brought up American children to hate England" (p. 6). Robert Schuyler (1918) agreed; he noted:

> Americans have been slow to overcome ancient prejudices inherited from the days of the American Revolution. They have cherished the belief that the British Empire, from which the United States revolted, is in a sense antagonistic to true Americanism. "Patriotic" school histories have fostered this notion, and until very recently twisting the British Lion's tail was a favorite diversion of one species of American "statesmanship." Few of us know how far the British Commonwealth of to-day has moved from the British Empire of George III. (p. 91)

Rather than perpetuating this historic sense of enmity, authors repeatedly argued that history teachers should help students see how the roots of U.S. democracy lay in English institutions. George B. Adams (1918) maintained that history teachers should

> show that in a truly historical sense we are what we are politically, in institutions and their interpretation, because the English are what they are. For in many ways and at many dates, directly and indirectly, he can bring out the fact that the democratic ideals, which are cherished for ourselves and desired for the world by both peoples alike, grow out of the same roots in our common past. (p. 424)

Similarly, Louise Capen (1918) noted, "Roots of sentiment are very old, and no people ever wholly forgets its past. Modern Americanism was born in the hopes, aspirations, ambitions, policies and purposes that were brought across the Atlantic, not in the hold of ships, but in the hearts of men" (p. 484). In arguments such as these, history's contribution to the war lay less in directly encouraging loyalty than in helping students understand the shared roots of British and American institutions, and thus implicitly justifying alliance with a traditional enemy.

Sometimes these authors and others explicitly contrasted U.S. and British democracy with the "autocratic" ideals of Germany and its allies; they cast the war not just as a defense of the former but an attempt to defeat the latter. Theodore Blegen (1918) concluded:

> Fundamentally, the ideals that we are now fighting for are the enduring ideals to which both Washington and Lincoln devoted their lives. Liberty, democracy, national honesty and integrity, the rights of humanity, respect for treaty obligations, justice between man and man as well as internationally, for small and great nations alike. (p. 464)

For Blegen, these contrasted with ideals bequeathed by German leaders: "oppression, intrigue, selfishness, national dishonesty, unscrupulousness, ruthlessness, the glorification of might, the defense of international wrong-doing, [and] autocratic government" (p. 464). This was a theme emphasized in a series of essays in *Michigan History Magazine* on the topic, "Why the United States is at War." These were written during the war (but published afterward) by elementary and high school teachers, and by students in normal schools, colleges, and universities.

In one such essay, Bernice Perry (1919) characterized the war as "the price paid by democracy for continued existence" (p. 93) and applauded Americans for coming to realize "that at last the supreme crisis in the age-long struggle between autocracy and democracy had been reached" (p. 94). Writing in *The Ohio History Teachers' Journal*, John Knipfing (1918) even argued that ancient history should be interpreted in terms of the difference between Hellenistic democracy and Roman autocracy, with students learning that the United States is the inheritor of Hellenistic ideals.

Ruth Kennen (1918) was careful, as Wilson was in his war speech, to note that "the United States had entered the war not against the German people, but German Government, over whose actions and policies the people had no control" (p. 288). But just as the larger national discourse increasingly elided this distinction, other articles implied a monolithic German society. Smith (1918), for example, decried the "refusal to believe that the Germans really differ in their political and social beliefs from ourselves" and argued,

> It is the business of every student of historical evidence to use his influence to make his pupils and his neighbors realize that the German people are absolutely under the control of political and social

beliefs which make it impossible for them to respect anything but superior force in international relations. (p. 380)

Duncalf (1918), meanwhile, argued that the German people "have never learned to govern themselves," and that in order to understand the war students must consider "why warlike ambitions developed in the minds of the German people" (p. 86). For most authors, the path to developing students' support for Britain and enmity toward Germany lay not in encouraging a blind loyalty toward their own government but in helping them understand that the Allies stood for both reason and democracy.

Even the argument for helping students evaluate evidence could be turned to such purposes, as when Hill (1918) suggested that students compare indefensible German statements concerning the war with Wilson's war speech, which is "a most creditable document." Comparing these, he thought, offered "an excellent tool, suitable for school purposes, to show concretely the differences between fact and opinion, between a supported conclusion and a mere assertion" (p. 13).

After the War: The United States as Guardian of World Democracy

After the war, the content and tenor of articles underwent a subtle but important shift. Some continued to focus attention on pedagogical techniques or traditional goals such as the evaluation of evidence, and some continued to stress historic connections with England, "the other great Anglo-Saxon people," or to take swipes at Germany's "national shame, dishonor, and dastardliness" (National Board for Historical Service, 1919, p. 95). But with the war over, neither German autocracy nor kinship with Britain was a compelling issue in itself. Instead, a more fundamental argument emerged: History teaching must adopt a new internationalism, so that the United States could assume its role as the world's protector of democracy.

Authors were clear that the days of isolationism were over, and that there could be no return to the country's provincial prewar status. As Calvin Davis (1919) observed, "Nothing is more certain than that any spirit of provincialism and aloofness which may have characterized America as a nation five years ago has either wholly disappeared, or else to-day is in the process of rapid disappearance" (p. 451).

Similarly, Warren Ayer (1919) noted, "Historians have long talked of world citizenship, now the American people have it thrust upon them and must immediately accept the responsibilities of that term in their entirety" (p. 11). And Charles Coulomb (1919) claimed that the lesson of the war was "that however much we may desire to live in splendid isolation it is impossible for us so to live, because of the interdependence, in these days, of one country upon another" (p. 501).

This meant moving away from the traditional emphasis on U.S. history and learning about the rest of the world, particularly the history of other countries. As Harding (1918) noted, "The war should teach us all to think more internationally"; in order to educate students with "a sense of world citizenship," schools must attend to the "history, aspirations, and institutions, of other people, as well as to factors and movements which in the past hundred years have made for a new internationalism" (p. 189).

History was indispensable to such international understanding; Ayer (1919) asked how students could "understand their relations to their European neighbors unless they have some knowledge of the struggles and labors through which those peoples have passed to reach the common ground upon which the whole civilized world now finds itself" (p. 11). K. S. Latourette (1919a, 1919b) also suggested that the internationalism resulting from the war also justified greater attention to the Far East, and Davis (1919) argued that "whether we will or not, we must in the future take full cognizance of the ambitions, plans, and activities of all peoples of the civilized world" (p. 451).

Learning about the world was not simply an academic exercise, nor did it imply a parity among the "ambitions, plans, and activities" of the world's peoples. International understanding, instead, was necessary in order for the United States to fulfill its historical destiny. As Ayer (1919) noted, "We are 'a chosen people,' selected by environment and temperament to work out the great plan of World Democracy whereby all the peoples of the earth may achieve their political and economic salvation" (p. 13). Similarly, Davis (1919) predicted:

> America, it seems probable, will be called upon to stabilize, guide and direct the activities of less fortunate and weaker nations of the world. Our democracy is the oldest, the strongest, the best organized, and the freest from radicalism of any of the self-governing nations of the world. Our governmental forms and practices have become the revered ideals of millions of less favored people. Our fraternal advice is being sought and our generous co-operation is expected. We are today, in a very literal sense, our weaker brother's keeper. Yes, more, we are coming very near to being the keeper of the fate of the entire family of nations. (pp. 451–452)

In order to better understand that role, students also had to understand the history of U.S. democracy. H. B. Wilson (1919) argued that "the emphasis in both our texts and teaching must be such as to support as strongly as possible the importance, improvement, and perpetuation of our American ideals and institutions" by "teaching more adequately and thoroughly than in the past the peculiar and characteristic genius of American institutions and the permanent and outstanding assets of our democracy" (p. 84).

Citizens must "genuinely realize," Wilson claimed, that the American Revolution had made the thirteen colonies safe for democracy; the Monroe Doctrine had made the American continents safe for democracy; and at the conclusion of the Great War, "the entire world has been made safe for democracy" (p. 85). The U.S. past, present, and future became unified in this quest to establish and protect democracy, not just for one country but for the world.

INTERNATIONAL CONFLICT AND CURRICULUM CHANGE

Analyzing articles for teachers cannot convincingly demonstrate how the history curriculum changed during this period; that requires more research into a wider variety of sources and over a longer timeframe. It would be particularly important to know whether authors' characterizations of curricular trends at the start of the war were accurate, as well as how textbooks, official curricula, and teaching practices evolved in the decades after the war. Nonetheless, the sources examined here illustrate how educators talked about history teaching at the time, and they may, therefore, provide insight into how national and global contexts influence curricular change.

First, the war spurred relatively little interest until the United States became directly involved. Although some authors thought that discussing an important current event such as the war would motivate students, there were no suggestions for fundamental revisions to the curriculum. This suggests that the potential for curriculum revision, absent a perceived crisis of national proportions, may be limited.

The curriculum—particularly in a decentralized educational system such as that of the United States—has an inertia that is not easy to overcome. In addition, some educators reported avoiding the topic altogether, because of the emotional involvement of students whose families came from countries at war. Resistance to addressing controversial issues reinforces curricular inertia; for many educators, then and now, stirring up trouble is the last thing they hope to accomplish.

Second, the war spurred a significant interest in internationalizing the curriculum, but in a particular way. During and after the war, authors noted that the curriculum could no longer be so inward-looking, and this meant that the United States must acknowledge its historical ties to Britain. That kind of internationalism simply involved recognizing other countries that were similar in values and institutions.

Interest in other countries broadened after the war, but the histories, cultures, and perspectives of other nations were important only insofar as they helped inform Americans how they could bring democracy—under U.S. direction—to the rest of the world. Broadening the curriculum to take account of other countries is not an inherently cosmopolitan undertaking, as Walter Parker (2008) has documented with regard to more recent efforts at international education.

Third, and perhaps most profoundly, curricular suggestions for history were conceived in distinctly nationalist terms—not usually the nationalism of jingoist patriotism, but nationalism as a political and intellectual project: the idea that states are, or should be, composed of people who share common cultures, languages, and national characteristics. This was a dominant political ideology of the time, but before becoming part of the world stage, U.S. history educators had not had to reflect extensively on their own national characteristics.

Ruth Elson (1972) argues that in 19th-century textbooks, for example, "liberty is a desirable but undefined and almost mystical entity" (p. 289). The war changed that; now all nations had to be portrayed in terms of clear and distinctive ideals. The United States and England came to be defined in terms of their commitment to democracy, justice, and self-determination; Germany by its commitment to autocracy.

This led to important simplifications. With regard to the United States, failure to live up to national ideals could be admitted, but only in the past; contemporary policies and perspectives that diverged from national ideals—such as domestic racism or foreign intervention—were never mentioned. Internationally, too, the need to contrast democracy with autocracy required distortions and omissions.

The imperialism of Britain, for example, was extolled as a model of idealism and restraint. Meanwhile, the autocratic government of Russia—an ally until the revolution—was ignored, and the complexities required to discuss national characteristics of Belgians, French, Italians, Ottomans, and others meant that those countries would hardly be mentioned. Nationalist history is inevitably simplified and idealized history; internationalizing the curriculum, that is, does not necessarily lead to greater complexity in thinking about nations and their relations with one another.

CONCLUSIONS

A quarter century later, as the Second World War drew to a close, P. L. Todd (1945) wrote, "In view of the grave problems that confront statesmen and educators in the years that lie before us, it may be of some use to look back upon our experiences in 1917 and 1918. It was then that the shadow of total war fell upon the nation" (p. 1). As we consider how the curriculum can and should respond to current international conflicts, we would do well to follow his advice. For those who hope to fashion curriculum that prepares students for the nation's place on the contemporary world stage, the changes that World War I wrought suggest both optimism and caution.

On the one hand, what we now consider long-standing patterns in U.S. history education—such as the focus on the nation and its democratic character—may not always have been part of the curriculum. Schlesinger (1918), in fact, complained that until the war, "our historians, being for the most part ultraconservatives by temperament, had failed to grasp the significance of the growth of democracy as the pivotal theme of American history" (p. 342). Schools' focus on the nation's uniquely democratic nature may have deep roots, but those appear to have been planted at a specific moment in time—and what was planted can be uprooted.

Uprooting patterns of curriculum that have been growing for a century, however, is no easy matter, particularly in a decentralized educational system. If ideas about history education changed at the time of World War I, it was not because of a committee report, the advice of educational scholars, or even the war itself. An emerging focus on the country's destiny resulted from a complex array of forces, including new patterns of immigration and international relations, publicity efforts of the government and other organizations, and perhaps most of all, the salience of nationalism as an ideological and political force.

These wider forces help explain why the nation was increasingly held up as the focus for historical study, and why the United States' democratic character was placed at the center of such study. World War I may have served as a catalyst for changes in the curriculum, just as the events of September 11 may inspire changes today, but any such transformations are rooted in worldviews and structural dynamics that shape and constrain how educators think about and implement curriculum. Educational scholars may be able to influence curriculum, but they must be prepared for their ideas to be reworked as they interact with other forces.

ACKNOWLEDGMENT

The author thanks Hana Jun of Indiana University for her indispensable help in collecting and analyzing evidence for this research.

REFERENCES

Adams, G. B. (1918). The English background of American institutions. *Historical Outlook, 9*, 423–425.
Altschul, C. (1915). *The American Revolution in our school text-books*. New York: George H. Doran.
Ames, H. V. (1917). Patriotism and the teaching of history and civics. *History Teacher's Magazine, 8*, 188–192.
Ayer, W. (1919). The teaching of European history after the war. *Ohio History Teachers' Journal, 12*, 11–15.
Barton, K. C. (2009). Home geography and the development of elementary social education, 1890–1930. *Theory & Research in Social Education, 37*, 484–514.
Beale, H. K. (1936). *Are American teachers free? An analysis of restraints upon the freedom of teaching in American schools*. New York: Charles Scribner's Sons.
Blakey, G. T. (1970). *Historians on the homefront: American propagandists for the Great War*. Lexington: University Press of Kentucky.
Blegen, T. C. (1918). Two standards of national morality. *History Teacher's Magazine, 9*, 457–466.
Burkholder, Z. (2012). "Education for citizenship in a bi-racial civilization": Black teachers and the social construction of race, 1929–1954. *Journal of Social History, 46*, 335–363.
Capen, L. I. (1918). Still another editorial man of straw. *Historical Outlook, 9*, 483–484.
Capozzola, C. (2008). *Uncle Sam wants you*. New York: Oxford University Press.
Chase, L. A. (1916). History course as an expression of the interests to-day. *History Teacher's Magazine, 7*, 21–24.
Coulomb, C. A. (1919). A decade of changes in elementary school history. *Historical Outlook, 10*, 500–501.
Davis, C. (1919). A course in world history. *Historical Outlook, 10*, 451–454.
Duncalf, F. (1918). A war textbook for Texas schools. *Texas History Teacher's Bulletin, 6*, 85–164.
Duncan, D. S. (1917). Use of magazines in history teaching. *Historical Outlook, 8*, 160–161.
Eckhardt, C. C. (1917). War and peace in the light of history. *Historical Outlook, 8*, 43–46.
Elson, R. M. (1972). *Guardians of tradition: American schoolbooks of the nineteenth century*. Lincoln, NE: University of Nebraska Press.
Gutsch, M. R. (1915). The teaching of current history in the high school. *Texas History Teachers' Bulletin, 3*, 33–37.
Hall, G. S. (1915). Teaching the war. *History Teacher's Magazine, 6*, 67–70.

Harding, S. B. (1918). Some geographical aspects of the war. *History Teacher's Magazine, 9*, 82.
Harris, W. C. (1916). The use of current literature in history class. *Ohio History Teachers' Journal, 2*, 72–77.
Hill, H. C. (1918). The war and teaching history. *History Teacher's Magazine, 9*, 10–13.
Hockett, H. C. (1917). The duty of history teachers during the war. *Ohio History Teachers' Journal, 11*, 155–157.
Kennedy, D. M. (2004). *Over here: The First World War and American society* (25th anniversary ed.). New York: Oxford University Press.
Kennen, R. (1918). Why the United States is at war. *Ohio History Teachers' Journal, 9*, 283–294.
Kibler, A. (2008). Speaking like a "good American": National identity and the legacy of German-language education. *Teachers College Record, 110*, 1241–1268.
Knipfing, J. R. (1918). The world war and the teaching of ancient history. *Ohio History Teachers' Journal, 9*, 295–304.
Knowlton, D. C. (1918). The epoch-making war in history. *History Teacher's Magazine, 9*, 261–263.
Latourette, K. S. (1919a). The Far East: A suggested addition to our reconstructed history curriculums. *Historical Outlook, 10*, 131–132.
———. (1919b). The synchronization of Chinese and Occidental history. *Historical Outlook, 10*, 238–239.
Lyman, C. S. (1914). The European war and its geography. *Popular Educator, 32*, 65–66.
———. (1915). Advantages and results of the study of Europe at the present time. *Popular Educator, 32*, 252–254.
McElroy, R. M. (1916). Class treatment of recent events in Europe and America. *History Teacher's Magazine, 7*, 85–88.
Mirel, J. (2010). *Patriotic pluralism: Americanization education and European immigrants.* Cambridge, MA: Harvard University Press.
National Board of Historical Service. (1919). Some British reconstruction views. *Historical Outlook, 10*, 95–111.
Parker, W. C. (2008). "International education": What's in a name? *Phi Delta Kappan, 90*, 196–202.
Paxson, F. L. (1918). The spirit of present history. *History Teacher's Magazine, 9*, 318–319.
Perry, B. A. (1919). America and the Great War. *Michigan History Magazine, 3*, 93–106.
Saxe, D. W. (1991). *Social studies in schools: A history of the early years.* Albany: State University of New York Press.
Schlesinger, A. M. (1918). Mobilizing Ohio's historical resources: A phase of Ohio's war activities. *Ohio History Teachers' Journal, 11*, 342–343.
Schuyler, R. L. (1918). The study of English history. *History Teacher's Magazine, 9*, 90–91.
Smith, T. C. (1918). The duty of the history teacher in forming public opinion during the war. *Historical Outlook, 9*, 379–380.
Swift, L. B. (1918). America's debt to England. *History Teacher's Magazine, 9*, 6–9
Todd, P. L. (1945). *Wartime relations of the federal government and the public schools.* New York: Bureau of Publications, Teachers College, Columbia University.
Violette, E. M. (1917). A renaissance in military history. *History Teacher's Magazine, 8*, 261–263.
Wilson, H. B. (1919). Guiding principles in American history teaching. *Historical Outlook, 10*, 82–85.
Wilson, W. (1917). Transcript of joint address to Congress leading to a declaration of war against Germany. Retrieved from http://www.ourdocuments.gov/doc.php?doc=61&page=transcript.
Ziegler, R. H. (2000). *America's great war: World War I and the American experience.* New York: Rowman & Littlefield.

Chapter Two

9/11 and the War on Terror in American Secondary Curriculum, Fifteen Years Later

Jeremy Stoddard and Diana Hess

During the first year following the terrorist attacks of September 11, 2001, numerous nonprofit education groups and professional organizations such as the American Bar Association created lessons and materials for teachers to use on the first anniversary of the attacks. Soon after, special sections were added to social studies textbooks, so that editions just coming out included these events. This was a remarkably fast timeline, given the usual six- to seven-year cycle of textbook revision.

This rush to develop curriculum reflected the power of the event and its potential to highlight the importance of social studies; one curriculum writer described it as "the ultimate teachable moment," and another referred to it as the "Sputnik event" for social studies education (Hess & Stoddard, 2007). From 2002 through 2012, we studied the curricular response to 9/11 and the subsequent War on Terror. Our goal was to understand how these events, which have shaped the American experience over the past fifteen years, have emerged in the "official record" that is the high school curriculum in U.S. government, U.S. history, and world history classes.

In particular, we analyzed high school–level supplemental curriculum developed by non-profit educational organizations and best-selling social studies textbooks in order to understand how these curricula represented the 9/11 attacks, terrorism in general, and the ensuing U.S. and international response to the attacks. We also sought to understand the kinds of intellectual work these curricula called for students to perform. We wanted to go beyond an analysis of the content of the curriculum to also analyze what activities the curriculum designers recommended that teachers use when engaging students in the written content and the extent to which those activities represented high-quality civic/democratic education (Gould, 2011).

We were specifically interested in identifying which issues the writers presented as live (i.e., "open") controversies and which were presented as questions for which there was a "settled" or "right" answer (Hess & McAvoy, 2015). For example, were the wars in Afghanistan and Iraq presented as matters of genuine controversy that students should deliberate, or did the curriculum materials suggest that they were either warranted or not? We were also interested in how topics, events, concepts, and issues were included in instructional materials and classroom activities and whether students were being asked to engage in any kind of inquiry or deliberative work.

In this chapter, we turn to an analysis of state academic standards, which serve as de facto curriculum guides across most of the country. In many states that have some form of high-stakes assessment in social studies, the standards and the curriculum frameworks that are developed from them outline *what* needs to be taught in high school social studies courses. These state standards, especially when assessed by multiple-choice, high-stakes tests, have also been found to affect *how* the content is taught; most often, this means that teachers emphasize memorization over inquiry or deliberation (Au, 2009; Grant, 2006).

Therefore, through analyzing how 9/11 and its aftermath are represented in state high school standards, we hope to contribute to the field's understanding of the importance assigned to these events across and between states, the essential questions or issues through which students are supposed to learn from or about 9/11, and where in the standards these topics are placed. For example, we were interested in whether the 9/11-related events or topics were included in all social studies subject areas or emphasized in one particular subject, such as world history or American government.

After providing a summary of our main findings from our earlier studies of supplemental curriculum and textbooks, we present our analysis of data collected in 2011 from the forty-nine states that had updated their academic standards documents at some point in the decade after the 9/11 attacks. The following questions drove our analysis of the high school standards:[1]

1. How is 9/11 represented in the high school standards? What level and kinds of detail are included? What relationship is there between general patterns in a state's standards and its standards particularly related to 9/11? For example, do the standards deal with 9/11 in broad or thematic ways, with little mention of details or related events, and does this correspond to the nature of the state's other standards?
2. How is the concept of terrorism presented, if it is included? What examples of terrorism are included? What are the implicit or explicit messages about who terrorists are?
3. What is the nature of the intellectual work students are asked to do related to 9/11 content?

Following our examination of the themes that emerged from this new round of analysis, we compare our findings about standards with those from our earlier, supplemental curriculum and textbook-based studies and also discuss the implications of studying how an event such as 9/11 is presented across different forms of curriculum. We also discuss the limitations of analyzing state standards documents because of the variety of ways in which standards are written and assessed across the country—and the need to be careful in how conclusions are made and warranted given the nature of the various forms of standards documents.

SUMMARY OF FINDINGS FROM THE FIRST TEN YEARS

From 2002 to 2010, we conducted three studies of how 9/11 and its aftermath were included in the high school social studies curriculum. Our analysis concentrated on a selection of the supplemental curricula produced for the first anniversary of the attacks in 2002 and two rounds of textbook analyses, the first using a set of nine textbooks published from 2004 to 2006 with a follow-up analysis of a subset of the 2009–2010 editions of those texts to answer the following questions:

- What happened on 9/11?

- What is 9/11—how is it being described?
- What caused 9/11?
- What is a terrorist/terrorism?
- What was the response to 9/11?

We became particularly interested in how the challenging and hard-to-define concept of terrorism was presented, and the extent to which the materials included any of the important controversies about the U.S. and international responses to 9/11. We also analyzed the kinds of thinking students were being asked to do about this content, and, finally, how the materials positioned the role of the citizen with respect to 9/11 and its aftermath.

MAJOR THEMES

The Ubiquity and Malleability of 9/11

We were surprised by the way in which one event could be used by curriculum and textbook providers toward such diverse curricular, pedagogical, and ideological ends (Hess & Stoddard, 2007, 2011). The use of the events generally reflected the goals of the producing organization, and the malleability of 9/11 was particularly prominent in the supplemental curriculum. For example, a video curriculum from the Close Up Foundation that focuses on energizing youth voters uses the attacks of 9/11 as the context for taking civic action—using the attacks as a call for citizens to vote.

Similarly, The Choices Program (formerly Choices for the 21st Century) from Brown University focuses primarily on developing curriculum on foreign policy decision making. Not surprisingly, they developed a post-9/11 curriculum that focuses on foreign policy decision making in the aftermath of the attacks. The curriculum from these organizations maintained goals consistent with other curricula they had produced, with each using some aspect of the 9/11 attacks in ways consistent with its own organizational mission.

For the textbooks, differences in the use of 9/11 depended on the course for which the textbook was written. Government texts, for example, often included 9/11 in the context of teaching about executive power or the judiciary, while world history texts placed the events within sections about the history of the Middle East or about global terrorism.

What Happened on 9/11?

To our surprise, despite the ubiquity of 9/11 and its aftermath across these curricula, there was a lack of detail about what happened that day and about what led to the attacks. For example, in our analysis of nine high school texts, only four included any reference to the number killed in the attacks, only three identified how many planes were involved, and only three identified the group responsible (Hess, Stoddard, & Murto, 2008). This lack of detail may be understandable in curricula made for the first anniversary or the initial revised textbooks, but we saw this trend continue even in the revised textbooks published in 2010, intended to be used with students who would have been quite young when the attacks occurred.

The Collective 9/11 Account and Imagery

Though we found a lack of detail as to what actually happened on 9/11, we also found a remarkable consistency in the rhetoric of what 9/11 was and should be remembered as, conveyed both in stories and visually. Across both the majority of supplemental curriculum and the first editions of textbooks we studied (published between 2004 and 2006), we found a remarkable similarity in how the events of 9/11 were presented. The incidents were portrayed as an "unprecedented attack" and as being of great importance to the world.

Eight of the nine textbooks in this portion of the study described the 9/11 attacks as historically significant both for the United States and for the world, going so far as to call it a "turning point" in world history and a "crime against humanity" (Hess & Stoddard, 2011). The United States was presented as the victim of an attack, an attack that brought Americans together and the rest of the world in support. These narratives were largely nationalistic and emphasized a collective memory rich in personal stories of heroism and survival. They also consistently used the now iconic images of rubble, firefighters, and the American flag.

This nationalistic narrative was largely absent, however, in the next edition of textbooks we studied (published between 2009 and 2010), which is perhaps indicative of the distance from the events, national weariness over fighting two wars, and the controversy over the economy at home. These later editions of textbooks also removed details, such as the presence of weapons of mass destruction as the key justification for the invasion of Iraq, that were present in some of the 2004–2006 editions, which reflects the challenge of updating history textbooks to include events that are dynamic and still unfolding (Stoddard, Hess, & Hammer, 2011).

What Is Terrorism?

One of our most compelling findings from the studies of curricula and textbooks concerned differences and inconsistencies in how the concept of terrorism is defined and applied. This finding transcends the events of 9/11, and even the past decade and a half, and has real implications for how young people understand what terrorism is and who is and is not labeled as a terrorist. One difference concerns how definitions of terrorism are portrayed; some of the curricula included very authoritative and settled definitions, while others suggested that the concept itself is contested.

Similarly, there was an inconsistency in how the label was applied within individual textbooks. For example, some textbooks would define terrorism as an attack against civilians and then include examples such as the attack on the USS *Cole*, a naval vessel, and the bombing of the marine barracks in Lebanon. In comparison to earlier texts, later texts placed more emphasis on examples of terrorist attacks outside the United States or committed by non-U.S. individuals or groups like al Qaeda, while putting less emphasis on domestic terrorism such as the bombing of the Federal Building in Oklahoma City.

Lack of Controversy

Little was presented in the early curricula and textbooks as being controversial; issues were not presented as having multiple and competing legitimate perspectives or answers. Further, we found that where open questions and tasks were included, textbooks in particular did not provide enough information for students to be engaged in an informed way. There were exceptions, such as the curriculum from The Choices Program, which was designed to engage students in deliberating foreign policy responses to the events of 9/11. The more recent textbooks have more opportunities for students to engage in thoughtful analysis of competing perspectives on issues related to 9/11.

Limited Opportunities for Intellectual Work

In addition to finding a limited number of activities in these curricula and few textbooks designed to foster students' engagement in controversy, we found that the opportunities to engage in higher levels of intellectual work overall were rare in curricula. This was particularly true of textbooks, which included items that focused on basic reading comprehension and that did not ask students to analyze, synthesize, or construct any new knowledge. We also found little opportunity for students to engage in critically examining the roots of terrorism or the 9/11 attacks in these curricula (Hess & Stoddard, 2007).

Similar to the example of controversy above, however, there were some examples of curriculum designed to engage students in open-ended questions and higher-order thinking. A task included in the textbook *Street Law* (Glencoe, 2005), for example, asked students to engage in the question "Is the war on terrorism similar to other wars where rights have been restricted? How is it the same? How is it different?" (p. 206). However, the majority of open-ended questions and tasks in the textbooks—that is, questions and tasks in which students were asked to construct new knowledge—related to personal opinions or conjecture without analysis or use of evidence.

CONCLUSIONS FROM STUDYING CURRICULUM AND TEXTBOOKS

Overall, we found that the supplemental curriculum provided a greater number of opportunities for students to engage in higher order intellectual work—especially in deliberation and controversial issues—than the textbooks. Textbooks, in part because of their restrictions on length and their neutral narrative tone, make it difficult for authors to include any discussion of contemporary events and issues. This is particularly true given the traditional publication schedules, approval processes, and six- or seven-year (or longer) replacement cycle in schools.

This relative lack of controversy can also be explained in part by the approval process that many state school boards or departments of education dictate for a textbook to be adopted. Finally, it is important to note the important role of standards and high-stakes assessments in shaping what content is included in social studies textbooks, as textbook companies modify or customize textbooks for states that represent large markets and have high-stakes assessments, such as Texas.

9/11 AND TERRORISM IN STATE STANDARDS DOCUMENTS

Given the role of state academic standards in influencing teachers' curricular decisions, particularly in states with high-stakes assessments, we wanted to examine how 9/11 and its aftermath were now being incorporated into this "official" curriculum. As in our earlier textbook studies, we wanted to know to what extent and in what ways 9/11 and its aftermath are included in post-2001 revisions of state high school standards. Our dataset included standards that were in use or were in the final stages of the approval process in 2011.[2]

What we found was that less than half of the states (n = 21) included the 9/11 attacks specifically in their standards. Six of these states included 9/11 as part of a content standard (i.e., as part of the main objective for that standard). Four states included 9/11 as part of a substandard (i.e., as one of several related events or topics under a broader standard). Eleven states included 9/11 as an example for a standard or as a substandard, usually in a series of possible examples to help guide teacher or curricular decision making.

At first glance, this statistic would likely lead one to believe that 9/11 is not viewed as important enough to be included in the high school social studies standards. However, of the twenty-eight states that had updated standards that did not include 9/11 specifically, twelve did include some reference to terrorism or another key term related to the War on Terror. This represents the level of detail in the standards for many of these twelve states; they tend to refer to larger concepts and do not include many specific details.

For example, only three of these twelve have a reference to Pearl Harbor, which we used as a comparable event. The remaining sixteen states that did not include a reference to 9/11 also did not include any of our other key terms, "Pearl Harbor," or terms related to general concepts such as globalization or foreign policy. These states therefore have standards with little to no specific content, being structured instead around broad themes similar to those of the National Council for the Social Studies.

For example, one of Iowa's high school social studies standards identifies aspects of historical thinking as the objective, calling for students to "Understand historical patterns, periods of time, and the relationships among these elements" (SS.9-12.H.1).[3] In these types of concept- and skill-based thematic standards, specific events such as the 9/11 attacks are not listed (table 2.1).

Though not as ubiquitous as in the supplemental curricula and textbooks, content related to 9/11 and the War on Terror appears across the social studies standards and is used for a wide variety of curricular goals. It is notable that in the majority of revised state standards documents, there are references to the 9/11 attacks or to modern terrorism. Our analysis focused on the standards of the thirty-three states that included some reference to 9/11 or terrorism and placed these standards in the context of their overall purpose to serve as a guiding document for teachers and for state assessments. Several themes emerged from this analysis and are presented below.

9/11 in the Standards

Where included, 9/11 is most often considered in a global context, as part of a standard related to foreign policy, or in a world history context. For example, the Texas standard for U.S. History II 11.4 asks students to "describe U.S. involvement in world affairs, including the end of the Cold War, the Persian Gulf War, the Balkans Crisis, 9/11, and the global War on Terror." Three states go a step further to describe 9/11 as a turning point in U.S. and world history.

Table 2.1. 9/11 and Terrorism in State Standards Documents, States with Standards Updated Since 2001 (N = 49)*

9/11 and Terrorism in State Standards	Number of States	% of States
States that do not mention the 9/11 attacks or any key content related to terrorism	16**	33%
States that include some aspect of terrorism or the war on terror (but not 9/11 specifically)	12	25%
States that include the 9/11 attacks specifically, as part of a standard, substandard, or as an example	21	43%

*Among all fifty states, plus the District of Columbia, only California and Montana had not updated their standards in the focus period.
** These states have broad thematic standards that do not include specific details.

The most widely included objective related to 9/11 is to be able to describe or identify the U.S. response to the attacks. For example, the District of Columbia's standards ask students to "Describe America's response to the September 11, 2001 terrorist attack on the World Trade Center and Pentagon, including the intervention in Afghanistan and the invasion of Iraq" (11.14.19). Other states frame the standards related to the effects of 9/11 from an inquiry perspective.

For example, Arkansas's standard states that students should "investigate the effects of the September 11, 2001 terrorist attack on the United States (19)," citing the Department of Homeland Security and Operation Enduring Freedom as examples. One of the most interesting examples of such standards comes from Georgia, which asks students to "analyze the response of President George W. Bush to the attacks of September 11, 2001" (USHSH25). This is unique, as it emphasizes the president's response while ignoring the response of the country, the world, or the people at large.

The majority of the standards in these thirty-three states ask students to know some aspect of the response to the 9/11 attacks, but most do not ask students to inquire into the causes and effects of these events or to deliberate the rationale for the response of the United States and its allies. Eight states do include standards that ask students to examine the roots of terrorism in general, at least to some degree. For example, South Dakota's standard simply requires that "students are able to explain cause-effect relationships and legacy" of key events (US 1.1), including 9/11 as a present-day example.

New Jersey's standard, on the other hand, requires more critical analysis: "Analyze why terrorist movements have proliferated, and evaluate their impact on governments, individuals, and societies" (6.2). Similarly, one of Washington's standards asks students to also evaluate the subsequent War on Terror, in particular to understand the "ramifications of mono-causal explanations" by evaluating "the validity of the attacks on 9/11 being the sole cause of the War on Terror" (4.3).

Some states also frame objectives related to 9/11 and the War on Terror as an examination of globalization as a cause of international terrorism. These standards ask that teachers engage students directly in analyzing the causal roots of 9/11 and the War on Terror and not simply cause-effect relationships in general.

Focus on International versus Domestic Terrorism

One trend in the standards that was also prominent in the textbooks was the emphasis on terrorism as an international phenomenon. Thirty of the states identify terrorism specifically in an international context, only identifying foreign terrorist groups and terrorist attacks occurring outside the United States. Therefore, terrorism is seen primarily in an international context, with a particular focus on the Middle East as a locus of terrorism.

For example, Hawaii's standards include terrorism as an example of one of the global challenges of the post–Cold War era. Arizona includes the study of the roots of terrorism in their standards, but includes only non-U.S. examples of terrorist groups and contexts. Indiana includes terrorism as an example for analyzing the "impact of globalization on U.S. economic, political and foreign policy" (USH.8.6). This theme of terrorism as having only foreign and not domestic roots represents a societal shift, post-9/11, away from examples of domestic terrorism such as the Unabomber and the attack on the Oklahoma City Federal Building.

In fact, only five states asked students to examine cases of terrorism with domestic roots. The Oklahoma City Federal Building bombing was the most prominent example. For example, Washington state includes the bombing of the Murrah Federal Building in Oklahoma City as an example within a standard that asks students to be able to examine how significant events lead to the development of historical eras (4.1.2). Oklahoma asks students to compare the causes and effects of the Oklahoma City bombing with the 9/11 attacks. This standard, in particular, places the focus of student study on both domestic and international examples of terrorism instead of associating terrorism directly with Islam or framing it as solely an international issue.

What Is Terrorism and Who Are Terrorists?

The word "terrorism" or the term "War on Terror" is used in thirty-two of the states' standards and is largely presented as if there were a fixed and concrete definition of what terrorism means. In reality, the concept of terrorism seems to be contested, based on our earlier research. Of course, standards primarily include only key terms, not going even as deep as a definition, which means that the framing of the concept of terrorism is then left up to the teachers and whatever sources they are using to engage their students.

This implicitly assumes that there is a clear and agreed-upon definition of the concept of terrorism to which the teacher can turn. When state standards do consider the meaning of terrorism (without defining it), they are often inconsistent with most widely accepted external definitions of terrorism, most of which define terrorism as a threat of violence against a civilian target for political goals—Georgia's standards identify modern terrorism, meaning twentieth century to current times, as a form of warfare (GA. HSWH. 20).

None of the standards provide enough detail, such as a definition, to identify their specific construction of terrorism, but several states' standards documents do recommend that students engage in *analyzing* how terrorism is defined. For example, a suggested activity in the Kansas Benchmark 4, which focuses on the examination of major events and turning points since 1990, asks students to examine how the media covers terrorism:

> Using newspapers and news magazines, read articles about acts of terrorism in the United States and around the world. Identify commonalities and differences in these attacks in terms of who, what, why, where, and how of the events.

While not explicitly identifying the contested definition of terrorism, this activity in essence asks students to conduct a concept formation lesson on terrorism through examining multiple cases and identifying the characteristics of what is labeled as a terrorist attack.

The Relationship between Islam and Terrorism

Given the lack of attention in the standards documents to the causes of terrorism, it is not surprising that there are few examples of standards intended to engage students in exploring the complex roots of terrorism and the complex histories of terrorist groups. Only eight of the states include standards that require students to analyze the causes of terrorism, and only four mention Osama bin Laden or al Qaeda.

Three states, however, specifically include Islam in the context of terrorism and 9/11. Massachusetts's standards place the focus of studying terrorism on Islamic fundamentalism and the Middle East without mentioning other examples of international terrorism, and they include no examples of domestic terrorism. Specifically, one of the world history standards asks students to "Explain the rise and funding of Islamic Fundamentalism in the last half of the 20th century" and, in particular, "the increase in terrorist attacks against Israel and the United States" (WHII.47).

Texas's standards promote a similar view of Islamic Fundamentalism and how it has impacted the United States. A world history standard focused on the rise of Islamic Fundamentalism and subsequent acts of terrorism includes two substandards: The first asks that students summarize the "development and impact of radical Islamic fundamentalism on events in the second half of the twentieth century, including Palestinian terrorism and the growth of al Qaeda," and the second asks students to "explain the U.S. response to terrorism from September 11, 2001" (14). Neither set of standards asks students to examine the root causes of terrorism within the context of the historical U.S. role in the Middle East.

By contrast, Louisiana's standards, which include the example of "Islamic terrorist organizations" (AH6.6), also include a standard that calls for the analysis of groups such as the Taliban and al Qaeda (WH7.6), placing the emphasis on the acts of particular groups and not in direct relation to religion. Louisiana's standards also include an item that asks students to compare the treatment of Japanese Americans during World War II to the treatment of Muslim Americans after 9/11 (AH1.2). The implicit message undergirding this standard is that stereotyping is wrong and dangerous. In other words, the message is that it is important not to link Islam explicitly with terrorism.

Contemporary Events, Open Questions, Deliberation, and Inquiry

Throughout our studies of how 9/11 and terrorism have been incorporated into curriculum, we have been especially interested in *how* students are being asked to engage with these events, and we sought to take our analysis beyond what content is included. We therefore examined the standards documents for how, or even if, issues and events related to 9/11 or terrorism are presented as open questions for students to inquire into or upon which to deliberate. In particular, we looked for open questions, which are presented as having multiple and competing legitimate answers.

We found that Washington's social studies skills standards, in particular, presented strong examples of open questions related to 9/11. One asks students to weigh evidence and "determine one's own stance on the war in Iraq" (5.4.1), and another directs students to critique different positions on the Patriot Act based on the Alien and Sedition Acts. In addition to the examples in the Washington standards, we found a number of states whose standards had at least the potential to promote inquiry and deliberation around issues related to the 9/11 attacks and the causes and effects of this event.

For example, West Virginia included a standard that asks students to "evaluate, take and defend a position involving a conflict between an individual freedom and the common good," with homeland security as one of the issues (12.01.09). These states did not explicitly include the standards as part of a goal of democratic citizenship, but we view these types of activities as critical to this goal.

In addition to deliberating controversial issues, there were other aspects of citizenship development related to 9/11 identified in some state standards. Four states explicitly addressed the role of citizens in the context of 9/11 and the War on Terror. Both Minnesota and Tennessee included standards that expressly linked citizenship to media literacy with respect to 9/11. In both of these standards, 9/11 was used as an opportunity for students to look at different forms of media (e.g., political cartoons, editorials, television news) and to critique these forms.

Minnesota's standard (Government & Citizenship VII.A.2) asked students to critically examine President Bush's address to the nation after 9/11, and Tennessee asked students to look at news media, to try to interview producers, and to author their own editorial critique (Culture 1). Here, students were asked to develop the skill of critically analyzing political messages in media, and, in the case of Tennessee, to also produce their own critique in a format commonly used in the political arena. Both of these skills are widely viewed as important for citizens in a democracy to possess. These standards also emphasize the need for citizens to be well informed about contemporary issues.

DISCUSSION: 9/11 AND ITS AFTERMATH IN STATE STANDARDS DOCUMENTS

Similar themes have emerged from our analysis of the state academic standards and our earlier studies of curriculum. However, the 9/11 attacks and their aftermath are less prominent in standards than they were in textbooks, in part because of the nature of standards in general—in particular, their low level of detail. However, the state standards explicitly called for students to engage in the examination of the causes and effects of the 9/11 attacks and other controversial aspects of the aftermath of 9/11 (e.g., the Patriot Act) more often than the curricula we examined in our earlier research, particularly in comparison to textbooks.

These findings are limited by state and regional variations; some states design standards that encourage student engagement in critical inquiry or analyzing the roots of terrorism, while others want students to engage in intellectual work that assumes that the roots of international terrorism lie in Islam. State standards reflect the political views of the bodies that produce them, and because they are more localized, they reflect a greater diversity in views of 9/11 and its aftermath than textbooks (which do their best to remain a more neutral source for all states) or curriculum developed by groups with specific niche audiences of teachers and schools in mind.

As most standards are written in the form of an objective, or an outcome that students are expected to reach at the end of the associated course or level of schooling, there is often little narrative structure and few explicit tasks or questions designed for student engagement. Instead, these documents are meant to outline the outcomes teachers should use to design their courses and lessons and to control the content being taught in those lessons. However, because they are written as objectives, some states' standards appear to provide more opportunities to engage in higher levels of intellectual work, inquiry, or analysis than other curricular forms, such as textbooks, provide.

Of course, the specificity of these objectives, as we noted above, also means that our analysis of the potential impact of standards on what is taught needs to be context specific and made with at least one major caveat. This is, in part, because some states are formally assessed and therefore teachers may have a higher level of accountability to align their lessons more closely with the standards than in other states, as we discuss further below.

Although our key terms related to 9/11 appeared relatively less often than in our previous curriculum and textbook studies, the nature of the thinking associated with many of these standards included more opportunities for students to engage in the causes and effects of 9/11, as well as to inquire into the controversies that emerged. This does not guarantee, however, that these will be taught in an open or deliberative way or in a way that necessarily requires higher order thinking.

For example, in Virginia, standards are written in a way that appears to require inquiry. However, because Virginia also requires students to pass Standards of Learning (SOL) exams at the end of high school, students may still be taught in a manner designed to transmit the correct answer to students. In the Virginia World History II SOL, standard 16 states that "The student will demonstrate knowledge of cultural, economic, and social conditions in developed and developing nations of the contemporary world" by, among other things, "analyzing the increasing impact of terrorism." Though the term "analyzing" is used, there is still a correct answer that will be needed when this particular standard is assessed on the end-of-course exam, a fact that may limit the kinds of open inquiry and deliberative pedagogy that, it is often claimed, promote democratic citizenship (Gould, 2011).

In states that have standardized, multiple-choice end-of-course exams, such as Virginia, there is a "correct" answer that teachers need to make sure that students know, and this may inhibit a teacher's ability to teach using inquiry or deliberation. Roughly half of all states have some form of standardized assessment for social studies. Among these states, there is a range of implementations, from optional assessments to graduation exams or yearly end-of-course assessments.

The assessments themselves also vary; with some, such as the New York Regents exams, including document-based question items in addition to multiple-choice items, and others assessing in a more limited way. For example, in Arizona, which recently adopted the test given to aspiring U.S. citizens as a graduation requirement, there would be no incentive to engage students in real inquiry or deliberation, as this might not help students to identify the kinds of "correct" answers the items in the test call for. The more standards are framed around specific events and people, the less room there is for teachers to address contemporary events and issues in class.

Even with this limitation, however, it is notable that ten years after the attacks, many states included an emphasis on engaging students in examination of post-9/11 policies, such as the Patriot Act. While this is positive, these items advocating critical inquiry or deliberation were far less common than we would hope, and it is difficult to assess the impact of these standards on actual teacher practice. One can imagine a teacher in a state without a state assessment using the Choices curriculum on foreign policy choices after 9/11 in order to work toward a standard that asks students to examine the causes and effects of the attacks. However, a teacher in the next classroom could be teaching a lesson that aligned with the same standard through a lecture on the causes and effects of the attacks and the U.S. response. The alignment of standards with key assessments at the local or state level, along with the school or district level adoption of particular pedagogical models (e.g., deliberation, inquiry), can greatly impact any real influence of these standards on classroom practice and the opportunity students have to engage in activities designed to promote civic/democratic education.

CONCLUSIONS

When we began our study of the curricular response to 9/11 over a decade ago, we found that state curricular frameworks, assessments, and textbooks used static content that provided little flexibility, let alone the motivation, for teachers to engage their students in contemporary issues that arose from a national crisis such as the terrorist attacks. We found that some of the organizations that produced supplemental curriculum were better able to respond to events like the 9/11 attacks than textbook producers. These organizations provided current, in-depth, and engaging curricula for the development of citizens.

The state standards offer a similar mixed bag of potential. Some present nationalistic themes related to 9/11 and terrorism similar to that which we observed in the textbooks, and few include thoughtful ways to engage students in inquiry into the causes of modern terrorism and deliberation of how we might respond to it. Many, however, appear to provide opportunities for students to go beyond rote memorization of facts about the events and provide teachers with the opportunity to engage their students in evaluating, critiquing, and deliberating post-9/11 policies and actions.

However, we have also made the point here that standards documents should not be examined in isolation, without an understanding of the relationship of the standard to any aligned assessments or the role that standards play in school or teacher curricular decision making. It is also important to limit any conclusions about the inclusion of any particular events, perspectives, or individuals to the nature of the standards documents themselves. This includes analyses that attempt to grade standards based on key terms that may promote the reduction of standards to a list of facts to be memorized.

We are not advocating for documents to list every single event, concept, term, or individual that should be taught in social studies classrooms, which would take away the ability of teachers to engage their students in events such as the 9/11 attacks and the domestic policy decisions and military actions taken since then. What we do advocate is the inclusion of performance objectives that align with the goals of democratic education and allow, or even require, teachers to address historic and contemporary public policy, social, and international issues that shape the world we live in, much like the events of 9/11 and its aftermath have.

ACKNOWLEDGMENTS

Thanks to the many former graduate students who contributed to the collection and analysis of data for the 9/11 curriculum and textbook studies, and specifically for the state standards portion of the study: Amy Kuenker, College of William & Mary, and Brian Gibbs and Taehan Kim, University of Wisconsin–Madison. Other graduate students who contributed to other portions of these studies are listed in footnote three of the *Social Education* article.

NOTES

1. We followed a similar protocol in our analysis of the standards as we did the curriculum and textbooks. We began by searching the standards documents for key terms used in the previous stages of the study (e.g., 9/11, terrorism/ist, al-Qaeda, Patriot Act). We then captured all of the standards or substandards with these references for qualitative analysis. In particular, we focused on how 9/11 and the concept of terrorism was represented, what examples of terrorism and terrorists were included, and the nature of the intended intellectual work in the standard. For this latter aspect of the analysis, we were particularly interested in what was being presented as controversial or as an open question with multiple and competing "correct" answers.

2. An earlier version of this dataset was released as a CIRCLE FactSheet (Stoddard & Hess, 2011). The data used here were updated in 2012 and reflect state standards at that time.

3. All states make their curriculum standards public through their respective department of education or public instruction websites. Readers interested in analyzing the standards for themselves can access them there through a simple google search (e.g., "Iowa secondary social studies standards").

REFERENCES

Au, W. W. (2009). Social studies, social justice: W(h)ither the social studies in high-stakes testing? *Teacher Education Quarterly, 36,* 43–58.
Glencoe. (2005). *Street law: A practical course in practical law*. New York: McGraw-Hill Education.
Gould, J. (2011). *Guardian of democracy: The civic mission of schools*. Philadelphia: Annenberg Public Policy Center of the University of Pennsylvania.
Grant, S. G. (Ed.). (2006). *Measuring history: Cases of state-level testing across the United States*. Greenwich, CT: Information Age Publishing.
Hess, D., & McAvoy, P. (2015). *The political classroom: Evidence and ethics in democratic education*. New York: Routledge.
Hess, D., & Stoddard, J. (2007). 9/11 and terrorism: "The ultimate teachable moment" in textbooks and supplemental curricula. *Social Education, 71,* 231–236.
———. (2011). 9/11 in the curricula: A retrospective. *The Social Studies, 102,* 175–179.
Hess, D., Stoddard, J., & Murto, S. (2008). Examining the treatment of 9/11 and terrorism in high school textbooks. In J. Bixby & J. Pace (Eds.), *Educating democratic citizens in troubled times: Qualitative studies of current efforts* (pp. 192–226). Albany: State University of New York Press.

Stoddard, J., & Hess, D. (2011). 9/11 and the war on terror in curricula and state standards documents. *The Center for Information Research on Civic Learning & Engagement (CIRCLE)*. Retrieved from http://www.civicyouth.org/911-is-now-in-textbooks-and-standards.

Stoddard, J., Hess, D., & Hammer, C. (2011). The challenges of writing "first draft history": The evolution of the 9/11 attacks and their aftermath in school textbooks in the United States. In L. Yates & M. Grumet (Eds.), *2011 world yearbook of education: Curricula in today's world: Identities, politics, work, and knowledge* (pp. 223–236). New York: Routledge.

Chapter Three

Including 9/11 in the Elementary Grades

State Standards, Digital Resources, and Children's Books

Elizabeth Bellows

Before 2001, time spent on social studies instruction in elementary schools was already on the decline as teachers were charged with imparting a restrictive curriculum that focused on literacy and mathematics (Boyle-Baise, Hsu, Johnson, Serriere, & Stewart, 2008). As an effect of the reauthorization of the 1965 Elementary and Secondary Education Act in the form of the No Child Left Behind legislation of 2001, the teaching of elementary social studies became even more of an infrequent occurrence.

Longer-lasting effects of this legislation include hotly debated topics such as what and whose history to include in the official curriculum, the promotion of capitalistic ways to teach economics concepts, and the use of disconnected social studies themed children's books to teach literacy in the spirit of content integration. Just as educators were preparing to shift their curricular focus, the nation was shaken to its core as teachers and schoolchildren across the nation witnessed and learned about the destruction of buildings, lives, and families on September 11, 2001.

Sander and Putnam (2010) found that on the heels of the (inter)national crisis of 9/11, those who experienced the crisis during their most impressionable years—known as the Millennials, or the post-9/11 generation—"seem[ed] to grasp their civic and mutual responsibilities far more firmly than [did] their parents" and that "the years since 9/11 have brought an unmistakable expansion of youth interest in politics and public affairs" (p. 11). Despite this promising finding, the authors acknowledge significant subtrends masked by the conflating of race and class in public discussion in the United States.

That is, most of the rise in political engagement among young people can be attributed to youth raised in more affluent homes and not those who are from lower- and working-class families. The researchers warn that "[i]f the United States is to avoid becoming two nations, it must find ways to expand the post-9/11 resurgence of civic and social engagement beyond the ranks of affluent young white people" (p. 14). This charge is especially important for elementary educators in an era of increasingly diverse public school populations, disparities between social class and neighborhood schools, and dichotomous political ideologies.

The elementary classroom is the first public space most children encounter that provides them with a microcosm of the larger civic space. In these tiny replicas of society students experience shared knowledge acquisition about cultural norms, what it means to be a "good" citizen, and what events or rituals are significant to mention (or abandon) in these shared spaces. Without clear aims and purposes for this shared knowledge, there exists a risk that the ways in which social studies content is contextualized could result in shallow and inconsequential learning experiences for children.

This chapter describes the challenges presented in teaching elementary children about 9/11 and its aftermath, the curricular abandonment of 9/11 as a worthy topic of inclusion in state standards, and the messages this sends to educators and students. Digital resources from reputable sources available for elementary teachers are then showcased before concluding with a brief analysis of children's books that can be used to teach 9/11 with purposes of highlighting civic action.

ELEMENTARY SOCIAL STUDIES POST-9/11

Social studies education experienced dichotomous reactions in the immediate aftermath of 9/11, and the chasm between these differences has only continued to grow. *Rethinking Schools* (2001) published a special report at the end of that year that posed compelling questions and encouraged critical thinking in the wake of this globalized event. The National Council for the Social Studies's (NCSS) journal *Social Education* responded similarly with an end-of-year issue whose contributors encouraged students to "learn, question, analyze, and think critically about the values and perspectives behind media messages" (Hobbs, 2001).

On the other side of this rift, Chester E. Finn, Jr. (2002) of the Thomas B. Fordham Foundation criticized lessons suggested by NCSS, Rethinking Schools, and other educational organizations for being "long on multiculturalism, feelings, relativism, and tolerance but short on history, civics, and patriotism" (p. 5). Finn further belittled teachers and their sense of agency and academic freedom to teach in multicultural ways to their diverse students. Finn's rationale for teaching after 9/11 was to

> buttress the civic values and enlarge the knowledge base of teachers and other educators—and to redress the balance between those who would have the schools forge citizens and those who would have them focus on students' own feelings and on doubts about America. (pp. 5–6)

For Finn, the teaching of multiculturalism and tolerance undermined the goals of patriotism within civic education after 9/11.

Though social studies scholars and stakeholders contributed ideas about teaching 9/11 couched within the theme of civic education during this time, I have discovered an alarming finding about the Millennial preservice teachers in my university classes. College students who were in grades one to eight on 9/11 can rarely recall any kind of meaningful lesson, discussion, or explanation by their K–12 teachers about the attacks. These data suggest that the curricular abandonment of 9/11 as a worthy social studies topic has provided teachers with less critical understandings of important terms such as patriotism and citizenship.

It seems, then, that the prevailing beliefs surrounding the teaching of 9/11 in the elementary grades should be reconsidered. The next section outlines the states that consider 9/11 a worthy social studies topic in their standards, what purposes those standards convey, and the messages these standards send to teachers and curriculum designers. After this discussion, digital resources are provided for teachers who desire to teach about 9/11 in more critical ways. The chapter then concludes with a brief analysis of several children's trade books focused on 9/11 that can help teachers broach these complex topics.

ELEMENTARY SOCIAL STUDIES STANDARDS: THE CURRICULAR ABANDONMENT OF 9/11

Considering social studies is currently perceived as insignificant and unimportant (Barton & Levstik, 2004; Brophy, Alleman, & Knighton, 2009), it is no surprise that only eight states in the nation have included the topic of 9/11 in their official elementary (K–6) social studies standards almost fifteen years after the events, and only one of these states includes the topic of 9/11 within the curricular strand of citizenship (Bellows & Groce, 2014). Table 3.1 shows each of these eight states and their respective standards that reference 9/11.

Elementary social studies state standards are organized into five strands: history, geography, civics and government (citizenship), economics, and culture, and these states have chosen

Table 3.1. Elementary Social Studies State Standards that Mention 9/11

State	Example Content Standard and Grade Level	Strand
Alabama	Grade 6: Explaining how conflict in the Middle East impacted life in the United States since World War II. Examples: oil embargoes; Iranian hostage situation; Camp David Accords; Persian Gulf Wars; 1993 World Trade Center bombing; terrorist attacks on September 11, 2001; War on Terrorism; homeland security.	History
Arkansas	Grade 6: Conflict and consensus: Discuss the ongoing conflicts between the United States and Southeast Asia, and the Middle East. Examine acts of modern-day terrorism (e.g., Oklahoma City bombing, World Trade Center attacks).	History
Georgia	Grade 5: The Student will trace important developments in America since 1975. Describe U.S. involvement in world events; including efforts to bring peace to the Middle East, the collapse of the Soviet Union, the Persian Gulf War, and the War on Terrorism in response to September 11, 2001.	History
Oklahoma	Grade 4: Identify the historic significance of major national monuments, historic sites, and landmarks including 9/11 memorials.	Geography
South Carolina	Grades 5–6: Challenges in Foreign Diplomacy: Explain the impact of the September 11, 2001, terrorist attacks on the United States, including the wars in Iraq and Afghanistan and the home front responses to terrorism.	History
Texas	Grade 3: Identify and compare the heroic deeds of state and national heroes, including Hector P. Garcia and James A. Lovell, and other individuals such as Harriet Tubman, Juliette Gordon Low, Todd Beamer, Ellen Ochoa, John "Danny" Olivas, and other contemporary heroes.	Culture
Vermont	Grades 5–6: 1. Identifying an important event in the United States and/or world, and describing multiple causes and effects of that event. 2. Explaining transitions between eras that occurred over time (e.g., the end of the Colonial era) as well as those that occurred as a result of a pivotal event (e.g., September 11, the writing of the Declaration of Independence).	History
West Virginia	Grade 6: Compare/contrast different forms of government worldwide and their influence on historic world events—Great Depression, WWI, WWII, 9/11; SS.6.C.5—examine and analyze various acts of patriotism and civil discourse in response to events throughout US history (support of American military during wartime . . . respect for the flag and response of Americans to 9/11); SS.6.H.CL6.3—identify the key figures in Middle Eastern conflicts and investigate the US reaction to these events (e.g., Saddam Hussein, Osama bin Laden, terrorism, 9/11, wars in Iraq and Afghanistan).	Civics

to frame their coverage of 9/11 differently. For example, Texas and Alabama include standards about 9/11 as early as third grade in the strands of culture and geography. The third-grade Texas standard states that students are expected to

> *identify and compare the heroic deeds of state and national heroes, including* Hector P. Garcia and James A. Lovell, and other individuals *such as* Harriet Tubman, Juliette Gordon Low, *Todd Beamer*, Ellen Ochoa, John "Danny" Olivas, and other contemporary heroes. (emphasis added)

Todd Beamer was aboard United Airlines Flight 93 (which crashed in Shanksville, Pennsylvania) and is known for stating, "Let's roll," while rallying other passengers to attempt to reclaim the flight from hijackers. In this curricular objective, the topic of 9/11 begins with a conversation about heroism but provides no context for discussing the events of 9/11 that led up to, or followed, this act of heroism. Because the language in this standard uses the term "such as" before listing Beamer's name, teachers are not required to use him as an example. Given that this is the only mention of any content related to 9/11, third-grade students might not learn about Beamer, Flight 93, or any other aspect of 9/11.

In Alabama, standards involving 9/11 are housed within the geography strand, expecting students to locate historical landmarks on maps: "the capitol of the U.S., the Alabama state capitol, *previous site of the twin towers of the World Trade Center in New York*, Statue of Liberty, Pearl Harbor" (emphasis added). Without providing historic or civic context in either of these examples, this inclusion of 9/11 promotes students' limited understanding of a global crisis while trivializing not only the events that occurred that day, but also the varied responses to governmental decisions that affected all citizens.

Other states that name 9/11 as a curricular topic in their K–6 standards include Arkansas, Georgia, Oklahoma, South Carolina, Vermont, and West Virginia. Besides West Virginia, however, the ways in which 9/11 is taught in elementary classrooms are not situated within the broader context of conflict resolution or citizenship. Rather, they fall under the strands of history, geography, and culture.

Messages in the Standards

As the curricular history of teaching 9/11 has only begun to be constructed, the standards reveal troubling messages to educators. The most alarming aspects of the language used in the elementary standards are the simple lists of decontextualized facts and information associated with 9/11. Five states—Alabama, Georgia, South Carolina, Vermont, and West Virginia—construct learning objectives as "justice narratives" (Duckworth, 2015) or narratives intended to justify U.S. military action, the limitation of freedoms within the United States, and "authoritarian patriotism" (Westheimer, 2009) in response to the attacks.

Given the troubling messages in the way state standards are considering (or abandoning) 9/11 as a topic of investigation, it is incumbent that teachers explore other resources before planning instruction. As anniversaries of the attacks come and go, children will stumble upon some television footage, radio mention, social media, or adult conversations about the event. This is the perfect time to allow students' questions to guide their inquiry into the topic of 9/11.

DIGITAL RESOURCES

The following digital resources for teaching about 9/11 in the elementary grades are easily accessible, proposed by organizations teachers might consider reputable, and offer alternatives to teaching 9/11 to children in the absence of the topic's mention in most state-sanctioned curricular documents. Though some of the resources cater more to a secondary audience (which I will discuss below), each provides at least a starting point for teachers whether it be for their own content knowledge, primary and secondary source access, or lesson plans.

Library of Congress: September 11, 2001, Documentary Project (http://www.loc.gov/teachers/classroommaterials/connections/september11/index.html)

This online project uses primary sources such as eyewitness accounts, photographs, drawings, audio and video interviews, and written narratives to contextualize the events and aftermath of 9/11. Teachers are guided through an overview of the collection and then introduced to a brief history of the event, which "captures the voices of men and women from diverse ethnic and socioeconomic backgrounds." In this section, the authors of the project offer caution to teachers:

> Teachers using the collection should be aware that some of the stories told in the interviews are disturbing reminders of the magnitude of the tragedy. Teachers should help students prepare to deal with the emotions that the interviews may evoke.

The sections in the Documentary Project are organized by eyewitness accounts of the attacks, the attacks as experienced via the media, public response to the attacks, and perspectives of first responders to the attacks.

Responses to the attacks are described in various ways, as experienced by people of different geographic locations, ethnic backgrounds, and ages. Most notable in this section is the collection's guidance in helping students understand the multiple responses that occurred immediately following the attacks. Considering that many of the aforementioned state standards want students to understand the War on Terror in response to the 9/11 attacks or home front responses to terrorism, the Documentary Project offers multiple perspectives that help students make this inquiry in more critical ways than are stated in these standards.

The suggested activity in this section requires students to make a three-column chart:

> In the first column, list three areas of disagreement among Americans following September 11. In the September 11, 2001 Documentary Project collection, find at least three different views on each area of disagreement identified. For each view, select a quote from an interview that represents that view and place it in the third column. What does this exercise tell you about Americans? Is this insight important? Why or why not?

Instead of teaching students that the U.S. response was to go to war, or that there were similar home front responses to the attacks, the Documentary Project uses historical thinking methods to allow students to make their own interpretations of how different people responded in different ways.

The September 11, 2001, Documentary Project uses sound social studies instructional methods and offers teaching ideas that highlight the importance of civic discourse, the consideration of multiple perspectives when studying a historical event, and encouragement of critical thinking. Additionally, the Documentary Project uses the voices of citizens that allow students, as critical citizens themselves, to develop their own interpretations of eyewitness accounts and views of those who may hold different beliefs than themselves.

Teaching History: In Remembrance: Teaching September 11
(http://teachinghistory.org/spotlight/september11)

Teaching History's remembrance website offers three sections for readers: Learning Resources, Teaching Resources, and a section called Remember and Reflect, which encourages visitors to "explore memories of 9/11 or contribute your own story." The Learning Resources section contains seventeen links to various resources that allow teachers to inform their own content knowledge before embarking on lessons with students. The first page of this section displays eight links, and each of these links leads teachers to a plethora of valuable resources. One helpful section offers web resources for controversial issues in order to spark healthy discussion in classrooms, and another addresses the use of structured academic controversy.

Though the resources provided by Teaching History are useful, they tend to cater to a secondary audience, which reveals a common problem for elementary educators. Oftentimes when my elementary preservice teachers seek out teaching resources in our methods course, they notice either meaningless, trite lessons geared for elementary students, or lessons that are not developmentally appropriate for young learners. Organizations such as Teaching History should recognize that elementary teachers also teach history, and desire to do so using appropriate methods that promote critical thinking and student discussion.

U.S. Department of Education: 9/11 Materials for Teachers
(http://www.ed.gov/911anniversary)

The U.S. Department of Education (ED) offers 9/11 materials for teachers and provides a disclaimer at the top of the website:

> These materials were developed by federal grantees and agencies in commemoration of the tenth anniversary of September 11, 2001. The materials are provided as a convenience for teachers and others seeking resources for teaching about September 11. ED does not control or guarantee the accuracy, relevance, timeliness, or completeness of these materials, nor does the inclusion of links to these materials represent an endorsement of these materials or organizations that created them.

Links on the site direct readers to various organizational websites before listing a collection of five links titled "Materials from Other Federal Agencies." The organizational websites include direct links to the Center for Civic Education (CCE), where teachers can find lessons about what it means to be an American, fundamental ideas about government that Americans share, and how well the government is fulfilling its purposes. These lessons are provided as a connection between Constitution Day and 9/11, though none of the lessons provided by the CCE mention September 11, the terrorist attacks, or legislation following the attacks (such as the Patriot Act).

Another resource provided on the ED website links readers to the Constitutional Rights Foundation Chicago (CRFC). The link to the CRFC does not include any lessons on 9/11; instead, the teaching materials on this site must be searched via grade level, topic, piece of the Constitution, and teaching strategy. A thorough search of all elementary teaching materials revealed an absence of any mention of 9/11. The clear message here is that if you are going to teach about 9/11, you need to be teaching about the Constitution.

The next section on the site's homepage lists "Materials from Other Federal Agencies," which might be the most helpful section of the site. The Corporation for National and Community Service provides teachers with a list of instances of people serving and ideas about how one might serve their local or national community to honor victims of 9/11. The ED lists the aforementioned Library of Congress Documentary Project followed by a link to the National

Archives where the 9/11 Commission Records are housed. Though recommended for teachers to contextualize their own content knowledge, these links would not be helpful for student use in an elementary classroom.

The final link in the "Materials from Other Federal Agencies" section leads teachers to the National Park Service Flight 93 National Memorial site. Though there are a few links at the bottom of this page, the site reads:

> The memorial is committed to the nation's youngest citizens and future stewards. The coming years will be a period of growth and change at the memorial and in its role as [a] place of learning. Guiding students to a deeper understanding of September 11 is not easy, but we are committed to working together to educate and inspire. Please check back as we expand our resources and program[m]ing. [http://www.nps.gov/flni/learn/education/index.html]

Once again, the silence around teaching about 9/11 with young children is deafening, as many sites ignore elementary learners in their collections of resources or leave their sites in an outdated state.

Rethinking Schools
(http://www.rethinkingschools.org/special_reports/sept11/index.shtml)

The organization has maintained its special report "War, Terrorism and Our Classrooms" in digital form on its website since 2001. The report serves as a critical first step for any educator with the desire to teach about 9/11, as it provides counternarratives to the stories that are already so well known about what happened fifteen years ago. There are no less than thirty-two editorials, articles, firsthand accounts, classroom activities, historical contextual pieces, image analyses, and other submissions to the report that help provide teachers and students with more nuanced views of 9/11 that showcase the complexities of this period of time in our history.

In addition to the variety of types of sources included, the report includes multiple perspectives via diverse author voices. For example, a rabbi answers the question "Where does the violence come from?" A victim's parents plead with the U.S. government not to engage in war in their son's name. Poet Suheir Hammad shares her "first writing since" the 9/11 attacks. The organization Educators for Social Responsibility discusses how to talk to children and help them cope with such tragedies.

Each of these contributions is unique, and each represents a different perspective or piece of the mosaic to help children understand the intricacies of difficult concepts such as terrorism, war, justice, humanity, and freedom. Though Rethinking Schools does not offer already-designed lesson plans for classroom use, the "War, Terrorism and Our Classrooms" report is an integral resource for any teacher who desires to broach the topic of 9/11 with his or her young learners.

9/11 Memorial: Teach + Learn
(https://www.911memorial.org/teach-learn)

The 9/11 Memorial and Museum opened its doors in May 2014 and provides education programs and workshops on site that are differentiated by grade level and aligned to Common Core Standards. There are three workshops offered for young learners (two for grades three to five and one for grades three to eight) and "are designed to challenge students to think critically about a wide range of topics related to 9/11." For those who cannot visit the museum in person, the Teach + Learn portion of the museum's website offers three sections for readers: Learn about 9/11, Teaching 9/11, and Talk to Children about 9/11.

The Learn about 9/11 portion offers:

- a brief history about the World Trade Center
- information about the rescue and recovery after 9/11
- 9/11-related terror, such as the World Trade Center bombing in 1993, bombing of the USS *Cole* in 2000, the bombing of four trains in Madrid in 2004, and the 7/7 bombings in London in 2005.

The reporting of these events helps give educators some context for what was going on in the world at this time but does not help teachers make sense of what happened on 9/11 in a way that might help them facilitate discussions with their young students.

Alternatively, the Teaching 9/11 section of the website offers a study guide (for middle school and high school learners) and a free download of materials intended for use before a visit to the museum. Lesson plans included in this section were conceived and designed by teachers and are aligned to Common Core Standards. There are lesson plans for young learners, and the museum's website suggests starting with a questioning of students' prior knowledge about the World Trade Center, what they think happened on 9/11, and what they wonder about with respect to that day. In this way, students' inquiry leads the teacher's design of the next lessons.

The website offers sixteen lesson plans for K–2 learners, and twenty-eight lesson plans for students in grades three to five. A handful of the lesson plans in both of these sections overlap. Many of the lesson plans for elementary students incorporate children's literature, namely, *The Man in the Red Bandana*, *September Roses*, *The Little Chapel That Stood*, *Bravemole*, and others. Along with the lesson plans, the museum offers an age-appropriate *9/11 Fact Sheet for Early Childhood Students*. This fact sheet helps students answer the following questions:

- What was the World Trade Center?
- What were the Twin Towers?
- What is 9/11?
- What happened to the Twin Towers and the World Trade Center?
- Why did the terrorists do this?
- How can we remember what happened on September 11, 2001?

With many years to think about and design these lessons before publishing them on their website, the resources offered by the 9/11 Memorial are extensive enough for elementary teachers to make choices based on their different purposes for teaching about 9/11. The website is easy to navigate and provides helpful interactive timelines for both teachers and students that incorporate images, audio, and video snippets. In addition to the timelines, the website has many primary sources, webcasts, images, and videos to help teachers and students contextualize 9/11.

Overall, searches within these five organizational websites reveal some similarities in the analysis of the state standards. For some available digital resources, not much is being discussed in terms of 9/11 and elementary instruction, and the messages revealed in them can potentially be erroneous or even harmful to children. On the other hand, some of the resources are rich with the inclusion of diverse voices, primary sources, and critical-thinking activities.

CHILDREN'S TRADE BOOKS ABOUT 9/11

Because elementary teachers must teach every content area, and every strand of the social studies, they are left with little time for curricular design and instructional planning. Oftentimes in their frustration they turn to lessons that are "cute" instead of lessons that "count" (Bauml, 2016), as is evident in elementary teachers' overuse of popular websites such as Pinterest and Teachers Pay Teachers. Other resources widely available to and frequently used by teachers, also seen as ways to integrate social studies with English language arts objectives, are children's books.

There are numerous children's books available that discuss or tell stories using 9/11 as the context. Table 3.2 provides a list of the books Bellows, Groce, and Frye (2015) analyzed and how they categorized each book's narrative purpose. This list was compiled based on popularity (books we have seen most often being used in elementary classrooms) and accessibility (whether the book was a print-on-demand or available from a nationally recognized publishing house).

Clearly, most children's books focus their narratives of 9/11 on symbolic representations of hope and resilience and sympathetic responses through some sort of community or social action. In a study of preservice teachers, only 4 percent of participants expressed their thoughts about teaching 9/11 through notions of civic practice (Bellows & Bodle, 2015). Initial findings from this study led the researchers to suggest the use of children's books in elementary social studies instruction to assist teachers in thinking about teaching 9/11 for a larger purpose of sympathetic response and civic action, six of which are described here.

Table 3.2. Children's Books about 9/11 and Their Narrative Purposes

Book Title	Narrative Purpose
Bravemole	Symbol of hope and resilience Demonizes the perpetrators*
Fireboat: The Heroic Adventures of the John J. Harvey	Sympathetic response through action Symbol of hope and resilience
14 Cows for America	Sympathetic response through action Symbol of hope and resilience International connection
It's Still a Dog's New York: A Book of Healing	Symbol of hope and resilience
On that Day: A Book of Hope for Children	Symbol of hope and resilience
September Roses	Sympathetic response through action Symbol of hope and resilience International connection
September 11, 2001 (a simple account for children)	Overt Patriotism/Belligerent Citizenship
The Day the Towers Fell: The Story of September 11, 2001	Symbol of hope and resilience
The Man in the Red Bandana	Symbol of hope and resilience
The Little Chapel that Stood	Sympathetic response through action Symbol of hope and resilience
The Survivor Tree: Inspired by a True Story	Sympathetic response through action Symbol of hope and resilience

*This category was added to the analysis completed by Bellows, Groce, and Frye (2015).

September Roses

The short, colorfully illustrated book *September Roses* tells the true story of two sisters who are commercial rose growers from South Africa preparing to attend a floral show in New York City. After arriving in the city on September 11, 2001, the sisters became stranded at the airport with their 2,400 roses. Help came in the form of a stranger who volunteered to drive the sisters to Union Square where the sisters wanted to offer their roses in response to the kindness extended to them.

The "homegrown memorial" (Kimmelman, 2001) provided a space for collective mourning, as family members searched and prayed for their missing loved ones. This book provides an international perspective to the attacks and adds a civic element that highlights the humanity of people and how they oftentimes feel compelled to give of themselves and collectively mourn in moments of crisis.

14 Cows for America

14 Cows for America tells the story of a young man, Kimeli Naiyomah, who returned to his Maasai village in western Kenya only a few months after he experienced 9/11 from the vantage point of New York City. Naiyomah emotionally recounts the terrorist attacks as the heartbroken villagers listen with sympathetic hearts. When an American diplomat visits the Maasai people, he is humbled to accept their gift to American citizens: fourteen cows that represent life.

The unexpected and thoughtful gift helps readers see there is power in sympathetic responses that can help others heal. As in *September Roses*, *14 Cows for America* provides an international perspective and a way to help students understand difficult content by relating to the role of a sympathetic witness who responds to tragedy through gracious action.

Fireboat: The Heroic Adventures of the John J. Harvey

Fireboat: The Heroic Adventures of the John J. Harvey introduces children to an old boat in the New York City Harbor that was retired in 1995. The boat was revived by a group of friends, and they were called upon on September 11, 2001, to help battle the fires ablaze in Manhattan. The book showcases the everyday hero and how small acts of a few can make a significant difference. The illustrations are colorful and poignant and help children make sense of a tragedy through the eyes of civic action.

It's Still a Dog's New York

As a parable of childhood bereavement, *It's Still a Dog's New York* presents two dog-buddies, Pepper and Rover, who are grieving over the losses of their city post-9/11. The book's author, Susan Roth, consulted three child psychiatrists before writing it. The mixed-media photographic collage approach to the book, along with its vertical spread, helps emphasize the height of the buildings and the cityscape in New York City. The book insinuates the collective identity that we are strong enough to survive, and it is alright to feel. In this way, the book serves as a symbol of hope and resilience, how citizens behave in moments of crisis, and how they overcome.

The Survivor Tree

A Callery Pear tree was discovered in the aftermath of 9/11, still alive but badly injured. The tree was rescued and taken outside of New York City to a nursery where it could be revived. *The Survivor Tree* tells the true story of this pear tree and its journey away from, and back to, New York City where it is planted and thriving today at the 9/11 Memorial site. *The Survivor Tree*—both the story and the tree—also serves as a symbol of hope, recovery, and resilience after an unthinkable tragedy. It also highlights the civic action of the tree's rescuers in order to keep this symbol alive.

The Little Chapel that Stood

Just east of Ground Zero stands St. Paul's Chapel, bordered by a wrought-iron fence. During the collapse of the towers, firefighters would use the fence to hang their shoes and pull on their fireman's boots, and some were not able to return to retrieve their shoes. The fence, and then the undamaged church it enclosed, became symbols of hope, resilience, and recovery for the workers at Ground Zero.

The Little Chapel that Stood describes the history behind this church and how workers eventually used it as a place of respite, a dining hall, and a gathering place in times of mourning. Today, the chapel has its own museum qualities, adorning patches and service hats of firemen and policemen. You can also see the markings and chipped paint on a preserved church pew where firefighters' flak jackets scarred up the benches as they took quick naps between rescue efforts.

CONCLUDING THOUGHTS

A teacher's self-reflection of her purposes for choosing any of these resources for inclusion in her classroom will no doubt color the student outcomes of investigating this topic. My intention was not to necessarily recommend any or all the websites and children's books analyzed here, but to showcase a handful of options most readily available for elementary teachers on the teaching of 9/11. Without a clearly articulated and driving purpose behind choosing any of these resources, however, the intentions of these resources' authors could just as easily be met or neglected.

As is true for the teaching of any social studies content, more than providing elementary teachers with ready-made instructional plans, they should be provided with opportunities to critically examine their purposes for teaching this content, as well as the resources available to them in order to design instruction based on the needs and interests of their students. In this digital age with more resources than one can possibly digest, it is important that teachers do not equate *more* with *better* when seeking out resources for teaching difficult content. Being aware of the usefulness of websites can help us in more critical quests for effective materials that will benefit our students (Salinas, Bellows, & Liaw, 2011).

Once a teacher can clearly identify and articulate a purpose (or purposes) for teaching about the topic of 9/11, I challenge the learning to expand beyond a lesson or a unit. For example, teaching with big ideas (Grant & Gradwell, 2010) can provide students with opportunities to revisit overarching questions even as the topics of study change. As elementary teachers approach the teaching of 9/11, I encourage them to carefully consider and create compelling questions that get at the heart of their purposes for teaching about this difficult topic and use these questions to frame an array of content throughout the year.

There is a present urgency to the messages that learning about 9/11 can potentially render to students. Since 9/11, our nation's political landscape has become increasingly polarized and decreasingly tolerant of those whose fundamental beliefs are in disagreement with culturally dominant ones. To cease perpetuation of the learning of broad, uncritical lists of content knowledge, there is a substantial need for elementary social studies teachers to investigate the teaching of difficult content, such as 9/11, in thorough and profound ways. An inquiry into 9/11 can create spaces for critical thinking, discussion, and multiple perspectives, all of which are essential to preparing students for life in a democratic society.

REFERENCES

Barton, K. C., & Levstik, L. S. (2004). *Teaching history for the common good*. Mahwah, NJ: Lawrence Erlbaum.

Bauml, M. (2016). Is it cute or does it count? Learning to teach for meaningful social studies in elementary grades. *Journal of Social Studies Research, 40*(1), 55–69.

Bellows, E., & Bodle, A. (2015, November). *Breaking the silence: The efficacy of teaching 9/11 in elementary school*. Paper presented at the annual meeting of the College and University Faculty Assembly of the National Council for the Social Studies, New Orleans, LA.

Bellows, E., & Groce, E. (2014, October). *An interruption in the official history: How U.S. state curriculum standards treat 9/11*. Paper presented at the annual meeting of the Organization for Educational Historians, Chicago, IL.

Bellows, E., Groce, E., & Frye, E. (2015, February). *Teaching 9/11 in the elementary grades: standards, trade books, and tough choices*. Paper presented at the annual meeting of the North Carolina Council for the Social Studies, Greensboro, NC.

Boyle-Baise, M., Hsu, M., Johnson, S., Serriere, S. C., & Stewart, D. (2008). Putting reading first: Teaching social studies in elementary classrooms. *Theory & Research in Social Education, 36*, 233–255.

Brophy, J., Alleman, J., & Knighton, B. (2009). *Inside the social studies classroom*. New York: Routledge.

Duckworth, C. L. (2015). *9/11 and collective memory in U.S. classrooms: Teaching about terror*. New York: Routledge.

Finn Jr., C. E. (2002). *September 11: What our children need to know*. Washington, DC: Thomas B. Fordham Foundation.

Grant, S. G., & Gradwell, J. (2010). *Teaching history with big ideas: Cases of ambitious teachers*. Lanham, MD: Rowman & Littlefield Education.

Hobbs, R. (2001). Media literacy skills: Interpreting tragedy. *Social Education, 65*, 406–411.

Kimmelman, M. (2001, September 19). In a square, a sense of unity; a homegrown memorial brings strangers together. *New York Times*, pp. E1, E5.

Rethinking Schools. (2001). War, terrorism, and America's classrooms: Teaching in the aftermath of September 11. *Rethinking Schools Special Report*. Retrieved from http://www.rethinkingschools.org/special_reports/sept11/index.shtml.

Salinas, C., Bellows, M. E., & Liaw, H. L. (2011). Preservice social studies teachers' historical thinking and digitized primary sources: What they use and why. *Contemporary Issues in Technology and Teacher Education, 11*, 184–204.

Sander, T. H., & Putnam, R. D. (2010). Still bowling alone? The post-9/11 split. *Journal of Democracy, 21*, 9–16.

Westheimer, J. (2009). Should social studies be patriotic? *Social Education, 73*, 314–318.

Children's Literature Bibliography

Aubin, C. S., & Harrington, S. (2011). *The survivor tree: Inspired by a true story*. Vienna, VA: Callery Press.

Curtiss, A. B. (2003). *The little chapel that stood*. Escondido, CA: Old Castle Publishing.

Deedy, C. (2009). *14 cows for America*. Atlanta, GA: Peachtree Publishers.

Fagan, H. C., & Crowther, J. (2013). *The man in the red bandana*. Nyack, NY: Welles Remy Crowther Charitable Trust.

Jonell, L. (2002). *Bravemole*. New York: G. P. Putnam's Sons.

Patel, A. (2001). *On that day: A book of hope for children*. Berkeley, CA: Tricycle Press.

Poffenberger, N. (2002). *September 11th, 2001: A simple account for children*. Cincinnati, OH: Fun Publishing.

Rodriguez, C. & Elliot, J. L. (2009). *I was born on 9/11*. Baltimore, MD: Publish America.

Roth, S. L. (2001). *It's still a dog's New York: A book of healing*. Washington, DC: National Geographic Society.

Santora, M. C. & Cardona, P. S. (2011). *The day the towers fell: The story of September 11, 2001*. Dallas, TX: SEGR Publishing.

Winter, J. (2004). *September roses*. New York: Farrar Straus Giroux.

Chapter Four

How Patriotism Matters in U.S. Social Studies Classrooms, Fifteen Years After 9/11

Mark T. Kissling

On the morning of Wednesday, September 12, 2001, I drove to Lebanon High School, where I was a student teacher, with goosebumps covering my body. I was on U.S. Interstate 89, crossing from Vermont into New Hampshire, and thanks to a local radio station, Lee Greenwood's song "God Bless the U.S.A." was blaring from my car's speakers. I clutched the steering wheel and repeatedly belted out Greenwood's recurring line: "and I'm proud to be an American."

The day before, four commercial U.S. planes were turned into missiles by hijackers. I learned of this at school when I was talking with my mentor teacher, Bill, between the first and second periods. Another teacher came into our room and reported a few of the early details about the tragic events. We simply could not comprehend what we heard, and my school's administration chose to remain silent.

Without easy access to instant news sources (i.e., our school had relatively few televisions with cable and computers with Internet connectivity), our incomprehension meant that we carried on rather normally with the day. It wasn't until I returned to my dorm room and spent the entirety of my evening watching television coverage that I began to understand the magnitude of the day's events.

Like so many Americans,[1] I was immediately caught up in a nationalistic fervor, as exemplified by my full-throated car singing, but I was confused about the events that had transpired. On top of this, I was processing the situation from a teaching perspective (i.e., how should I teach about this?), and such processing was still rather new to me. I had an immediate impulse to shout that I was proud to be an American.

But I also had an impulse to recoil from such a proclamation. This was not a simple *United States: right-or-wrong* situation. I had a growing commitment to teaching for social justice, one that had me increasingly thinking critically about "the nation."[2] Just two weeks earlier, Bill had introduced me to the writings of Howard Zinn, including *A People's History of the United States* (1980/2003), which was one of two main texts we were using in our advanced placement U.S. history course (Kissling, 2014).

I was immediately captivated by Zinn's work, including his take on patriotism. Zinn (1991) writes:

> If patriotism were defined, not as blind obedience to government, not as submissive worship to flags and anthems, but rather as love of one's country, one's fellow citizens (all over the world), as loyalty to the principles of justice and democracy, then patriotism would require us to disobey our government, when it violated those principles. (p. 118)

I had an emerging theoretical commitment to Zinn's ideas, but I also had lived through twenty-two years of a large dosage of American exceptionalism in which critical thought about the United States was neither taught nor encouraged.

PATRIOTISM IN SOCIAL STUDIES

Schools in the United States have a long history of teaching—or at least attempting to teach—students to *love their country*, which is a common notion for patriotism. Noah Webster (1790/1965), one of the earliest proponents of public schooling in the United States, argued that if the young, fledging country was going to succeed, a schooling system that foremost taught love for the country needed to be in place. Although formal education during Webster's life was far from any widespread public program, this patriotic mission of schools for which he advocated became, and in many ways continues to be, a reality (Westheimer, 2007a).

But what does it mean to love one's country? Social studies, the school subject area where patriotic teaching is most pronounced, has at times grappled with this question in the subject's nearly one-hundred-year existence (Evans, 2004). Indeed, social studies pioneer Harold Rugg was attacked for supposedly undermining U.S. patriotism while espousing a pedagogical philosophy focused on studying the "American problem," which was rooted in a deep love for the United States (Evans, 2007).

Yet the contemporary field is relatively silent on the explicit teaching of patriotism. Citizenship education is the overt focus of social studies (e.g., National Council for the Social Studies [NCSS], 2010), and this is reflected on a massive scale in social studies teaching and research, but patriotic education lurks in its shadow. Like the daily recitation of the Pledge of Allegiance in so many schools, patriotic education is ubiquitous while largely unscrutinized in the social studies curriculum.

Westheimer (2009) importantly asks if social studies should be patriotic. But given that social studies—and its precursor, history—always has been a mix of explicit and implicit patriotic indoctrination (e.g., Bohan, 2005; Kissling, 2015; Loewen, 2007), Westheimer's question reads like a patriotism-focused offshoot of Stanley's (2005) question about social studies and the social order: transmission or transformation?

More than asking whether social studies should be patriotic, or whether the tradition of teaching patriotism in social studies should be transmitted or transformed, I see Westheimer asking a different question. Akin to his prominent work with citizenship education (Westheimer, 2015), I think he is prompting us to consider: What kind(s) of patriotism should be taught in social studies education?

The purpose of this chapter is to answer this question, mindful that patriotism is far more complex than what students learn about it (mostly implicitly) in schools. I argue that social studies education—particularly now, fifteen years after September 11, 2001—must be patriotic in two important ways.[3] First, study of patriotism must be "explicit" in the social studies curriculum; it cannot be relegated to the "implicit curriculum" (Eisner, 1985), where it often resides.

Students must wrestle with patriotism, being challenged explicitly to answer the question, "What does it mean to be patriotic?" As part of this inquiry, students must wade into the complexity of patriotism, its many and differing notions and expressions. Second, social studies education must *be* patriotic. That is, it must teach students to be patriotic—but only in some ways and not in others. Below I argue for the particular importance of *place-based patriotism*.

KINDS OF PATRIOTISM

Much has been written about patriotism—historically and recently, in the United States and elsewhere, by governmental officials and critics, explicitly and implicitly, and embedded within or in relation to many other topics. Amid this massive sea of thought and work, I rely most on several sources that focus particularly on patriotism in the United States (Bodnar, 1996; Cohen, 1996; Westheimer, 2007a). Across these sources—as well as many more—one can find scores of adjectives modifying patriotism. Yet, patriotism is often presented as a banal, innocuous, matter-of-fact topic in popular culture and schools.

Westheimer (2007b, 2009) outlines two "umbrellas" for differing ideas of patriotism in the United States. They are umbrellas because they are not meant to be an exhaustive overview of all of the kinds of patriotism. Rather, they are meant to broadly categorize the main discourses. "Authoritarian patriotism" features the belief that the United States is inherently better than other countries, and, as a result, its citizens should support and follow, without questioning, the policies of the officials who run the country.

Democratic principles are viewed as automatically rooted in the actions of the government. Loyalty and obedience are markers of patriotic sentiment. Rallying cries of authoritarian patriotism are "my country, right or wrong" and "America: love it or leave it" (Westheimer, 2007b, p. 174). Apple (2002) refers to patriotism under this umbrella as "uncritical and unquestioning" (p. 1767), as well as "compulsory" and "mandated" (p. 1769). Orr (2005) names it "cheap, bumper-sticker patriotism" (p. 26).

Westheimer's (2007b) other umbrella, "democratic patriotism," is marked by allegiance to a set of principles that are seen as foundational to the United States (e.g., freedom and justice for all) but not necessarily always enacted by the government or its people. Deliberation and dissent are valued over certainty and conformity. Critical scrutiny and demanding governmental action that is in accord with democratic principles are hallmarks of this patriotic sentiment.

Rallying cries of democratic patriotism are "dissent is patriotic" and "you have the right to *not* remain silent" (Westheimer, 2007b, p. 174, emphasis in original). Along these lines Apple (2002) writes, "social criticism is the ultimate act of patriotism . . . [as] rigorous criticism of a nation's policies demonstrates a commitment to the nation itself" (p. 1768). Similarly, Foner (2001), writing just nine days after September 11, said "the most patriotic act of all is the unyielding defense of civil liberties, the right to dissent and equality before the law for all Americans" (para. 9). Both authoritarian patriotism and democratic patriotism can be said to express love for and loyalty to country, but the ways in which these expressions are enacted (as well as taught and learned) are quite different.

FOUR EXAMPLES OF PATRIOTISM

Mindful of Westheimer's patriotism umbrellas, I share here four brief stories of contemporary expressions of patriotism related to schooling in the United States during the 2014–2015 academic year.

Legislating "Traditional American History" in the U.S. Senate

In July 2015, the U.S. Senate overwhelmingly passed a bill to reauthorize the Elementary and Secondary Education Act of 1965. This major, comprehensive piece of legislation, titled "Every Child Achieves Act of 2015," was intended to fix some of the problems of the No Child Left Behind Act of 2001.

Buried in the bill, Section 2302 provided for the U.S. secretary of education to award competitive grants to local education agencies "to promote the teaching of traditional American history in elementary schools and secondary schools as a separate academic subject (not as a component of social studies)" (U.S. Senate, 2015, p. 314). The secretary could also administer grants to develop, implement, and strengthen programs that serve this purpose of teaching "traditional American history."

The Senate's legislation clearly seems to be grounded in a love for the country. The key word, though, is "traditional." What does it mean? Does it refer to studying the wars throughout American history? Is it about using a pedagogical approach, like a teacher telling a story through lecture? Does it put forth a particular theme or message, like the rise to greatness of the United States?

All of these possible conceptions of "traditional" are powerful traditions in the history of American history education, and they have all been used to teach a love for the country. But why, then, is it imperative for the Senate to highlight the need for teaching traditional American history? Is there a "nontraditional" threat to the teaching of American history? The legislation simply omits any nuance here; it offers something that seems relatively benign.[4]

Requiring Student Passage of Citizenship Tests in Arizona

In January 2015, the Arizona legislature enacted legislation requiring students to pass the U.S. citizenship test in order to receive a high school diploma. While Arizona was the first state to mandate this requirement, North Dakota's house of representatives quickly followed suit as other state legislatures charted similar courses. Some advocates of this national legislative effort hoped that all fifty states would feature similar legislation by 2017, the 230th anniversary of the U.S. Constitution.

The Arizona-based Joe Foss Institute, whose motto is "Patriotism matters," is the major driver behind this nationwide effort. In its mission statement, the Foss Institute (ThankYouForYourService.US, 2013) states, "Schools, driven by an increasing emphasis and funding for proficiency in the hard sciences . . . and standardized testing are producing students who are learning less and less about how our freedoms were earned and why they matter" (para. 2).[5] The Foss Institute makes clear that its push for the state-mandated student passage of the U.S. citizenship test is patriotic.

The institute's mission statement embeds a video clip from President Ronald Reagan's farewell address.[6] In the segment the president warns of the lack of "informed patriotism" that he felt had taken hold in the country. Explaining the problem, he says, "Younger parents aren't sure that an unambivalent appreciation of America is the right thing to teach modern children."

The president goes on to state: "I'm warning of an eradication of the American memory that could result, ultimately, in an erosion of the American spirit. Let's start with some basics: more attention to American history and a greater emphasis on civic ritual." After the video clip, the institute's mission statement reads, "President Reagan's words of warning are as important to hear today as they were on January 11, 1989" (ThankYouForYourService.US,

2013, para. 5). This is the context for the nationwide push for students to pass the citizenship test in order to graduate high school.

Reviewing the U.S. History Curriculum in Jefferson County

In September 2014, the school board for Jefferson County, Colorado (JeffCo)—the state's second largest school district—approved a plan to establish a committee to review the district's U.S. history curriculum, particularly focusing on advanced placement United States history (APUSH). The focus on APUSH was due to the fact that the college board, which administers all advanced placement testing, had recently revised the APUSH course and examination.

The intent behind the college board's revisions centered on two main changes: spelling out the specifics of the curriculum in greater detail (to help teachers better know what to teach and how to prepare their students for the culminating exam) and aligning the course with college credit requirements and the new Common Core State Standards. Nationwide, critics of the revisions decried how the new framework "emphasizes negative aspects of the nation's history and downplays 'American exceptionalism'" (Heitin, 2015, para. 1).

Sharing similar concerns, JeffCo school board member Julie Williams (2014a) explained the intent of the history curriculum review was to ensure that curricular materials

> promote citizenship, patriotism, essentials and benefits of the free enterprise system, respect for authority and respect for individual rights. Materials should not encourage or condone civil disorder, social strife or disregard of the law. Instructional materials should present positive aspects of the United States and its heritage. Content pertaining to political and social movements in U.S. history should present balanced and factual treatments of the positions. (para. 2)

When Williams (2014b) was asked about this proposed review, she responded, "APUSH rejects the history that has been taught in the country for generations. It has an emphasis on race, gender, class, ethnicity, grievance and American-bashing while simultaneously omitting the most basic structural and philosophical elements considered essential to the understanding of American History for generations" (para. 4). She viewed the curricular review as a patriotic act, one that would make sure that patriotism was restored in the history curricula and that "American-bashing" was eliminated.

Pledging Allegiance in State College

In February 2015, on a cold school day in State College, Pennsylvania, where I live, I did something rather unusual for my daily routine. Just before 7:00 a.m., I tuned into a local radio station that likes to begin weekdays with recorded recitations of the Pledge of Allegiance by classes of nearby elementary schoolchildren. I listened because I knew one of the second-grade students in the class whose recitation was aired that day.

After the conclusion of a typical song that the station plays, the disc jockey said, "It's time for the Pledge of Allegiance brought to you by [name of local sponsor]." The DJ made a brief plug for the products of that sponsor, and then he played the recording of my friend's class. It started with the teacher introducing her students, their classroom and grade level, and their school.

Then eighteen seconds of methodical, monotone student recitation of the Pledge followed. It sounded like every other Pledge recitation that I have heard in my experiences as a student and as a teacher. At the Pledge's conclusion, after a split-second pause, the students excitedly made a noise that is associated with this particular radio station. Then a series of commercials ensued and it was back to regular programming.

Recitation of the Pledge is a commonplace school civic ritual, of the kind that President Reagan talks about in his address embedded in the Foss Institute's mission statement. On the day that these students were recorded saying the Pledge, they were doing something that countless other students across the country were doing: communicating their allegiance to the U.S. flag and republic. Further, when the radio station played their recording, which was sanctioned by the school, this traditional practice that most U.S. adults know very well from their own schooling was extended to the mainstream public.

PATRIOTISM IN THESE STORIES

Considering Westheimer's umbrellas, authoritarian patriotism is on display in these stories: there is obedience, loyalty, and touting (or defense of) American exceptionalism. But mindful of the mission of social studies to educate effective citizens (NCSS, 2010), I see these actions as a disturbing form of patriotism: *nationalism*.

Writing near the end of the Second World War, the English novelist and commentator George Orwell (1945) argued that nationalism and patriotism are distinct because "opposing ideas are involved." Patriotism is "devotion to a particular place and a particular way of life," whereas nationalism "is inseparable from the desire for power" for one's nation (para. 2). Thus, Orwell contends that a patriot is defensive of his country, whereas a nationalist is offensive on behalf of it.

The American farmer and writer Wendell Berry picks up on this latter point, saying, "Nationalism always implies competition, always the wish that your nation might thrive, even at the expense of other nations" (cited in Ritter, 2011, thirty-eight-minute mark). Nationalism, as I define it, is the uncritical, forceful touting of exceptionalism of one's nation. Mindful of Billig's (1995) work, I see nationalism as a narrow, reactionary discourse within the larger discursive field of patriotism. I recognize Orwell's important distinction, but I think the nationalist desire for power is a distorted offshoot of patriotic devotion.

In the United States, nationalism is expressed as people position their country to be unequivocally greater and unquestionably more exceptional than any other country. President Reagan's statement about the need for parents to teach their children "an unambivalent appreciation of America" is an example of this. Thus, in pushing for mandated student passage of citizenship tests, the Foss Institute is propelled by President Reagan's nationalist call.

Likewise, the U.S. Senate's support for "traditional American history" is an implicit nationalist project, touting the unequaled greatness of America under the guise of a nondescript bill section. Similarly, in JeffCo and elsewhere, objections to the new APUSH course are reflective of the same nationalist positioning: The United States is exceptional and must be taught as being such.

The nationalism of the Pledge in State College is subtler. Students everywhere who recite the Pledge daily are participating in a commonplace ritual of ideological reproduction of the nation, what Billig (1995) refers to as "banal nationalism." The power of the United States as a nation is both taught and reinforced in the typically mindless recitation of the Pledge (and other rituals, like the playing of the national anthem before sporting events).

In terms of procedure, the Pledge is disturbingly similar to the daily "Two Minutes Hate" from Orwell's (1949) novel *1984*. Sanctioned by the school, it is rarely a critical act; it is usually an obedient one. It is part of the school's curriculum, although its banal quality usually relegates any learning associated with it to the hidden, implicit curriculum. Bigelow (2007) calls this approach to schooling "nationalistic indoctrination" and "wagon-circling patriotism."[7]

In an essay written after the events of September 11, Michael Apple (2002) speaks to how patriotism has been co-opted by nationalism, as in the four stories above. Patriotism and other concepts—like freedom—are sliding signifiers, inherent constructions with no fixed meanings, and yet they "are part of a contested terrain in which different versions of democracy exist on a social field of power in which there are unequal resources to influence the publicly accepted definitions of key words" (p. 1767). Powerful people and corporations stand to benefit when a slippery concept like patriotism is effectively fixed in the minds of the public.

David Orr (2005), writing in a book titled *The Last Refuge*—as in Samuel Johnson's famous 1775 quote, "patriotism is the last refuge of a scoundrel"—makes a similar argument. Orr contends that words like *patriot*, *liberal*, and *taxation*, which have noble linguistic histories, have been corrupted: "The manipulation of words and symbols by extremists has become an art form designed to confuse, baffle, and exploit public gullibility in order to further enrich the already wealthy" (p. 26). As does Apple, Orr argues that powerful elites with deep pockets have succeeded in shaping and narrowing the hegemonic ideals of these words in order to serve their own interests.[8]

The Foss Institute's push to have all states adopt mandatory high school student passage of the U.S. citizenship test in order to earn a diploma is an example of what Apple and Orr are talking about. Powerful financial and political resources are used in order to institutionalize a nationalistic notion of patriotism. Both Apple and Orr call for public struggle with this supposedly fixed patriotism, and Apple (2002) says such a struggle is inherently an act of patriotism (p. 1768). I contend that this struggle—for the sake of effective citizenship—must play out, at a minimum, in social studies classrooms.

Mindful of this struggle, in my telling of the four stories above, I purposefully ended the JeffCo story prematurely. In response to the school board's approval of the proposed curricular review, many JeffCo students, teachers, and parents protested publicly and vigorously. Students walked out of their schools, rallied and marched in busy, prominent public places, and displayed signs that had messages such as "Civil Disobedience is Patriotism."

Teachers and parents publicly resisted the curricular review, too. Five months later, due to the significant pushback, the JeffCo school board dropped its review plan. Whereas the curricular review proposal was an example of authoritarian patriotism (specifically nationalism), the student, teacher, and parent protests were a form of democratic patriotism, and the latter won out in this instance.

THE COMPLEXITY OF PATRIOTISM

Westheimer's umbrellas hinge on whether patriotism should be *critical*, asking questions about power and challenging existing power relationships: authoritarian patriots say "no," while democratic patriots say "yes." I find the umbrellas, with this particular hinge, to be an important construct, especially as I work with preservice teachers and ask them to wrestle with the two umbrellas. My students almost always find some merit in both umbrellas, while also recognizing clear distinctions between the two, particularly with respect to dissent and civil disobedience.

Yet, I find the umbrellas problematic with respect to how land is positioned within Westheimer's framework. One of the ideological features described for authoritarian patriotism is "Primary allegiance to land, birthright, legal citizenship, and government's cause" (Westheimer, 2007b, p. 174). With no further discussion of the role of land, I take Westheimer's point to be that land is understood by an authoritarian patriot as one way of delineating between "us" and "them."

That is, "we" are on "our" land, "they" are on other land, and thus "we" are loyal and obedient to "our" land. But as land is a far more robust concept—as well as an essential reality for the sustenance of all life—it is with respect to land that I highlight a particular kind of patriotism that disturbs the binary of Westheimer's umbrellas: place-based patriotism.

PLACE-BASED PATRIOTISM

Wendell Berry conceives of a notion of patriotism that is founded on one's fidelity to the land that is under one's feet *and* sustains one's life and community (Berry, 2003; Ritter, 2011). Berry understands patriotism to be "the love of a home country that's usually much smaller than a nation" (cited in Ritter, 2011, thirty-eight-minute mark). The term *home country*, here, refers to one's local place of dwelling, not a national political state, which is what Berry implies with the word *nation*. Patriotism means caring for and cultivating one's surrounding "land community" (Leopold, 1966): all the creatures—human and nonhuman—that share a common place.

Berry's patriotism recognizes the primary role of land in the lives of humans (and nonhumans). It is not, though, founded on the idea of ownership of land. Rather, it asserts the responsibility of humans to the land: to care for it and cultivate it. This perspective aligns with traditions of indigenous American cultures for which respect for the land is foundational (e.g., Deloria & Wildcat, 2001), and it also bears a resemblance to strands of U.S. and world history in which communities organized around public, "common" lands (e.g., Bowers, 2006).

From this perspective, Berry contends that patriotism "recognizes the obligation of charity towards other places, to other people. It recognizes that the prosperity of your place need not come at the expense of the prosperity of other places" (cited in Ritter, 2011, thirty-nine-minute mark). Thus, patriotism is affection for one's place that is rooted in one's ability to imagine other places and connections to them, and this affection is contextualized by an understanding that the prosperity of one's place improves as the prosperity of other places improves.

Importantly, Berry's notion of patriotism—a landed, more-localized patriotism—is not uncritical. Writing in direct response to the White House's new national security strategy that was unveiled in response to the events of September 11, Berry (2003) asserted:

> Thomas Jefferson justified general education by the obligation of citizens to be critical of their government: "for nothing can keep it right but their own vigilant *and distrustful* superintendence." An inescapable requirement of true patriotism, love for one's land, is a vigilant distrust of any determinative power, elected or unelected, that may preside it. (p. 5, emphasis in original)

Akin to the critical umbrella of democratic patriotism, Berry envisages a patriotic distrust that operates at multiple scales, extending from his Kentucky farm to all the lands and peoples of the United States—and beyond.

Scales of Patriotism

Local lands are far removed from the patriotism in the four stories above. While this is not surprising given the contemporary discursive field of patriotism, which is largely fixed on nationalism, it is surprising upon consideration of the Latin roots of patriotism. Patriotism is derived from the Latin words *pater* ("father") and *patria* ("fatherland").

Other English derivatives include "patriarch," "paternal," "compatriot," and so on. Importantly, *patria*, the most direct root of patriotism, is associated with notions of ancestry, birthright, culture, land, and tradition. It is not specific to political citizenship or the overarching political state, the Latin words for which are *civis* and *civitas*, respectively, from which English derives "civic" and "civility."[9]

Despite the ancestral, localized notions of this etymology for patriotism, it is rare in the United States that the signifier of patriotism slides beyond "the national." Even though the Latin roots of patriotism give no reason to concern oneself mightily with the national, or national patriotism, in the course of U.S. history, patriotism *is* the national (Bodnar, 1996).[10]

Focused on the national, President George Washington spoke of "patriot," "patriotic," and "patriotism" in his presidential farewell address in ways similar to President Barack Obama and his recent predecessors. Critics who have decried patriotism—in the United States and beyond—have also framed it as national patriotism (e.g., Bigelow, 2007; Goldman, 1911). Yet this national focus is still not so simple, as even the national is quite complex. Indeed, what, exactly, is the national?[11]

In the examples above, the national is about allegiance to U.S. history (JeffCo; Senate), U.S. citizenship (Arizona), and the flag and republic of the United States (State College). It is not about a global patriotism, like Nussbaum's (1996) notion of "cosmopolitanism," which is premised on the idea of "allegiance . . . to the worldwide community of human beings" (p. 4). It is also not about affinity-group patriotism (at least not overtly, although some might argue it is a kind of Christian patriotism). Of most interest to me, here, is that it is not about more local notions of patriotism, ones that do not require such distant imagining of the national (Anderson, 2006).

Beyond its own complexity, the national is merely one scale of patriotism. One reason why I chose the stories at the onset is that they involve different scales of geopolitical association. While they all engage a national patriotism, they implicate associations at the scale of the national (U.S. Senate), state (Arizona), county (JeffCo), and city (State College). If we think about these scales in terms of a place-based patriotism, we have a whole spectrum of landed affections, some of which might be explicitly connected, but others of which might be less directly connected.

There are many other scales, geopolitical and otherwise. The most prominent scale outside of national patriotism is cosmopolitanism, which has received considerable acclaim and criticism (e.g., Cohen, 1996). Yet Mitchell and Parker (2008) showed through study of middle- and high-school students that students have complex, shifting loyalties that are far more dynamic than the false-binary containers of national patriotism and cosmopolitanism.

While patriotism does involve the national, it must be understood in deep relation to other scales of association. Following this notion, I contend that patriotism must be understood, or at least contended with, as place-based. Thus, I define patriotism as loving one's shared lands and communities—that is, one's *place*—by working for the betterment of all living beings within those lands and communities. The starting point for this patriotism is our places: our local lands and the communities of beings who inhabit them.

However, our place-based patriotism then scales outward to other places and their communities, as well as larger, imagined scales that span places. But we must remember that we are always reconstructing this patriotism through our personal experiences, not by having predetermined containers of patriotism placed around us (which schools and social studies too often are quick to do).

Therefore, acquiring wealth at the expense of one's fellow community members—near or far—is unpatriotic. Likewise, acquiring wealth through the degradation of one's (and, by public definition, others') lands is unpatriotic. War, lethal and destructive to lands and communities, whether near or far, is unpatriotic. Touting one's nation-state as the best in the world for the purposes of power and politics is unpatriotic. Whitewashing the history of one's communities is unpatriotic. Squashing dissent and avoiding democratic deliberation is unpatriotic. These notions need to be contended with in the explicit social studies curriculum.

THE FUTURE OF PATRIOTISM IN SOCIAL STUDIES

The complexity of patriotism must be encountered directly and taught explicitly in social studies classrooms across the K–12 grade spectrum. What passes for patriotic education in most social studies classrooms is similar to the nationalism of the stories above: implicit, uncritical, and entirely focused on the national. Not connecting students to where they live and to who and what surrounds them (civically, communally, ecologically, economically, geographically, historically, politically, etc.) *displaces* them from the realities of their living, which, in a word, is unpatriotic.

Let's start with what social studies must not be: nationalist. Social studies must teach students to identify with their communities, but in anti-oppressive, justice-oriented ways. Nationalism is neither anti-oppressive nor justice-oriented. Any identification is developed on coercive grounds. A critical, place-based patriotism starts from the premise that one is a citizen of communities—not just a national citizen—and possesses a responsibility to work on behalf of all in those communities, from the most local to the most global.

How Social Studies *Must* Be Patriotic

First, social studies teachers and curriculum planners must make patriotism an explicit part of the curriculum, right alongside citizenship.[12] Further, the complex, interwoven relationship between citizenship and patriotism must be explored. Patriotism cannot continue to dwell in mundane school practices or everyday aspects of the social studies curriculum. Students must understand that they are learning about patriotism.

Second, social studies education must present patriotism as a complex and dynamic concept. Students must understand that patriotism is not fixed, that there is no one conception of patriotism to which all people and groups adhere. Presented with multiple, competing notions and examples of patriotism, students are required to be critical thinkers about patriotism. In this sense, patriotic education must be "critical."

Third, and related to the second point, social studies education must allow for students to construct—through significant thought and study—what patriotism is and what it means to them. Students should not simply be forced into the container of national patriotism. Within this construction, students must have the ability to enact fluid, hybrid, and shifting patriotism. As a part of this work, students must examine past and present discourses and examples of patriotism. Examples should be local, regional, national, and global to the students, and they should also come from nonlocal places and other countries.

Finally, social studies education must attend to the ways in which patriotism is place-based. There must be a concerted effort to show that patriotism includes (if not comes from) one's fidelity to the local land under one's feet. This is about scale: patriotism is commonly understood with respect to the national and rarely with respect to more local communities. All people are at the mercy of the *placed* nature of experience and the limits of human understanding.

This point about the imperative of teaching place-based patriotism is also about solidarity, particularly in the face of the borderless issue of environmental sustainability and the immense, unavoidable problem of human-induced climate change. While we can imagine locally, nationally, and globally, it is very difficult to understand beyond our lived experiences. Thus, we must act locally in ways that benefit other local places all over the world.

What Patriotic Social Studies Can Look Like

A starting *place* is learning and teaching about the places that students and teachers—and schools and communities—inhabit. Students can learn the natural history of where they live, including the names and characteristics of plants and animals indigenous to their area and the history of how that landscape has evolved. Alongside this place-based, earthen knowledge, students can intentionally experience the natural history of their place, taking hikes through and across the terrain and growing gardens from which they can make meals.

Beyond the natural history of their place, students can learn the human history of the people who have inhabited their local place, going back to the earliest inhabitants. This can include learning about the cultures and industries—past and present—of the area. As part of this inquiry they can visit museums, talk to elders, and study archival information and other artifacts. Students also can engage deeply but critically in local public activities, developing skills of effective citizenship and community membership while cultivating community.

While this place-based study might be conceived of as students looking into a *mirror*, it's equally important for students to look through a *window*, to other places. Students can learn the natural and human history of other places, ones that are nonlocal to them, and in this they can consider the ways in which these places and their place are interconnected, across time and space. While such "window" learning is quite common in social studies, it takes on an important—and I would argue essential—framing when it is contextualized and prompted through "mirror" learning.

Importantly, this learning is not solely scaled at the local level, be it local places or nonlocal places. It is imperative for students to learn constantly in and across the scales of their living, making connections all the while and understanding how they have many and fluid affinities. In some ways this is a geographic approach to social studies, thinking about history, civics, and economics across the continuum of personal-local-regional-national-global, but also doing this from different perspective vantage points—understanding that one's scale continuum is always pointed in a different direction from everyone else's—needs to be emphasized.

To be sure, the scale of the national needs to be included—and even be quite prominent—in social studies because so many of the structures that organize our daily lives are formed under the logic of the national. The national should not be omitted in social studies, but it (like everything else) should be explored through critical inquiry.

NOTES

1. "Americans," here, refers to residents of the United States, but I place the term in quotes because I am mindful that America includes all of the countries in North, Central, and South America and Americans are all of the people who reside in the countries of North, Central, and South America. Yet, in U.S. popular discourse, "America" and "Americans" commonly refer solely to the United States and its residents. Given this oversimplification, I refer to the United States in this chapter and not "America."

2. In this chapter I typically use (unless noted otherwise) the terms *country*, *nation*, *nation-state*, and *state* interchangeably. While much more discussion is needed in order to name the relationships between these distinct-but-related terms, I do not have the space to take up that discussion here.

3. The reader will note that my focus is specific to social studies in the United States. This boundary is not meant to exclude the rest of the world; rather, it is meant to work with patriotism in the *place* of the United States.

4. This part of the legislation is also troubling because social studies, by and large, *is* the teaching of traditional American history (Loewen, 2007). To extract history from social studies is like extracting geometry from mathematics. Further, there are other disciplines in social studies—civics, economics, geography; sometimes anthropology, sociology, and social psychology—and there are topics outside the United States, but even in these courses, the backdrop is the teaching of American history. This emphasis was true in the earliest years of schooling in the United States (e.g., Bodnar, 1996; Bohan, 2005), and even though the subject of social studies arose largely as an antidote to this traditional American history teaching, the latter never stopped being the focal point as it morphed into social studies.

5. The Foss Institute changed their website between the time this chapter was written and when it went to press. However, readers can see the text that was on the Foss Institute website at that time at the ThankYouForYourService.US website listed in the reference. The Foss Institute's current website can be accessed at http://www.joefossinstitute.org.

6. The ThankYouForYourService.US website only contains the text that was on the Foss Institute's website at the time this chapter was written. However, readers can access President Reagan's farewell address at https://www.youtube.com/watch?v=UKVsq2daR8Q.

7. The recording and airing of the students' Pledge of Allegiance by the radio station is also an act of indoctrination. At its worst, it is banal indoctrination into capitalism and the culture of celebrity, both of these wrapped in nationalism. At its best, it is a public service—but one of nationalistic indoctrination. The radio station attracts listeners (like me, a first-time listener, on that day my friend's class was aired) and sponsorship money, both facilitated by the cuteness of local schoolchildren. For listeners who are tuning in for reasons other than hearing the voices of youth they know, the banal experience is not very different from the actual act of reciting the Pledge in a classroom. It's a thirty-second nationalism break, and then on with the day.

8. The same was true when Rugg's social studies textbooks were attacked in the 1930s and 1940s.

9. Interestingly, the main Latin root of nationalism is *natio*, which means "birth," among other things.

10. I use "the national" to refer to all representations of association at the national level: country, federation, nation, nation-state, state, and so forth.

11. Perhaps the national *is* the U.S. president and other political leaders. Perhaps it *is* "we the people," the collective residents of the United States. Perhaps it *is* the principles on which the government rests. Perhaps it *is* the land within the geopolitical boundaries of the country. In short, the national can be, and often uncritically is, many things.

12. Elsewhere I have written (Kissling, 2016; Kissling & Calabrese Barton, 2013) about "ecological citizenship," which I see as nearly identical to place-based patriotism.

REFERENCES

Anderson, B. (2006). *Imagined communities: Reflections on the origin and spread of nationalism*. London: Verso.

Apple, M. W. (2002). Patriotism, pedagogy, and freedom: On the educational meanings of September 11th. *Teachers College Record, 104*, 1760–1772.

Berry, W. (2003). *Citizenship papers*. Berkeley, CA: Counterpoint.

Bigelow, B. (2007). Patriotism makes kids stupid. In J. Westheimer (Ed.), *Pledging allegiance: The politics of patriotism in America's schools* (pp. 87–88). New York: Teachers College Press.

Billig, M. (1995). *Banal nationalism*. London: Sage.

Bodnar, J. (Ed.). (1996). *Bonds of affection: Americans define their patriotism*. Princeton, NJ: Princeton University Press.

Bohan, C. H. (2005). Digging trenches: Nationalism and the First National Report on the elementary history curriculum. *Theory & Research in Social Education, 33*, 266–291.

Bowers, C. A. (2006). *Revitalizing the commons: Cultural and educational sites of resistance and affirmation*. Lanham, MD: Lexington Books.

Cohen, J. (1996). *For love of country: Debating the limits of patriotism*. Boston: Beacon Press.

Deloria, V., & Wildcat, D. R. (2001). *Power and place: Indian education in America*. Golden, CO: Fulcrum.

Eisner, E. (1985). *The educational imagination: On the design and imagination of school programs* (2nd ed.). New York: Macmillan.

Evans, R. W. (2004). *The social studies wars: What should we teach the children?* New York: Teachers College Press.

———. (2007). *This happened in America: Harold Rugg and the censure of social studies*. Charlotte, NC: Information Age.

Foner, E. (2001, September 20). The most patriotic act. *The Nation*. Retrieved from http://www.thenation.com/article/most-patriotic-act/.

Goldman, E. (1911). *Anarchism and other essays* (2nd ed.). New York: Mother Earth Publishing.

Heitin, L. (2014, May 7). Advanced placement U.S. history to undergo changes. *Education Week*. Retrieved from http://blogs.edweek.org/edweek/curriculum/2014/05/advanced_placement_us_history.html.
———. (2015, March 3). Rewrite of AP framework for U.S. history criticized. *Education Week*. Retrieved from http://www.edweek.org/ew/articles/2015/03/04/objections-spread-to-ap-us-history-rewrite.html.
Kissling, M. T. (2014, September 8). Grappling with multiple histories: Teaching critical inquiry with Zinn's *A People's History of the United States*. *Zinn Education Project*. Retrieved from http://zinnedproject.org/2014/09/grappling-with-multiple-histories.
———. (2015). Complicating patriotism in the elementary grades: An examination of Rugg and Krueger's overlooked textbooks. *Social Studies, 106*, 264–273.
———. (2016). Place-based social studies teacher education: Learning to teach for ecological citizenship while investigating local waste issues. In A. Crowe and A. Cuenca (Eds.), *Rethinking social studies teacher education for 21st century citizenship* (pp. 321–338). Gewerbestrasse, Switzerland: Springer International Publishing.
Kissling, M. T., & Calabrese Barton, A. (2013). Teaching social studies for ecological citizenship. *Social Studies Research and Practice, 8*, 128–142.
Leopold, A. (1966). *A Sand County almanac*. New York: Oxford University Press.
Loewen, J. W. (2007). *Lies my teacher told me: Everything your American history textbook got wrong* (rev. ed.). New York: Touchstone.
Mitchell, K., & Parker, W. (2008). I pledge allegiance to . . . Flexible citizenship and shifting scales of belonging. *Teachers College Record, 110*, 775–804.
National Council for the Social Studies. (2010). *National curriculum standards for social studies: A framework for teaching, learning, and assessment*. Washington, DC: National Council for the Social Studies.
Nussbaum, M. C. (1996). Patriotism and cosmopolitanism. In J. Cohen (Ed.), *For love of country: Debating the limits of patriotism* (pp. 2–17). Boston: Beacon Press.
Orr, D. W. (2005). *The last refuge: Patriotism, politics, and the environment in an age of terror*. Washington, DC: Island Press.
Orwell, G. (1945). Notes on nationalism. Retrieved from http://orwell.ru/library/essays/nationalism/english/e_nat.
———. (1949). *1984*. New York: Signet.
Ritter, S. (2011). Interview with poet, essayist, farmer, and novelist Wendell Berry. *Profiles*. Indiana Public Media (WFIU). Retrieved from http://indianapublicmedia.org/profiles/wendell-berry/.
Stanley, W. B. (2005). Social studies and the social order: Transmission or transformation. *Social Education, 69*, 282–286.
ThankYouForYourService.US. (2013, October 26). Joe Foss Institute students served-1,224,682. Retrieved from http://thankyouforyourservice.us/issue/february-2016/article/joe-foss-institute-students-served-1-224-682.
U.S. Senate. (2015). Every Child Achieves Act of 2015. Retrieved from https://www.congress.gov/114/bills/s1177/BILLS-114s1177es.pdf.
Webster, N. (1790/1965). On the education of youth in America. In F. Rudolph (Ed.), *Essays on education in the early republic* (pp. 41–78). Cambridge, MA: Belknap Press.
Westheimer, J. (Ed.). (2007a). *Pledging allegiance: The politics of patriotism in America's schools*. New York: Teachers College Press.
———. (2007b). Politics and patriotism in education. In J. Westheimer (Ed.), *Pledging allegiance: The politics of patriotism in America's schools* (pp. 171–188). New York: Teachers College Press.
———. (2009). Should social studies be patriotic? *Social Education, 73*(7), 316–320.
———. (2015). *What kind of citizen? Educating our children for the common good*. New York: Teachers College Press.
Williams, J. (2014a). Board committee for curriculum review. *Jefferson County Board of Education*. Retrieved from http://www.boarddocs.com/co/jeffco/Board.nsf/files/9NYRPF6DED70/$file/JW%20PROPOSAL%20Board%20Committee%20for%20Curriculum%20Review.pdf.
———. (2014b). Press release for APUSH. *Jefferson County Board of Education*. Retrieved from http://www.jeffcopublicschools.org/media/web_news/2014/Press%20Release%20for%20APUSH.pdf.
Zinn, H. (1980/2003). *A people's history of the United States*. New York: Perennial Classics.
———. (1991). *Declarations of independence: Cross-examining American ideology*. New York: HarperPerrenial.

Chapter Five

National Identity and Citizenship in a Pluralistic Society

Educators' Messages Following 9/11 and Charlie Hebdo

Lisa Gilbert

Around lunchtime in Paris on January 7, 2015, brothers Saïd and Chérif Kouachi entered the offices of *Charlie Hebdo*, a French satirical weekly magazine known for its caricatures and crude humor often aimed at religious and ethnic minorities. The often-controversial magazine had refused to apologize for publishing cartoons of the Prophet Mohammed and mocking Muslim clerics, even after its editor-in-chief, Stéphane Charbonnier, had been placed on a hit list by al Qaeda in the Arabian Peninsula in March 2013.

Armed with assault rifles, the brothers killed twelve people and wounded eleven more before fleeing. France raised its "Vigipirate" terrorism alert rating to its highest level and a manhunt ensued. Two days later, the brothers took hostages at a signage company in Dammartin-en-Goële. An accomplice, Amedy Coulibaly, took hostages at a Jewish supermarket in Porte de Vincennes.

After a standoff that lasted nearly nine hours, the Kouachi brothers, who had expressed a desire to die as martyrs, were killed during a shootout with police. In the kosher supermarket, Coulibaly killed four people before he was killed by police. That same day, a cleric speaking for al Qaeda in the Arabian Peninsula claimed the *Charlie Hebdo* attack as "revenge for the honor" of the Prophet Mohammed.

The international outcry that followed was overwhelming. Perceived to be an assault on free speech itself, the streets of Paris were flooded with over two million people in a rally of national unity on January 11. Similar protests across France amounted to an estimated 3.7 million attendees, making the display of solidarity the largest public rally in France since the end of World War II. Similar vigils were held in countries across Europe and North America. The phrase *Je suis Charlie* ("I am Charlie") became a rallying cry, emblazoned on signs held in the streets and trending on social media as #jesuischarlie.

An important symbol of solidarity was the cartoonist's pencil, evoking the freedom of the press—pictured variously as broken and resharpened, dripping with blood, or aimed like a gun. In one editorial cartoon by Dutch artist Ruben Oppenheimer, two pencils stand erect like towers against the sky with a silhouette of a plane headed toward them in the lower right corner. The message was clear: with the country reeling from its deadliest terror attack since 1961,[1] *Charlie Hebdo* was France's 9/11.

This chapter accepts the cartoonist's invitation to consider these two events as parallel cases. In some ways, the dominant discourses of the countries' responses were similar: Both spoke of the need to "protect our liberties" as a free society. Both felt it was important to define themselves, to set boundaries on what was—and wasn't—"American" or "French."

In other ways, the countries' responses were dissimilar: whereas Americans rallied around firefighters, police, and military for their roles in responding to the events of September 11, 2001, the French did not do the same, despite an officer from the National Police being among the victims of the attack. Thus, the French response to *Charlie Hebdo* offers a similar, yet different, example for American social studies educators interested in considering an alternate national response. The goal is not to suggest France's approach is superior, but that such reflection can be helpful in theorizing best practices for American social studies in a post-9/11 world.

This chapter traces a pattern of educators' responses in both countries. First, teachers were concerned with making sure students learned important lessons about national identity from these events. The way they sought to make tragedies into "teachable moments" tended to present national ideals as acquired characteristics rather than commonly held values, an approach that narrowed the boundaries of national identity.

Thus, the second section of this chapter will consider those students who were excluded from this identity or labeled as troublemakers for their failure to respond the way adults expected. Finally, the third section will consider what lessons educators might learn from these cases today. For educators interested in disrupting this pattern, a key lesson is that, when teaching about patriotism following a national tragedy, ideals key to national identity should be taught as aspirations rather than static characteristics that have been achieved.

USING EDUCATION TO DEFINE AND LIMIT NATIONAL IDENTITY

As each country interpreted these events, powerful voices in American and French societies moved to protect that which they perceived to have been attacked. Mainstream American political discourse following 9/11 repositioned "freedom" as a static attribute of American national identity.[2] It was no longer enough to say that Americans loved freedom as a shared cultural value. Rather, it was important to assert that freedom was a defining characteristic of American society that had been achieved and could be assumed to be present in America's civic institutions.

Likewise, values important to French national identity, such as freedom, equality, and brotherhood, were repositioned as static qualities that defined the French national character. The mainstream discourse offered a sense of assurance that these shared values had been achieved, and if any part of French society were to be examined, an expression of these values would be found. In this context, the dominant discourse in French society suggested that the very offensiveness of the *Charlie Hebdo* magazine was a demonstration of France's rigorous implementation of the value of freedom, whether of speech, of religion, or of press.

Uniformity as Patriotism

For both societies, the inherent assertion that such values had been achieved bred a sense of insecurity. Those who did not fit into this rigid framework—for example, Americans who raised concerns about the Patriot Act, or French citizens who saw *Charlie Hebdo*'s rhetoric as an affront to their shared values of equality and brotherhood—were branded as unpatriotic. In this context, schools became a clarifying ground for the messages adults wanted children to receive about national identity in a pluralistic society. These messages could be communicated both explicitly and implicitly as part of the schools' "hidden curriculum."

This is a common role for schools to play. In a historical overview of American schooling, Reuben (2005) found that "Americans have looked to schools to foster individuals' identification with the nation" (p. 1) since the 1790s, and indicated that today "[e]ducation remains a key means of 'enacting' ideals of citizenship" (p. 21). In an examination of civic education in American schools in the years between 1900 and 1950, Mirel (2002) noted that "schools are a major battleground in the struggle to define national identity and good citizenship" (p. 144).

American exceptionalism is frequently promoted in American social studies curricula (Nash, Crabtree, & Dunn, 1997). Camicia and Zhu (2011) found that nationalism dominates citizenship education in the United States, with cosmopolitan approaches relegated to the realms of critique and reform (p. 611). In one such promotion of global citizenship education, Myers (2006) found that social studies in the United States is geared toward national identity and patriotism rather than a global view of history.

Following 9/11, American schools became zones of conflict where the country's divided politics played themselves out in debates over ideals key to national identity. For example, Apple (2002) recounted the populist outrage that followed a Wisconsin school board's 2001 rejection of a proposed requirement that students be taught patriotism by being required to sing the "Star-Spangled Banner" and recite the Pledge of Allegiance. In the emotionally charged time that followed September 11, both supporters and opponents of the proposal felt their very freedom as Americans was at stake.

Following the *Charlie Hebdo* attacks, French schools similarly became a place to ensure that children adhered to a uniform sense of French identity. However, an important distinction between American and French educational systems should be noted here. Whereas local control has been a hallmark of the American educational system, French schools are under the central government's authority. This allowed for a particularly clear message to be sent about national identity and the role schools were to play in the nation's recovery from a disaster.

This role is neatly encapsulated in an open letter sent to schools the day after the attack from the head of France's education ministry, Najat Vallaud-Belkacem:[3]

> The murderous attack against the magazine *Charlie Hebdo* struck at the heart of our Republic. The essential values of our Republic were targeted. Freedom of speech is at the foundation of all our freedoms. Freedom of conscience and respect for personal opinions are principles that allow us to live together. Our schools' role is to demonstrate and transmit the Republic's values and principles. Since its inception, the Republic has entrusted its schools with the mission of shaping citizens and transmitting the fundamental values of freedom, equality, brotherhood, and secularism. The Republic's schools transmit to students a shared culture of mutual tolerance and respect. Each student learns to reject all forms of intolerance, hate, racism, and violence. Our schools teach freedom: freedom of conscience, freedom of expression, and the freedom to choose the meaning one finds in life, as well as openness toward others and reciprocal tolerance. Our schools teach equality and brotherhood by teaching students they are all equal. They allow them a direct experience of this truth by welcoming them all without any discrimination. Now more than ever, as our country demonstrates its national unity in the face of this challenge, our schools must embody the ideal of the Republic itself. (Vallaud-Belkacem, 2015)

In some ways, the "fundamental values" of French identity as outlined by Vallaud-Belkacem stand in contrast to American discourses around "citizenship" in the immediate aftermath of 9/11, which focused heavily on patriotism as characterized by support for military, the national government, local firefighters and police, and capitalist economic policies (Giroux, 2002). Osanloo (2011) wrote that the climate post-9/11 "created cohesion, solidarity, and togetherness in a vulnerable, attacked American people. It also led to strong patriotism that has gone beyond pride and honor in country and may be described as jingoism anchored in xenophobia" (p. 64).

This attitude poses challenges to civic education as it obscures "deeper meanings of freedom, democracy, and independence" (p. 66). At first glance, Vallaud-Belkacem's call to French schools to "embody the ideal of the Republic itself" by promoting mutual tolerance, freedom of conscience, and equality seems the opposite of the narrow definition of citizenship often found in American schools after 9/11.

Yet the American and French meanings of the same terms can be quite different. For example, "free speech," an issue at the heart of the *Charlie Hebdo* story, represents two very different ideas. The United States interprets the First Amendment to protect all forms of speech, no matter how repugnant; in contrast, France has laws against hate speech.

Following the attacks, France's tolerance of *Charlie Hebdo*'s offensive speech was elevated to a celebration of Western freedoms. Yet, the same society would imprison those whose offensive speech did not fit into societal norms. For example, a nineteen-year-old student at l'Arc à Orange high school was sentenced to twelve months in prison and 210 hours of community service after another student found his posts on social media praising the attackers (La Provence, 2015).[4]

The countries also diverge on the meaning of freedom of religion, especially in terms of the separation of church and state. Whereas Americans tend to view the expression of religious sentiment in public spaces as essential to the freedom of religion, in France, the value of "secularism" denotes how the public sphere is conceived of as a nonreligious space. As such, French schools do not allow students or teachers to wear religious symbols of any kind, whether the hijab, a yarmulke, or a "large" cross necklace. When Vallaud-Belkacem referred to schools offering students a "direct experience" of equality, she was making a veiled reference to this policy.

These examples of free speech and freedom of religion show that what Vallaud-Belkacem called the schools' "mission of shaping citizens and transmitting the fundamental values of freedom, equality, brotherhood, and secularism" meant adopting a specific set of norms that govern what it means to be properly French in a pluralistic society. A similar sense of specificity operated in American social studies educators' approaches to citizenship and patriotism in the aftermath of 9/11.

For example, Weaver-Hightower (2002) found that the omnipresent American societal discourse around the "heroes of 9/11" construed these individuals almost exclusively as white males who took action as firefighters, police officers, and soldiers. As students were encouraged to look up to these "American heroes," students implicitly learned that women and people of color took few heroic actions on that day.

CURRICULUM MATERIALS AND RESOURCES

The way 9/11 has been memorialized in the curriculum also carries messages about American identity. Reyes-Torres (2014) analyzed the discourses in post-9/11 children's books and found that they encouraged children to adopt an "us versus them" mindset that demanded sameness as central to American national identity. Saleem and Thomas (2011) found middle and high school textbooks' 9/11 narratives consistently associated Islam itself with violence and provided little to no positive representations of Muslim Americans. Following 9/11, citizenship education was a tool used to narrow the borders of what it meant to be American.

Similarly, in France, an examination of pedagogical materials prepared by the Ministry of Education supports the interpretation that the attack was recognized as a "teachable moment" to be put in service of citizenship education. Central to these materials was a document containing advice for managing classroom discussions in a time of emotional upheaval, in which a list of "themes likely to come up" included freedom of speech, freedom of the press, plurality of opinions, secularism, and human rights (Ministère de l'éducation nationale, 2015a).

The resources tied to these themes implicitly suggested that they were descriptors of French society, both in its history and the present day. Students were not expected to engage in critical inquiry around these themes (e.g., "When has the French Republic lived up to its shared value of brotherhood? When has it failed to do so?"). Instead, the pedagogical materials positioned students as people who needed to learn, internalize, and live up to values that were already fully realized in French society.

The Ministry of Education also provided French educators with lists of children's literature, films, paintings, and pieces of music that might be used as part of classroom reflections on the *Charlie Hebdo* attack (Ministère de l'éducation nationale, 2015b, 2015c). Taken as a whole, these suggestions connected to the events only in an abstract way, evoking a vague set of principles tied to national identity.

For example, the musical pieces suggested were *La Marseillaise* (the French national anthem) and Beethoven's *Ode to Joy* (the European Union's anthem). Artistic works included Delacroix's 1830 painting *Le 28 juillet: La liberté guidant le people* (July 28: Liberty Leading the People), in which Marianne (the French counterpart to Lady Liberty) leads the French people forward, holding a revolutionary flag aloft in one hand and a musket in the other, with the bodies of the fallen underfoot. Selected seventeenth-century fables by Jean La Fontaine, long used for a cherished and distinctly French tradition of memorization and recitation, were suggested as ways to evoke certain themes, such as "Individual Liberty and Its Limits."

In both authorship and subject, the selections on the ministry's list evoked a sense of nationalism and nostalgia. For example, films included a sentimental Truffaut classic from 1976, *Argent de poche*, whereas more recent and more clearly related films were not included. The effect of these choices is that the complexity of French society and history was collapsed and streamlined into a consistent, monovocal narrative. Further, despite France's current status as the European country with the largest Muslim population in Europe, the list reflected a national vision in which Muslim authors, artists, and musicians are wholly absent and do not merit artistic exploration or celebration.

These materials were prepared quickly, under intense pressure, and with a great sense of national urgency. They might have looked quite different if they had been compiled under different circumstances, with more time to seek out additional voices and feedback. Yet at their most basic level, the ministry's approach to providing resources showed that teachers were tasked with more than making sure students understood the facts of what had happened and giving them support in their emotional processing of a traumatic national event.

Rather, teachers were also supposed to make sure that students interpreted the events in a specific way. In this context, students' conformity demonstrated how well they lived up to the national identity set out for them: To refuse to "be Charlie" was to be excluded from "being French." Just as American students who felt uneasy with displays of enforced patriotism at their schools after 9/11 were nevertheless often taught to conform, these French students who found it difficult to say "I am Charlie" were flagged as troublemakers.

VIVE LA RÉSISTANCE?: DEVALUING STUDENT DISSENT[5]

While the education systems of the United States and France had goals for what students would learn, think, and do following the respective attacks on their countries, the students themselves exercised their own agency as they responded to these intended messages. When they did so in a way that threatened teachers' sense of appropriateness, they faced reprisals.

Teachers' Interactions with Students

In the United States, even as some teachers emphasized that dissent was a prized right of American citizenship, they limited the exercise of this right among students of immigrant backgrounds. Abu El-Haj (2010) provided an example of Palestinian-American boys who were suspended for drawing pictures of planes flying into buildings, despite the fact that many other elementary schoolchildren across the country drew such pictures as they attempted to process the events in an age-appropriate way. Yet when the boys' teacher saw the drawings on *their* desk, she assumed they were drawing them in support of the attacks.

In France, the students who resisted the *Je suis Charlie* mantra that flooded the streets and social media alike were often seen as suspect. With the manhunt for the Kouachi brothers continuing for two days, and the international media's attention firmly fixed on Paris, the country was at an emotional fever pitch. Teaching with this backdrop of events would already be difficult, but two stories from schools that were widely circulated no doubt added to teachers' sense of stress: a fake bomb with a sign reading "*Je ne suis pas Charlie*" ("I am not Charlie") was found in the teachers' lounge of a Paris high school (Battaglia & Floc'h, 2015), and an incident of an eighth-grader in Lille who threatened his teacher by saying "I'll end you with a Kalashnikov" (Verduzier & Beyer, 2015).

Nevertheless, some teachers reported that conversations went smoothly. One teacher in a private high school described his day this way:

> [The students] started by describing their shock, their raw emotions, as well as their fear. I was happy with their reaction on that count: very quickly and on their own, they distinguished between terrorists and Muslims . . . they even expressed their fear that extremism would be able to rise and we would see intolerant or discriminatory reactions to these events. (Brouze, 2015)

Yet, the media coverage suggests that many teachers were often shocked at statements students made as they attempted to process the events (L'Express, 2015). Divergence from the official narrative was not perceived as reasoning but rather was frequently interpreted as insubordination.

This line of thought was especially evident when students wrestled with whether the magazine bore any responsibility for possibly having provoked the attack. In one such comment, a sixth-grade girl named Erica said, "Both sides did things wrong. To take away the lives of twelve people is a crime against humanity—even if they did kind of ask for it. But that's not an excuse" (Battaglia & Floc'h, 2015). Even those accustomed to leading classroom discussions frequently found it difficult to respond to such statements: a high school philosophy teacher stated that it was "impossible" to have a conversation with students on the subject (Verduzier & Beyer, 2015).

Attempts at classroom engagement often gave way to a need to control what was said. A social studies teacher in a private middle school recounted showing *Charlie Hebdo* caricatures to her students and giving them time to draw, during which she explained, "I decided not to allow talking during this exercise. . . . It's hard to admit, but I was afraid of hearing things I didn't want to hear. I work in a school where many pretty racist things can get said. . . . I didn't want it to get too emotional" (Brouze, 2015).

An eighth-grade teacher described feeling as though she had "lost control" of her class when students didn't accept her explanations about free speech in response to a group of students who agreed with a girl who said, "Madame, we're not going to allow ourselves to be insulted by drawings of the Prophet. Of course we're going to avenge ourselves. It's not just teasing, it's an insult!" (Dupont, 2015).

Even as France congratulated itself for supporting free speech in any circumstances (the common response to those who questioned the derogatory messages that graced the cover of *Charlie Hebdo* each week), such statements, when made by students, were difficult for many teachers to take. Responding to a call for testimonials, teachers flooded *Le Monde* with anonymous reports of Muslim students saying they thought "*Charlie Hebdo* really asked for it" and "Good for them. All they had to do was not insult the Prophet" (Nunès, 2015). Many teachers, who were still processing the attacks themselves, clearly felt ill at ease with students whose life experiences led them to process the events differently.

The responsibility to serve as a representative of the Republic clearly made many teachers' tasks even harder. Some students demanded that teachers recognize the double standard they perceived in French society. A middle school class is reported to have asked why there was a moment of silence for *Charlie Hebdo* but not "for the Palestinians or Africa" (Nunès, 2015). A comparison was frequently made with Dieudonné, a controversial comedian who has received several convictions for hate speech.

As Yacine, a student in sixth grade, told a reporter, "A lot of young people compare it to Dieudonné. He got fined for making anti-Semitic hand gestures, but when *Charlie* draws them, suddenly it's about freedom of speech" (Battaglia & Floc'h, 2015). For some teachers who keenly felt their responsibility to represent the Republic, this demand to recognize injustice in society could result in feeling cornered.

Reprisals Following a Moment of Silence

A flash point occurred around a moment of silence scheduled for Thursday, January 8, at noon. While the majority of schools observed the moment without incident, some students engaged in civic disobedience by refusing to participate. At an elementary school in Seine-Saint-Denis, 80 percent of the children refused to participate in the moment of silence (Verduzier & Beyer, 2015). Students at a middle school in Toulouse sang Algeria's national anthem (Bossard, 2015).

In certain schools, teachers were surprised to find themselves needing to respond to students who did not wish to participate. A student in Grenoble asked, "Why should I respect a moment of silence for people I didn't know?" The teacher said, "I found that reaction to be violent. His classmates were just as shocked as I was. . . . He was trying to provoke me" (Dupont, 2015).

With many adults aghast at students' refusal to observe a moment of silence for victims of a terrorist attack, the press asked some students to explain their reasoning. A seventeen-year-old named Marie-Hélène explained, "I didn't want to do the moment of silence. I didn't think it was right to honor people who had insulted Islam, along with other religions" (Battaglia & Floc'h, 2015).

An unnamed student told reporters, "I can't stand up for people like that" and "you reap what you sow—they brought this on themselves" (Verduzier & Beyer, 2015). A fourteen-year-old named Abdel did participate, but had mixed feelings about it: "I did [the moment of silence] for those who were killed, but not for Charlie, the guy who did the drawings. I don't feel sorry for him at all. He had no respect for us as Muslims. But they didn't have to kill twelve people. They could have just killed him" (Battaglia & Floc'h, 2015).

Often, these students were not perceived to be engaging in free speech. Rather, they were perceived to be out of order. One teacher reported that children who didn't respect the moment of silence were sent to the school principal or nurse "to hear a different perspective than the one they must have been hearing at home" (Dupont, 2015). The Ministry of Education, embarrassed on the national stage by the students' acts of civic disobedience, responded by announcing a three-point plan for the nation's schools (Magnenou, 2015):

- the creation of a booklet that educated teachers on radicalization
- increased inspections and observations in certain schools
- a study of France's citizenship education program, with a goal of understanding why some students weren't internalizing its messages

With the media eagerly repeating such inflammatory stories, some teachers and students did express concern about the impact the nation's response to the attacks might have on Muslim students and families. A sixteen-year-old named Maryam told the newspaper *Le Monde* she was worried about girls her age who wear the veil and might be "assaulted by skinheads in the 9-4 [slang for Val-de-Marne, a department to the southeast of Paris]" (Battaglia & Floc'h, 2015). One teacher worried that some might lose sight of the way Muslim students are vulnerable (Nunès, 2015):

> You have to hear these students when they say they're afraid people will point fingers at them, how many times they say Islam has absolutely nothing to do with terrorism, that the terrorists aren't Muslim . . . and to hear them say how sincerely shocked they are by certain *Charlie Hebdo* drawings.

These worries proved justified: According to the National Observatory Against Islamophobia, there were nearly as many anti-Muslim incidents reported within two weeks of the *Charlie Hebdo* attacks as for the entire previous calendar year (quoted in *Le Monde*, 2015). These included eighty-eight threats and twenty-eight instances of violence, including gunshots and training grenades fired at mosques, at least one bomb detonated at a Muslim-owned restaurant, and the defacing of mosques and prayer centers by leaving severed pigs' heads on doorsteps, hooking pigs' intestines over doorknobs, and painting graffiti on walls with phrases like "Death to Arabs" and "Arabs Get Out" (Stone, 2015).

Students were not exempt from these incidents; during the moment of silence, a seventeen-year-old Muslim immigrant from Maghreb was assaulted by a group of five people in the town of Bourgoin-Jallieu (Verduzier & Beyer, 2015). Such reports did not garner the same kind of dismay and were not consumed as eagerly as stories where Muslims were presented as aggressors, a phenomenon that parallels American media after 9/11. In American schools as well, Muslim students were subjected to bullying that included actions taken by students, teachers, and administrators following the attacks of 9/11 (Abu El-Haj, 2010).

Further, despite reporting that made overtures toward being "colorblind," the students whose voices the media highlighted as shocking were nearly all members of France's Muslim population. Many teachers too seemed to find deficits in Muslim students and their culture. Feeling destabilized and grasping for explanations, some teachers theorized that the students' families were the problem. A middle school teacher described how she felt at odds with her students' parents:

Schools are there to transmit our values, but sometimes we're undermined a bit by the parents. We can teach republican principles to the children, but once they're at home, they'll do whatever they want with them. They don't trust teachers anymore. They think we're enemies rather than allies. (Dupont, 2015)

A teacher identifying herself as "Marie" wrote a blog entry to defend "the vast majority" of her students in Seine-Saint-Denis, an area with a high Muslim immigrant population. She emphasizes that it was only a "handful" of students who were the problem:

Curiously—or not—these are the same students who, all throughout the year, respect neither the school nor the teachers. These are the same students who come to class unprepared, who don't do their work or learn their lessons, who disrupt their classes. These are the same ones whose parents don't come to parent-teacher conferences, whose families don't answer the telephone. The same ones we're worried about dropping out. It's not a coincidence. (Tailspin, 2015)

Examples like these show that, when students diverged from the "correct" interpretation of the *Charlie Hebdo* attack, their families and home cultures could be devalued along with their perspectives.

Taken as a whole, these examples of dissenting students suggest that, even as schools sought to inculcate civic values, they ceased to fulfill their civic purpose. Instead of providing a place for students to encounter one another and consider diverse ideas, schools served as sites of social reproduction. As countries hardened their sense of national identity, minority students were further marginalized at school through implicit and explicit messages that their life experiences and perspectives were not valid grounds for questioning values promoted as acquired characteristics of national identity.

ASPIRATIONAL APPROACHES TO NATIONAL VALUES

The examples of 9/11 and *Charlie Hebdo* suggest that an important ballast against nationalistic tendencies may be to teach national ideals as aspirational rather than acquired values. That is, Americans may love freedom and aspire toward a free society, but it cannot be taken for granted that Americans always experience freedom or always act in ways that increase freedom at home or abroad.

Indeed, a shared love of freedom would demand that citizens not attempt to deny times when their country failed to live up to its values, but rather to recognize and actively work against such instances. This approach may manifest itself in teachers' mindsets, their approach to the curriculum, and pedagogical strategies more broadly.

Approaching values as aspirational inherently opens a space for critical inquiry, as the suggestion that a value is not fully acquired means there are situations in which we might discover its absence or partial presence. In recognizing that a value does not have to be acquired to be shared, this stance provides a space for what Merry (2009) called "critical patriotism," a form of loyalty and attachment to one's homeland which carries the following advantages:

[T]he critical patriot will embrace what is wonderful about one's homeland on the understanding that its ideals extend to all citizens irrespective of one's color, sexual orientation, creed or political affiliation. Where it is sensibly allowed, critical patriotism will foster the capacity to express dissent and moral outrage, and this arises from the fact that citizens may sometimes feel the best ideals of American democracy are being betrayed if not effectively undermined. Moreover, critical

> patriotism will consider the welfare of those outside of one's borders and understand one's role as citizen in ways not confined by national borders or geopolitical expediency. (p. 379)

Such a definition of patriotism is distinct from the way the term often functions; in a systematic look at American high school seniors' definitions of patriotism, Kahne and Middaugh (2007) found that students felt stifling critique was part of their patriotic duty. However, philosophers have often argued that unquestioning patriotism is not a virtue and have either argued against the concept entirely or proposed alternate definitions that value the role of dissent in a democratic society. Among these are cosmopolitan patriotism (Nussbaum, 1996), ethical patriotism (Primoratz, 2008), moderate patriotism (Nathanson, 1989), and progressive patriotism (Green, 2004).

This aspirational approach to national identity has several benefits. First, it prepares children to make contributions to their democratic society by recognizing problems and challenging those times and places we do not live up to our national ideals. For example, as the world engaged in an outpouring of support for the slain *Charlie Hebdo* cartoonists, another protest was held in Paris on January 18, seeking to draw attention to the thousands of victims of the Islamist militant group Boko Haram.

These victims included a group of nearly three hundred girls in Nigeria, kidnapped from their school and subjected to sexual assault in captivity. Little was done on the part of the international community to find the girls, much less rescue them and return them to their families; at the one-year anniversary of their kidnapping, they remained in captivity.[6]

Among the signs held by protestors that day in Paris was one that pictured a broken, bloody pencil and the slogan "Let Us Not Forget the Victims of Boko Haram" (Bettinelli, 2015). The implicit message was clear: some victims matter more than others. In some classrooms, a student who raised this issue might be seen as challenging not only the teacher, but also the dominant sense of French national identity that existed after the attacks. In a classroom where the teacher was working from a framework of critical patriotism, the same student would be recognized as animated by a spirit of love for freedom, equality, and brotherhood.

Second, aspirational approaches to national values open a space for more voices to be heard. When national identity is defined in a rigid way that is not open to challenge, various groups of people who should be included in a nation are excluded. This diminishes the possibility of a pluralistic society, even as it ostensibly celebrates diversity.

Hess and Ganzler (2007) detailed the benefits that come from exposing students to diverse points of view and wrote that steps should be taken to "create schools and classes that are as politically heterogeneous as possible" in order to prepare students to "become patriots of the *deliberative* sort" (p. 138; emphasis in original). Parker (2006) advocated for "inclusive deliberation," in which "marginalized voices are encouraged to speak" and "listening is generous" (para. 8).

Further, as they hear more voices, students become more able to parse the various societal factors that influence who is included and excluded within a normative national identity. As Patton (2008) suggested:

> Allowing human crises to serve as teachable moments can help students raise issues of race and class and help them understand how and why such issues matter in this country. Educators can also use human crises to examine how ideologies, philosophies, and traditions can adversely affect those considered "other" in the United States and abroad. (p. 12)

As educators seek to achieve this goal, they should remember that their students are not homogenous, and "such issues" matter in their classrooms. In France, students who found it difficult to say *Je suis Charlie* were often socially positioned as marginal. The narrowed definition of French identity that was promoted and enforced through the mainstream national discourse, including in pedagogical materials created by the Ministry of Education, only served to alienate them further.

Their voices deserved to be heard, and their classmates would have grown from hearing them speak. Yet observing silence can be a measure of self-protection, and breaking that silence sometimes carries risks that cannot be mitigated simply by a teacher's good intentions. Effective teaching in a pluralistic society requires a high level of fluency in recognizing and navigating these dynamics.

Third, taking an aspirational approach to national values helps teachers continue to grow through self-questioning, reflection, and challenge by students. This stance is expressed in a poignant, soul-searching open letter written by three French teachers who worked in schools in Saint-Denis, an area with a high Muslim population. They reflected on the divide between themselves as socially privileged individuals, and their students, whose voices were often viewed with suspicion or seen as only marginally French.

Drawing on the French value of brotherhood, they wrote that sadness and anger are easier emotions to bear than shame, and reflected on the responsibility of French educators to recognize *all* students as children of the French Republic:

> The people of *Charlie Hebdo* were our brothers. We mourn them as such. Their assassins were orphans, placed under our care as students of our nation and children of France. Our children killed our brothers . . . let us open our eyes to understand how we arrived at this situation, so that we can take action to build a society that will be secular and cultivated, more just, more free, more equal, more brotherly. (Boussard, Louys, Richer, & Robert, 2015)

The stance articulated by these teachers is resonant with what Zembylas and Boler (2002) termed a "pedagogy of discomfort," one that encourages students to engage with the emotions they feel, to critically evaluate and resist the conflation of nationalism and patriotism, and to learn to "inhabit ambiguity, discomfort and indeterminism" (para. 56). Educators who adopt this approach in their own professional development, as well as in their classrooms, may become more able to engage in authentic conversations with students and colleagues around the presence and limitations of shared national values, even in times of crisis.

Fourth, taking an aspirational approach to national values is a strategy for preventing ideals from enforcing their opposites. If students cannot question whether the American value of "freedom" has been fully achieved, they are not free in the ways they think about, talk about, challenge, and perhaps even love the idea of freedom. Likewise, if "free speech" is taken to be an acquired asset in France, students who question the way it is implemented are apt to be seen as potentially dangerous in their dissent.

This stifles students who might otherwise express themselves, wondering why they are seen as aberrant for refusing to participate in a moment of silence while they are simultaneously told that the very offensiveness of *Charlie Hebdo* represented proof of the tolerance of French society. Further, just as students are unequally positioned in society, this silencing operates unequally as well. A value which on the surface seems to promote something positive for one group can be experienced as negative by another. When students are able to engage in critical inquiry around these values, they can increase the chances that a given value will in fact function in a positive way.

Finally, taking an aspirational approach to national values includes some measure of protection for students. The roles that students and teachers play in schools—as learners and experts, respectively—mean that students inherently occupy a disadvantaged position in classrooms, with their perspectives subject to a teacher's review.

When a teacher attempts to teach about national values as acquired, students whose life experiences challenge this interpretation are deemed to be providing the "wrong" answers. When social studies educators suggest a given ideal is an important shared value and allow students to engage in critical inquiry around how that shared value is expressed or limited in society, educators can take a step toward positioning students as fellow citizens and critical compatriots.

CONCLUSION

Writing after September 11, Giroux (2002) suggested that "[i]n a time of crisis, unity is a powerful force, but it is not always innocent" (p. 1142). The pedagogical decisions of both American and French educators frequently used the attacks on their respective countries as an opportunity to define, and in some cases enforce, a specific sense of "proper" national identity. This collapsed the complexity of a pluralistic society into something that felt more manageable and safe for some, while increasing a sense of exclusion and danger for others.

The ways educators emphasized certain ideals key to national identity suggested that these ideals were not commonly held values, but rather static characteristics that could not be questioned. Discussion of possible flaws in these definitions was tacitly or explicitly suppressed. These approaches to patriotism conflict with the proper goals of education (Merry, 2009). Instead, taking an aspirational approach toward values associated with national identity can help social studies educators navigate the challenges of teaching about citizenship in a post-9/11 world.

NOTES

1. This chapter was written before the November 13, 2015, attacks in Paris, which, sadly, replaced this record.
2. For an example, see Bratta's (2009) powerful analysis of this phenomenon focused on flag imagery.
3. All translations from French are by the chapter author. References to French grade levels have been modified to reflect their American equivalents.
4. It should be noted that American schools can limit the speech of both teachers and students in certain circumstances. See suurtamm and Darden (2007) for an overview. Westheimer (2007) details instances of students and teachers who were reprimanded in the months following 9/11 for speech that failed to conform to an authoritarian form of patriotism.
5. Out of necessity, this section depends on media coverage to represent student voices; indeed, this chapter may be seen as a qualitative content analysis of this media coverage. Because the media tend to report things that are exceptional, the incidents relayed here should not be seen as average experiences in French schools following the attacks. However, this same principle makes media coverage particularly well suited to finding dissenting voices: during times with a keen perceived need for national unity, any voices that disrupt that unity will be flagged as aberrant. A close reading of media coverage tells us who was considered newsworthy for failing to fit in and whose words were perceived to be shocking.
6. *Charlie Hebdo* itself had "satirized" the situation by running a headline of "Anger Among Boko Haram's Sex Slaves" on the cover of the October 22, 2014, issue, with a caricature of four pregnant girls in headscarves portrayed as "welfare queens," one shouting, "Don't touch our benefits!"

REFERENCES

Abu El-Haj, T. R. (2010). "The beauty of America": Nationalism, education, and the war on terror. *Harvard Educational Review, 80*, 242–274.

Apple, M. W. (2002). Patriotism, pedagogy, and freedom: On the educational meanings of September 11th. *Teachers College Record, 104*, 1760–1772.

Battaglia, M., & Floc'h, B. (2015, January 10). A Saint-Denis, collégiens et lycéens ne sont pas tous "Charlie." *Le Monde*. Retrieved from http://www.lemonde.fr.
Bettinelli, M. (2015, January 18). A Paris, un rassemblement en hommage aux milliers de victimes de Boko Haram. *Le Monde*. Retrieved from http://www.lemonde.fr.
Bossard, C. (2015, January 16). L'école face au défi républicain. *La Nouvelle République*. Retrieved from http://www.lanouvellerepublique.fr.
Boussard, D., Louys, V., Richer, I., & Robert, C. (2015, January 13.) Comment avons-nous pu laisser nos élèves devenir des assassins ? *Le Monde*. Retrieved from http://www.lemonde.fr.
Bratta, P. M. (2009). Flag display post-9/11: A discourse on American nationalism. *Journal of American Culture, 32*, 232–243.
Brouze, E. (2015, January 8). Témoinages: Beaucoup d'élèves sont choqués par les dessins de Charlie Hebdo. *Rue89*. Retrieved from http://rue89.nouvelobs.com.
Camicia, S. P., & Zhu, J. (2011). Citizenship education under discourses of nationalism, globalism, and cosmopolitanism; Illustrations from China and the United States. *Frontiers of Education in China, 6*, 602–619.
Dupont, L. (2015, January 9). Le désarroi d'une prof qui parle de "Charlie" à ses élèves. *Le Point*. Retrieved from http://www.lepoint.fr.
Giroux, H. A. (2002). Democracy, freedom, and justice after September 11th: Rethinking the role of educators and the politics of schooling. *Teachers College Record, 104*, 1138–1162.
Green, M. (Ed.). (2004). *What we stand for: A program of progressive patriotism*. New York: New Market.
Hess, D., & Ganzler, L. (2007). Patriotism and ideological diversity in the classroom. In J. Westheimer (Ed.), *Pledging allegiance: The politics of patriotism in America's schools* (pp. 131–138). New York: Teachers College Press.
Kahne, J., & Middaugh, E. (2007). Is patriotism good for democracy? In J. Westheimer (Ed.), *Pledging allegiance: The politics of patriotism in America's schools* (pp. 115–126). New York: Teachers College Press.
La Provence. (2015, January 10). Un lycéen condamné pour apologie des attentats. *La Provence*. Retrieved from http://www.laprovence.com.
Le Monde. (2015, January 19). Les actes antimusulmans ont doublé en janvier. *Le Monde*. Retrieved from http://www.lemonde.fr.
L'Express. (2015). Charlie Hebdo: Que faire quand des eleves defendent des terroristes? Retrieved from http://www.lexpress.fr/actualite/societe/charlie-hebdo-que-faire-quand-des-eleves-defendent-des-terroristes_1639423.html.
Magnenou, F. (2015, January 14). "Charlie Hebdo": après les incidents en classe, que prépare le ministère de l'Education? *France TV Info*. Retrieved from http://www.francetvinfo.fr.
Merry, M. S. (2009). Patriotism, history and the legitimate aims of American education. *Educational Philosophy and Theory, 41*, 378–398.
Ministère de l'éducation nationale, de l'enseignement supérieur et de la recherche. (2015a). Liberté de conscience, liberté d'expression: outils pédagogiques pour réfléchir et débattre avec les élèves. Retrieved from http://eduscol.education.fr.
———. (2015b). Liberté de conscience, liberté d'expression—ressources pour le premier degré: education artistique. Retrieved from http://eduscol.education.fr.
———. (2015c). Liberté de conscience, liberté d'expression—ressources pour le premier degré: la littérature de jeunesse. Retrieved from http://eduscol.education.fr.
Mirel, J. (2002). Civic education and changing definitions of American identity, 1900–1950. *Educational Review, 54*, 143–152.
Myers, J. (2006). Rethinking the social studies curriculum in the context of globalization: Education for global citizenship in the U.S. *Theory & Research in Social Education, 34*, 370–394.
Nash, G. B., Crabtree, C., & Dunn, R. E. (1997). *History on trial: Culture wars and the teaching of the past*. New York: Knopf.
Nathanson, S. (1989). In defense of "moderate patriotism." *Ethics, 99*, 535–552.
Nunès, E. (2015, January 14). Dans les collèges et lycées, le soutien à "Charlie Hebdo" loin de faire l'unanimité. *Le Monde*. Retrieved from www.lemonde.fr.
Nussbaum, M. (1996). Patriotism and cosmopolitanism. In J. Cohen (Ed.), *For love of country* (pp. 2–20). Boston: Beacon.
Osanloo, A. F. (2011). Unburying patriotism: Critical lessons in civics and leadership ten years later. *High School Journal, 95*, 56–71.
Parker, W. (2006, March 9). Public schools are hotbeds of democracy. *Seattle Post-Intelligencer*. Retrieved from http://www.seattlepi.com.
Patton, L. D. (2008). Learning through crisis: The educator's role. *About Campus, 12*(6), 10–16.
Primoratz, I. (2008). Patriotism and morality: Mapping the terrain. *Journal of Moral Philosophy, 5*, 204–226.
Reuben, J. (2005). Patriotic purposes: Public schools and the education of citizens. In S. Fuhrman & M. Lazerson (Eds.), *The public schools* (pp. 1–24). New York: Oxford University Press.
Reyes-Torres, A. (2014). Essentialism in children's literature: The emergence of retrogressive discourses in post-9/11 picture books. *ATLANTIS: Journal of the Spanish Association of Anglo-American Studies, 36*, 123–137.
Saleem, M. M., & Thomas, M. K. (2011). The reporting of the September 11th terrorist attacks in American social studies textbooks: A Muslim perspective. *High School Journal, 95*, 15–33.

Stone, J. (2015, January 14). Firebombs and pigs' heads thrown into mosques as anti-Muslim attacks increase after Paris shootings. *The Independent*. Retrieved from http://www.theindependent.co.uk.

suurtamm, k. e., & Darden, E. C. (2007). Toeing the line and the law: First Amendment rights in schools. In J. Westheimer (Ed.), *Pledging allegiance: The politics of patriotism in America's schools* (pp. 139–144). New York: Teachers College Press.

Tailspin [blog]. (2015). Pour mes eleves de Seine Saint-Denis. Retrieved from http://tailspin.fr/post/107696839163/pour-mes-%C3%A9l%C3%A8ves-de-seine-saint-denis.

Vallaud-Belkacem, N. (2015, January 8). Lettre à la suite de l'attentat contre l'hebdomadaire "Charlie Hebdo." Ministère de l'éducation nationale, de l'enseignement supérieur et de la recherche (DGESCO). Retrieved from http://www.education.gouv.fr.

Verduzier, P., & Beyer, C. (2015, January 9). Charlie Hebdo: ces minutes de silence qui ont dérapé dans les écoles. *Le Figaro*. Retrieved from http://www.lefigaro.fr.

Weaver-Hightower, M. (2002). The gender of terror and heroes? What educators might teach about men and masculinity after September 11, 2001. *Teachers College Record*. Retrieved from http://www.tcrecord.org/Content.asp?ContentID=11012.

Westheimer, J. (2007). Politics and patriotism in education. In J. Westheimer (Ed.), *Pledging allegiance: The politics of patriotism in America's schools* (pp. 171–188). New York: Teachers College Press.

Zembylas, M., & Boler, M. (2002). On the spirit of patriotism: Challenges of a "pedagogy of discomfort." *Teachers College Record*. Retrieved from http://www.tcrecord.org/Content.asp?ContentID=11007.

Chapter Six

The Courage of Hopelessness

Creative Disruption of Everyday Life in the Classroom

E. Wayne Ross

The world after the events of September 11, 2011, is depressing for anyone who values freedom and equality. In the wake the heinous 9/11 attacks, we have experienced assaults on civil liberties and human rights in the name of protecting freedom. The Patriot Act in the United States significantly expanded the authority of government to enhance surveillance of individual behavior and communication, seize assets, conduct warrantless and secret searches, and detain individuals indefinitely without charge.

The War on Terror has produced horrors such as the extraordinary rendition program (e.g., the case of Maher Arar), the Guantanamo Bay Detainment Camp, U.S. citizens held as "enemy combatants," criminalization of refugees, among others (Freedom House, 2008). In a recent MSNBC interview, retired general and former democratic presidential candidate Wesley Clark even called for the revival of internment camps for "disloyal Americans," advocating for a return to one of the most shameful chapters in American history, the forced relocation and incarceration of Japanese Americans, most of whom were U.S. citizens.

Post-9/11 policy shifts are not limited to the United States. Canada's Anti-terrorism Act of 2015 (aka Bill C-51) follows in the Patriot Act's footsteps by drastically expanding the definition of "security" originally outlined in Ottawa's 2001 anti-terror law. The bill contains the following provisions:

- lowers the threshold for preventative arrest and detention of citizens
- criminalizes speech acts that have no connection to acts of violence
- provides new, sweeping powers to police and prosecutors
- turns the national intelligence agency, Canadian Security Intelligence Service, into a police force
- engages in domestic spying on citizen groups who oppose resource extraction and then turns the information over to the energy industry
- allows secret court proceedings to use secret evidence to compile secret no-fly lists
- allows federal courts to limit the Charter rights of Canadian citizens, including the right to return to Canada after traveling abroad

The human, social, environmental, and economic costs of the wars in Iraq, Afghanistan, and Pakistan since 2001 are astronomical. Nearly 400,000 people (including over 200,000 civilians) have died due to direct war violence. One million U.S. veterans have been disabled. Veterans also suffer from psychological and cognitive problems at an astronomical rate, including what has been described as an epidemic of post-traumatic stress disorder–induced suicides, nearly 8,000 per year (Tanielian, & Jaycox, 2008).

Indirect deaths of people in war zones, related to malnutrition, damaged health infrastructure, and environmental degradation, are likely many times more. Eight million people have been displaced and are living in inadequate conditions, and Iraq's health and education systems have been devastated. These wars have produced major human rights and civil liberties violations including "a program of indefinite secret detention and the use of brutal interrogation techniques in violation of U.S. law, treaty obligations, and our values" (U.S. Senate Select Committee on Intelligence, 2014, p. 2).

The environment is another casualty of the war in Iraq. Radiation from the depleted uranium in hundreds of thousands of tons of bombs and other ordnance dropped on Iraq has created a toxic environment, poisoning soil and water, making the environment carcinogenic, and creating abnormally high cancer rates (Busby, Hamdan, & Ariabi, 2010). The toxic legacy of the U.S. assault on Fallujah has been described as "worse than Hiroshima" (Cockburn, 2010). After the "shock and awe" bombing campaign in Iraq, a fourfold increase in the levels of depleted uranium was measured in the atmosphere in Europe, transported on air currents from the Middle East and Central Asia (Gould & Ungoed-Thomas, 2006).

Estimates suggest these wars have cost $4.4 trillion, a figure that will double in the next forty years as a result of government borrowing to finance wars that not only failed to bring democracy to these countries, but have produced even more death and destruction as war spread into Syria and Yemen. No expense is spared when it comes to the warfront. Meanwhile, income and wage inequality continues to grow with the 1 percent leaving everyone else in the dust.

We are now in a new Gilded Age, with massive concentrations of wealth at the top, while the people in the bottom 40 percent are becoming poorer (Organization for Economic Cooperation [OECD], 2014; Piketty, 2014). The gap between the rich and poor in developed countries is at its highest level in three decades. In the United States, the wealthiest 0.1 percent are worth as much as the bottom 90 percent combined (Saez & Zucman, 2014). Oxfam (2014) reports that the eighty-five richest people in the world are as wealthy as the poorest half of the world.[1]

A 2014 OECD report confirms what the rest of have long known—trickle-down and austerity economics only make the rich richer. The OECD reports data that neoliberal economic policies have not only failed to create economic growth, they have also "curbed economic growth significantly" (p. 4). OECD argues that inequality matters because it undermines education opportunities, lowers social mobility, and hampers skill development for the disadvantaged.[2]

Oxfam (2014) points out that the concentration of economic resources presents a significant threat to inclusive political and economic systems, specifically that "people are increasingly separated by economic and political power, inevitably heightening social tensions and increasing the risk of societal breakdown" (p. 2). The world is at a crisis point we have never seen the likes of before.[3] The French theorist Guy Debord often cited a letter written by Karl Marx in which he says: "The hopeless conditions of the society in which I live fill me with hope."[4] Philosopher Giorgio Agambem adds:

Any radical thought always adopts the most extreme position of desperation. Simone Weil said "I do not like those people who warm their hearts with empty hopes." Thought, for me, is just that: the courage of hopelessness. And is that not the height of optimism? (cited in Skinner, 2014, para. 8)

We certainly have plenty of fuel for our hopes. The challenge we face as social studies educators is to not warm our students' hearts with empty hopes, but rather confront what are seemingly hopeless times for freedom and equality with a pedagogy and curriculum that come from a courage of hopelessness.

DEMOCRACY IN CRISIS

In *Brave New World Revisited* (1958) Aldous Huxley wrote:

> [B]y means of ever more effective methods of mind-manipulation, the democracies will change their nature; the quaint old forms—elections, parliaments, Supreme Courts and all the rest—will remain. The underlying substance will be a new kind of non-violent totalitarianism. All the traditional names, all the hallowed slogans will remain exactly what they were in the good old days. Democracy and freedom will be the theme of every broadcast and editorial—but democracy and freedom in a strictly Pickwickian sense. Meanwhile the ruling oligarchy and its highly trained elite of soldiers, policemen, thought-manufacturers and mind-manipulators will quietly run the show as they see fit. (Chapter 12, "What Can Be Done?" para. 4)

From Democracy to Plutocracy

Huxley was prescient. His description accurately captures the landscape of post-9/11 politics. A landscape where democracy, as a concept and as a thing, has less to do with its actual content as an egalitarian system of political-economic values than it does with the neglect of this content for its mere form. "More simply put, the concept of democracy in the West is the mere distillate remaining after the actual content (equality, egalitarianism, justice, rights, etc.) has been boiled away" (Smith & Sperber, 2014, p. 1).

In the *Society of the Spectacle*, Debord (2014/1967) argues, "in societies dominated by modern conditions of production, life is presented as an immense accumulation of spectacles. Everything that was directly lived has receded into a *representation*" (p. 1). That is, our democratic experiences have degraded from being, to having, to merely appearing to have.

The lofty, Deweyan (1916) ideal of democracy as a social phenomenon, what he called an "associated way of living," which he understood as an end-in-view, something to be striven for, is first reduced to a political phenomenon (e.g., weak conceptions of democracy, such as representative government) then is degraded further to a spectator democracy, where a specialized class of experts identifies what our common interests are then acts accordingly, leaving the rest of us spectators, rather than participants, in democracy.

Today the United States behaves nothing like a democracy. As Noam Chomsky (2013) explains:

> Roughly 70% of the population—the lower 70% on the wealth/income scale—have no influence on policy whatsoever. They're effectively disenfranchised. As you move up the wealth/income ladder, you get a little bit more influence on policy. When you get to the top, which is maybe a tenth of one percent, people essentially get what they want, i.e. they determine the policy. So the proper term for that is not democracy; it's plutocracy. (para. 5)

In 2014, Marin Gilens and Benjamin Page reported an empirical study in the highly respected journal *Perspectives on Politics* that attempts to answer the questions: Who governs? Who really rules? To what extent is the broad body of U.S. citizens sovereign, semi-sovereign, or largely powerless? This work is particularly significant because, despite a large body of empirical research on the policy influence of one or another set of actors, until recently it has not been possible to test contrasting theoretical predictions against one another in a single statistical model. Using a unique dataset that included measures of the key variables for 1,779 policy issues, Gilens and Page (2014) were able to accomplish this task. Their analysis indicates economic elites and organized groups representing business interests that have substantial independent impacts on U.S. government policy, while average citizens and mass-based interest groups have little or no influence.

Overall, evidence strongly favored political theories of economic elite domination and biased pluralism, where corporations, business associations, and professional groups dominate. There was little evidence to support descriptions of the United States as a majoritarian electoral democracy. These findings contradict the central tenet of the social studies curriculum.

The evidence confirms that the United States is not a functioning democracy; rather, it is a plutocracy, as Chomsky has claimed. Do we need statistical analysis to tell us this? For example, the 2010 U.S. Supreme Court ruling *Citizens United v. Federal Election Commission* cemented the false doctrine of "Money = Speech" that allows the richest to buy government influence and set policy agendas (Dangl, 2010). *Citizens United* is merely the latest way in which the United States protects itself from too much democracy.

The framers of the U.S. Constitution were keenly aware of the threat of democracy. According to James Madison, the primary responsibility of government was "to protect the minority of the opulent against the majority." Madison believed the threat of democracy was likely to increase as "the proportion of those who will labor under all the hardships of life and secretly sigh for a more equal distribution of its blessing" (cite in Elliot, 1888, p. 243).

In crafting a system giving primacy to property over people, Madison and the framers were guarding against the increased influence of the unpropertied masses. As expressed by John Jay, first chief justice of the U.S. Supreme Court, "the people who own the country ought to govern it" (cited in Monaghan, 1935, p. 323).[5]

As Paul Street (2014) argues in *They Rule: The 1% v. Democracy*, Washington runs on corporate and financial cash, connections, reach, and propaganda, not public opinion. The "unelected dictatorship of money" is not interested in crafting policy that responds to public opinion polls (Scheiber & Sussman, 2015) that show:

- two-thirds (66 percent) of Americans think that the distribution of money and wealth should be more evenly distributed among more people in the United States.
- sixty-one percent of Americans believe that in today's economy it is mainly just a few people at the top who have a chance to get ahead.
- eighty-three percent of Americans think the gap between the rich and the poor is a problem.
- sixty-seven percent of Americans think the gap between the rich and the poor needs to be addressed immediately, not as some point in the future.
- fifty-seven percent of Americans think the U.S. government should do more to reduce the gap between the rich and the poor in the United States.
- almost three-quarters (74 percent) of respondents say that large corporations have too much influence in the country, about double the amount that said the same of unions.
- sixty-eight percent of Americans favor raising taxes on people earning more than $1 million per year.

- fifty percent of Americans support limits on money earned by top executives at large corporations. (Street, 2015)

The disconnect between the rhetoric and reality of democracy (and equality, justice, rights) in North America is a direct challenge to our work as social studies educators. We can no longer rely on the old tropes of democracy and freedom that have dominated the curriculum and classroom discourse; to do so is to sell students a lie about history and contemporary life.

DANGEROUS CITIZENSHIP

> Citizenship implies *freedom*. . . . Citizenship is not obtained by chance: It is a construction that, never finished, demands we fight for it. It demands commitment, political clarity, coherence, decision. (Freire, 1998, p. 90)

Our challenge, particularly in a time of standardized curriculum and heightened surveillance of teachers' work, is to have the courage to reimagine our roles as teachers and find ways to create opportunities for students to create meaningful personal understandings of the world. What we understand about the world is determined by what the world is, who we are, and how we conduct our inquiries. Social studies education is not about showing life to people, but rather bringing them to life.

The aim is not getting students to listen to convincing lectures by experts, but rather to get them to speak for themselves in order to achieve, or at least strive for, an equal degree of participation and a more democratic, equitable, and justice future. This requires a new mindset, something I call dangerous citizenship (Ross & Vinson, 2014).

The practice of critical, or dangerous, citizenship requires that people, individually and collectively, take on actions and behaviors that bring with them certain necessary dangers; it transcends traditional maneuvers such as voting and signing petitions. Citizenship today, from this perspective, requires a praxis-inspired mindset of opposition and resistance, an acceptance of a certain strategic and tactical stance. The implication is that dangerous citizenship is dangerous to an oppressive and socially unjust status quo, to existing hierarchical structures of power. In a post-9/11 world, however, it is also a risky practice for teachers, students, and citizens.

Dangerous citizenship is a radical critique of schooling as social control and a collection of strategies used to disrupt and resist the conforming, anti-democratic, anti-collective, and oppressive potentialities of society and schooling that includes:

- political (non)participation
- critical awareness, what Freire called *conscientization* and class consciousness, which is something to be achieved (Lukács, 1971)
- intentional action—behaviors designed to instigate human connection, the true engagement with everyday life, meaningful experience, communication, and change

Philosopher Michel Foucault (1988) argued that a critique is not merely a matter of saying that things are not right as they are. Rather:

> It is a matter of pointing out on what kinds of assumptions, what kinds of familiar, unchallenged, unconsidered modes of thought, the practices that we accept rest. Criticism is a matter of flushing out that thought and trying to change it: to show that things are not as self-evident as one believed,

to see that what is accepted as self-evident will no longer be accepted as such. Practicing criticism is a matter of making facile gestures difficult. (p. 154)

Dangerous citizenship challenges assumptions about the state of the world and requires exploration of questions that make some uncomfortable: Given what we know about the lack of democracy in the United States and world today, is it even possible to teach for a democracy that is not dominated by capital? Do we want to teach for capitalist democracy? Is there an alternative? Is the concept of democracy bankrupt? Is democracy as a concept and practice even salvageable?

If democracy is salvageable then that teaching about and for democracy in contemporary times cannot be done without engaging the complexities and contradictions that have come to define what really existing (or nonexisting) democracy is. It is a practice that must be understood as difficult, risky, and even dangerous.

Premises of Dangerous Citizenship

How do we break free of the tropes that have come to dominate our conceptions of democracy and define what it means to be a democratic citizen? Four fundamental premises inform dangerous citizenship. First, democracy and capitalism are incompatible. There is a fundamental contradiction between the ideals of democracy (people rule) and what capitalist democracy actually delivers (rule of the rich).

Too often democracy and capitalism are conflated in our discussions and teaching of both. In short, democracy does not dominate capital; it submits to capital. Many people work to make capitalism less hostile to democracy (e.g., social democrats), but as the history of the United States illustrates, capital will always trump democracy.[6]

The second premise is teachers and curriculum have been subject to ever intensifying policy regimes that attack academic freedom and discourage critical social analysis. No Child Left Behind and Race to the Top are U.S. variations on a worldwide phenomenon that includes (Gibson & Ross, 2015; Ross & Vinson, 2014):

- marketization and privatization of education
- human capital policies for teachers
- regulation of what people know and how they come to know it

The third premise is neatly captured in the words of historian Howard Zinn (1970):

> Civil disobedience is not our problem. Our problem is civil obedience. Our problem is that people all over the world have obeyed the dictates of leaders . . . and millions have been killed because of this obedience. . . . Our problem is that people are obedient all over the world in the face of poverty and starvation and stupidity, and war, and cruelty. Our problem is that people are obedient while the jails are full of petty thieves . . . the grand thieves are running the country. That's our problem. (para. 5)

Lastly, dangerous citizenship is meant to call attention to the need for new pedagogical imaginaries for teaching because traditional conceptions of democratic citizenship are bankrupt, perverted by capitalism's triumph over interests of the public(s). The balance of this chapter sketches out some of these possibilities for dangerous citizenship in the classroom.

MAKING TROUBLE: CREATIVE DISRUPTION OF EVERYDAY LIFE IN THE CLASSROOM

I have long been intrigued by the public pedagogy of politically inspired performance artists who aim to creatively disrupt everyday life through creative resistance (e.g., Thompson & Scholette, 2004). In this section I briefly present some theories and tactics relevant to teaching social studies that can serve as imaginaries for a pedagogy of dangerous citizenship.

Tactics of Everyday Life

French scholar Michel de Certeau (1984) is a great place to start when thinking about the creative disruption of everyday life in the classroom. De Certeau argued that developing strategy is the purview of power; strategy assumes some measure of control (e.g., management, administration, governmental authorities). Tactics, on the other hand, are the purview of the nonpowerful (e.g., teachers, students), an adaptation to the environment that has been created by strategies of the powerful (Goff, 2012). The practice of everyday life is about responding to the immediate situation with tactical agility, not long-term transformation of circumstances.

There is no reason to wait for the "the revolution" or for "better" colleagues or more supportive circumstances before you take action. Observe your surroundings, orient the most important developments in the environment, decide on a course of action, and repeat. This is termed the OODA-Loop; it is a way to take advantage of unpredictable situations and destroy obstacles to meaningful learning while creating spaces that are responsive to the interests and desires of students instead of external imposed goals (Boyd, 1976).

Consider what de Certeau called *la perruque* (translated as *wig*), the diversionary practice of using the employer's resources for personal use. In other words, the workers own work is disguised as work for the employer. It differs from pilfering in that nothing of value is stolen. The worker who indulges in *la perruque* diverts time from the factory for work that is free, creative, and precisely not directed toward profit. De Certeau's illustrations include the secretary who uses company time and equipment to write a love letter and the cabinet maker who "borrows" a lathe to make a piece of furniture for his living room.

La perruque is a subversive mode of resistance in which schooling can be seen as "our time" and not simply a managed or enculturating time, unquestioned labor-work, controlled by authorities. The rationale for enacting *la perruque* ought to be consistent with promoting democracy, collectivity, and authenticity and opposed to oppression. Lastly, *la perruque* should be about capabilities and solidarity, that is, it should empower teachers and students to chase their interests, desires, skills, and abilities while simultaneously encouraging them to connect and form communities with one another—within and across classrooms and within and across schools (Vinson & Ross, 2003).

How can we use the resources (time and materials) of the school to teach social studies in ways that are directed toward interests and desires of students and local communities, rather than privileging the narrow and often exploitative interests of the elite, which are embedded in standardized curriculum, corporate textbooks, and examinations that regulate what students learn and restrict teachers' autonomy as decision makers?

Temporary Autonomous Zones

The idea of Temporary Autonomous Zones (TAZ), created by Hakim Bey (2003), is closely related to de Certeau's conception of tactics. TAZ are alternatives to traditional models of revolution. TAZ are not a revolutionary moment; they are an uprising that creates free, ephemeral enclaves of autonomy in the here and now, avoiding direct confrontation with the state or authorities (Jordan, 2012). Bey describes TAZ as mobile and stealthy—appearing, disappearing, then reappearing.

While the physical classroom may be fixed, we can think about creating temporary "liberated" spaces within (and beyond) the classroom. TAZ are "an eruption of free culture where life is experienced at maximum intensity. It should feel like an exceptional party where for a brief moment our desires are made manifest and we all become the creators of the art of everyday life" (Jordan, 2012, p. 270). What can we learn, pedagogically, from liberated spaces like Occupy, Burning Man, Fiume, or Freetown Christiania?[7]

Society of the Spectacle

Debord's theory of the spectacle is at the heart of the idea of dangerous citizenship and much of my thinking about education and schooling (e.g., Ross & Vinson, 2014; Vinson & Ross, 2003). The key idea is that capitalism exercises social control through images, mass media that turn us into spectators:

> What we feel, what we believe, how we express desire, what we believe is possible—all are filtered through, and constrained by, the media we consume and produce. (Mitchell, 2012, p. 266)

Détournement is one of tactics that Debord and his colleagues created in the Situationist International. It involves capturing images and turning them around in a new presentation to subvert the authority of the sign and the significations it sets in order.

In other words, *détournement* is a variation on a previous media work, in which the newly created one has a meaning that is antagonistic or antithetical to the original. What would happen if a teacher taught a lesson or two using what Marker (2005) called "the most dangerous social studies textbook in America," Jon Stewart's (2004) *America (The Book): A Citizen's Guide to Inaction*?

What images, artifacts, objets d'art, and texts might be rerouted, misappropriated, hijacked or otherwise put to something beside its normal purpose in order to raise questions or disrupt conventional ways of thinking about social issues?[8] For example, how might a concept such as war (or empire, freedom, capitalism) be explored through the detourned image in figure 6.1?

The Propaganda Model

Developed by Edward Herman and Noam Chomsky (1988; Herman, 1996) to examine the behavior of corporate media, the propaganda model explains how the mass media consistently produces content that reflects the interests of economic and political elites. The basic hypothesis of the propaganda model is that corporate media will generally produce news content that serves elite interests.

Corporate media serve these interests not as a result of direct control or censorship of the media, but as the result of filters existing within the institutional structure of corporate media organizations. The model proposes five filters through which the "raw material of the news" passes:

1. concentration of media ownership and the profit-seeking imperative of the dominant media corporations
2. advertising as the primary source of income

Figure 6.1. Detourned photo of "Raising the Flag on Iwo Jima." Image created by UnManuel and used with permission.

3. sourcing of news relies on "expert" and official sources (the "moral division of labor" where officials give the facts and the reporters merely get them)
4. negative commentary to a news story (flak) disciplines journalists and news organizations
5. an external enemy or threat creates fear (e.g., anti-communism, anti-terrorism, anti-Islam)

By measuring the volume, sourcing, and tone of news output the model attempts to empirically demonstrate how the political economy of the mass media generally serves the centers of power that own and control the media and related interests.

> In terms of international affairs, the propaganda model predicts that media coverage will favor the U.S. and its allies, hiding or downplaying their crimes and emphasizing their plights, while doing exactly the opposite for enemy states or regimes. The model, which has been well tested, has been a valuable contribution to media studies and has helped scholars better understand the propaganda function of the media. (Corcoran, 2012, p. 3)

The propaganda model argues that corporate media function to "manufacture consent." It allows us to understand, in part, how diverse societies can be dominated by a ruling class, how beliefs, explanations, perceptions, and values are manipulated to justify the social, political, and economic status quo, what Chomsky has called "thought control in democratic societies."

The propaganda model in and of itself is an excellent way to engage students in critical media analysis of current issues (e.g., wars in Iraq, Afghanistan, Yemen, Syria). The model is also a useful framework for analyzing official curriculum documents, textbooks, and the entire enterprise of schooling, exposing hegemonic curriculum that serves the same centers of power and interests as corporate media. Consider how students might employ the propaganda model to reveal the political economy of textbooks or government-mandated curriculum.

How might the propaganda model reveal the political economy of education reform? Examples of existing studies that employ the analytic spirit if not the rigid application of the model include:

- Montaño and Aoki's (2011) analysis of charter schools in Latino communities
- Alan Singer's (e.g., Singer & Thompson, 2016) ongoing critique of educational publisher Pearson
- Susan Ohanian's (2016) deconstruction of education reform discourse in the *New York Times*
- the *Critical Education* article series "The Media and the Neoliberal Privatization of Education"[9]
- a series of articles in *Z Magazine* from 1999 to 2003, deconstructing the creation and impact of the corporate-driven education reform in the United States (e.g., Ross, 2000; Ross & Mathison, 2001; Ross & Vinson, 2002; Vinson & Ross, 2001)

The Alienation Effect

Teaching and drama/acting certainly share some commonalities. Dramatist Bertolt Brecht's idea of making the familiar strange has great potential as a strategy for disrupting the alienating routines that can dominate classroom experiences. As teachers we are almost always engaged in an effort to provoke responses from students. Brecht's criticism of theater was that it took the audience on "an uncritical emotional roller coaster ride, crying when the main character cried, laughing when s/he laughed—identifying with him/her even when the character had nothing in common with them or their interests" (cited in Bogad, 2012, p. 210).

The alienation effect aims to disrupt emotional manipulation with a "surprising jolt," such as when actors break down the imaginary "fourth wall" by speaking directly to the audience. Another technique is *social gest*, "an exaggerated gesture or action that is not to be taken literally, but which critically demonstrates a social relationship or power imbalance. For example, workers in a corporate office may suddenly and quickly drop to the floor and kowtow to the CEO, or the women in a household may suddenly start to move in fast-motion, cleaning the house, while the men slowly yawn and loaf around" (Bogad, 2012, p. 211).

This tactic can be used to illustrate how social studies education (and schooling in general) functions less as a democratizing influence and more as a means of social control. Imagine interrupting your own civics lesson to inform your students that what they have learned about democratic citizenship is merely an attempt to convince them to be loyal, obedient, dutiful, and useful servants to the ruling class under a variety of lies such as:

- "we are all in this together"
- "this is a multicultural society"

- "democracy trumps inequality" (e.g., anyone can be president or prime minister)

Making the familiar strange opens the door for students (and teachers) to confront the emotional manipulation that is part and parcel of traditional narratives presented in social studies curriculum (e.g., democracy trumps capitalism and inequality) and at the same time create a classroom that is surprising, critical, and appealing to students.

What happens when the familiar social studies narrative of American exceptionalism—national policy guided by an interest in protecting freedom, democracy, and justice worldwide—is exposed as policies of advancing empire and global domination economically and militarily?[10] In most cases, I think it is fair to say students would experience Brecht's "surprising jolt." Brecht's challenge as dramatist, as described by Bogad, has pedagogical implications too: How do we confront emotional manipulation while creating a stimulating, surprising, radically critical, and appealing social studies classroom?

The Ethical Spectacle

Andrew Boyd (2012), the editor of *Beautiful Trouble*, argues that to be politically effective we need to engage in spectacles that are ethical, emancipatory, and faithful to reality.[11] Drawing inspiration from Debord and the Situationists as well as Zapatistas, Yes Men, and Iraq Veterans Against the War, Boyd describes the ethical spectacle as striving to be:

- Participatory: seeking to empower participants and spectators alike, with organizers as facilitators
- Open: responsive and adaptive to shifting contexts and the ideas of participants
- Transparent: engaging the imagination of spectators without seeking to trick or deceive
- Realistic: using fantasy to illuminate and dramatize real-world power dynamics and social relations that otherwise remains hidden in plain sight
- Utopian: celebrating the impossible—and therefore helping to make the impossible possible (Boyd, 2012, p. 230)

According to Debord, boredom is always counterrevolutionary. A classroom that incorporates the ethical spectacle should then have revolutionary potential. Imagine what a social studies classroom would look like when it is participatory, open, transparent, realistic, and utopian. What principles, tactics, and strategies would be necessary to achieve the ethical spectacle in a classroom? What would go by the wayside? What risks are involved in striving for an ethical and spectacular social studies curriculum? Is it worth the risk? Is the safe alternative worth pursing?

BEING HOPEFUL IN HOPELESS TIMES

The post-9/11 world does much to encourage hopelessness. It is crucial for social studies educators to engage students in learning about our world in ways that are realistic, but that also fashion hope. Yet, this hope should not take the form of the false hope that is embedded in the tired tropes of democracy and freedom that only exist in social studies textbooks and other propaganda outlets.

In his latest book, *Wages of Rebellion: The Moral Imperative of Revolt*, Chris Hedges (2015) argues we are in a revolutionary moment, and while the status quo is doomed, it is unclear whether the future will be progressive or reactionary. The one certainty in this world is that things change. Finding courage in hopelessness means teaching and acting in ways that support participatory democracy, freedom, and equality, even when the opposition is ruthless.

> To be hopeful in bad times is not just foolishly romantic. It is based on the fact that human history is a history not only of cruelty, but also of compassion, sacrifice, courage, kindness. . . . And if we do act, in however small a way, we don't have to wait for some grand utopian future. The future is an infinite succession of presents, and to live now as we think human beings should live, in defiance of all that is bad around us, is itself a marvelous victory. (Zinn, 2006, p. 270)

To teach now as we think we should teach, in defiance of all that is bad in society (and schools), is to be courageous in the face of hopelessness.

NOTES

1. Yes, you read that correctly, eighty-five individuals have wealth equal to over 3.5 billion people.
2. It is interesting to note this OECD report also argues that tackling inequality through tax and transfer policies does not harm economic growth; that redistribution of wealth should focus on families with children and youth and promotes skills development and learning across people's lives. OECD's perspective is one of enhancing human capital, these are decidedly not the recommendations of a left-wing, socialist outfit.
3. This section does not begin to encompass all of the concerns we face. For example, there is the climate crisis; serial police violence, especially against people of color; and an apathetic electorate, 82 percent of which disapprove of Congress.
4. Letter from Marx to Arnold Ruge (May 1843): "You will hardly suggest that my opinion of the present is too exalted and if I do not despair about it, this is only because its desperate position fills me with hope." Retrieved from https://www.marxists.org/archive/marx/works/1843/letters/43_05-alt.htm.
5. Donald Trump updated this principle in the August 2015 Republican presidential debate when, in his two-minute exchange with Fox News' Brett Baier, he said the rich own the political process: Baier: "And when you give [money to politicians], they do whatever the hell you want them to do." Trump: "You'd better believe it" (Whitney, 2015).
6. For more on this argument see Gibson and Ross (2015) and Szymanski (1978).
7. Occupy is a social movement against social and economic inequality worldwide that was sparked by the Occupy Wall Street movement that began in the United States in 2011. Burning Man is an annual gathering in the Black Rock Desert in Nevada in which participants celebrate self-expression, decommodification, and community, among other principles. The event culminates in the burning of a wooden effigy that is supposed to represent "The Man." Fiume was an independent free state in Europe from 1920 to 1924, and Freetown Christiania is a an autonomous neighborhood of approximately 850 residents located in Copenhagen, the capital of Denmark.
8. See Trier (2014) for descriptions of *détournement* as pedagogical praxis, primarily in the context of teacher education. Find other examples by searching images for "detournement" or visiting http://detournementexhibition.org/.
9. See a full listing of the articles in the *Critical Education* series "Media and the Neoliberal Privatization of Education" here: http://ices.library.ubc.ca/index.php/criticaled/article/view/185091.
10. Social studies educators interested in trying to answer this question will find that the American Empire Project has many resources: http://www.americanempireproject.com/booklist.asp.
11. *Beautiful Trouble* is a book and an interactive website (http://beautifultrouble.org/) that I have cited extensively in this section.

REFERENCES

Bey, H. (2003). *The temporary autonomous zone, ontological anarchy, poetic terrorism* (2nd ed.). New York: Autonomedia.
Bogad, L. M. (2012). Alienation effect. In A. Boyd (Ed.), *Beautiful trouble: A toolbox for the revolution* (pp. 210–211). New York: O/R Books.
Boyd, A. (2012). The ethical spectacle. In A. Boyd (Ed.), *Beautiful trouble: A toolbox for the revolution* (pp. 230–231). New York: O/R Books.
Boyd, J. R. (1976). *Destruction and creation*. Ft. Leavenworth, KS: U.S. Army Command and General Staff College, Center for Army Tactics. Retrieved from http://www.goalsys.com/books/documents/DESTRUCTION_AND_CREATION.pdf.

Busby, C., Hamdan, M., & Ariabi, M. (2010). Cancer, infant mortality and birth sex-ratio in Fallujah, Iraq 2005–2009. *International Journal of Environmental Research and Public Health, 7*, 2828–2837.

Chomsky, N. (2013, August 17). The U.S. behaves nothing like a democracy. *Salon*. Retrieved from http://www.salon.com/2013/08/17/chomsky_the_u_s_behaves.

Cockburn, P. (2010, July 24). Toxic legacy of US assault on Fallujah "worse than Hiroshima." *The Independent*. Retrieved from http://www.independent.co.uk/news/world/middle-east/toxic-legacy-of-us-assault-on-fallujah-worse-than-hiroshima-2034065.html.

Corcoran, M. (2012). The propaganda model, class struggle, and new media technology: An analysis of the propaganda model in an age of social uprising and social media. Boston: University of Massachusetts. Retrieved from http://crhsgg-studentresources.wikispaces.umb.edu/file/view/Corcoran_MichaelCAPSTONE.pdf.

Dangl, B. (2014, November 20). Who rules the world? How a concentration of wealth and political undermines democracy. *CounterPunch*. Retrieved from http://www.counterpunch.org/2014/11/20/who-rules-the-world-2/.

Debord, G. (2014/1967). *The society of the spectacle*. Berkeley, CA: Bureau of Public Secrets.

de Certeau, M. (1984). *The practice of everyday life*. Berkeley, CA: University of California Press.

Dewey, J. (1916). *Democracy and education*. New York: Macmillan.

Elliot, J. (Ed.). (1888). *Debates on the adoption of the federal constitution*. New York: Burt Franklin.

Foucault, M. (1988). *Politics, philosophy, culture*. New York: Routledge.

Freedom House. (2008). Today's America: How free? Retrieved from https://freedomhouse.org/report/special-reports/todays-american-how-free#.VcJ3kpNVhBc.

Freire, P. (1998). *Teachers as cultural workers*. Boulder, CO: Westview.

Gibson, R., & Ross, E. W. (2015). Education and empire: Education for class consciousness. In P. R. Carr & B. J. Porfilio (Eds.), *The phenomenon of Obama and the agenda for education: Can hope (still) audaciously trump neoliberalism?* (2nd ed., pp. 251–278). Charlotte, NC: Information Age Press.

Gilens, M., & Page, B. I. (2014). Testing theories of American politics: Elites, interest groups, and average citizens. *Perspectives on Politics, 12*, 564–581.

Goff, S. (2012). Tactics of everyday life. In A. Boyd (Ed.), *Beautiful trouble: A toolbox for the revolution* (pp. 268–269). New York: O/R Books.

Gould, M., & Ungoed-Thomas, J. (2006, February 19). UK radiation jump blame on Iraq shells. *The Sunday Times*. Retrieved from http://www.thesundaytimes.co.uk/sto/news/uk_news/article205368.ece.

Hedges, C. (2015). *Wages of rebellion: The moral imperative of revolt*. New York: Nation Books.

Herman, E. S. (1996). The propaganda model revisited. Retrieved from http://www.chomsky.info/onchomsky/199607--.html.

Herman, E. S., & Chomsky, N. (1988). *Manufacturing consent: The political economy of the mass media*. New York: Pantheon.

Huxley, A. (1958). *Brave new world revisited*. Retrieved from http://www.huxley.net/bnw-revisited/.

Jordan, J. (2012). Temporary autonomous zones. In A. Boyd (Ed.), *Beautiful trouble: A toolbox for the revolution* (pp. 270–271). New York: O/R Books.

Lukács, G. (1971/1923). *History and class consciousness*. Cambridge, MA: MIT Press.

Marker, P. (2005). The most dangerous social studies "textbook" in America. *Theory & Research in Social Education, 33*, 292–294.

Mitchell, D. O. (2012). Society of the spectacle. In A. Boyd (Ed.), *Beautiful trouble: A toolbox for the revolution* (pp. 266–267). New York: O/R Books.

Monaghan, F. (1935). *John Jay*. New York: Bobbs-Merrill.

Montaño, T., & Aoki, L. (2011). Manufactured consent: Latino/a themed charter schools in whose interests? In P. R. Carr & B. J. Porfilio (Eds.), *The phenomenon of Obama and the agenda for education* (pp. 121–145). Charlotte, NC: Information Age Publishers.

Ohanian, S. (2016). Against obedience. In N. E. McCrary & E. W. Ross (Eds.), *Working for social justice inside and outside the classroom* (pp. 29–45). New York: Peter Lang.

Organization for Economic Co-operation and Development. (2014, December). Focus on inequality and growth: Does income inequality hurt economic growth? Retrieved from http://www.oecd.org/els/soc/Focus-Inequality-and-Growth-2014.pdf.

Oxfam. (2014, January 20). Working for the few: Political capture and economic inequality (178 Oxfam Briefing Paper—Summary). Retrieved from https://www.oxfam.org/sites/www.oxfam.org/files/bp-working-for-few-political-capture-economic-inequality-200114-summ-en.pdf.

Piketty, T. (2014). *Capital in the twenty-first century*. Cambridge, MA: Belknap Press.

Ross, E. W. (2000, March). The spectacle of standards and summits. *Z Magazine, 12*(3), 45–48. Retrieved from https://zcomm.org/zmagazine/the-spectacle-of-standards-and-summits-by-e-wayne-ross/.

Ross, E. W., & Mathison, S. (2001). No child left untested? *Z Magazine, 15*(3), 14–15. Retrieved from https://zcomm.org/zmagazine/no-child-left-untested-by-site-administrator/.

Ross, E. W., & Vinson, K. D. (2002, January). The schools we want. *Z Magazine, 15*(1), pp. 45–48. Retrieved from https://zcomm.org/zmagazine/the-schools-we-want-by-e-wayne-ross/.

———. (2014). Dangerous citizenship. In E. W. Ross (Ed.). *The social studies curriculum: Purposes, problems, and possibilities* (4th ed., pp. 93–125). Albany, NY: State University of New York Press.

Saez, E., & Zucman, G. (2014, October). *Wealth inequality in the United States since 1913: Evidence from capitalized income tax data*. Cambridge, MA: National Bureau of Economic Research. Retrieved from http://gabriel-zucman.eu/files/SaezZucman2014.pdf.

Scheiber, N., & Sussman, D. (2015, June 3). Inequality troubles Americans across party lines. *New York Times*. Retrieved from http://www.nytimes.com/2015/06/04/business/inequality-a-major-issue-for-americans-times-cbs-poll-finds.html.

Singer, A., & Thompson, E. (2016). Pearson, Inc.: Slashing away at Hercules' Hydra. In N. E. McCrary & E. W. Ross (Eds.), *Working for social justice inside and outside the classroom* (pp. 47–57). New York: Peter Lang.

Skinner, J. (2014, June 17). Thought is the courage of hopelessness: An interview with philosopher Giorgio Agamben. Retrieved from http://www.versobooks.com/blogs/1612-thought-is-the-courage-of-hopelessness-an-interview-with-philosopher-giorgio-agamben.

Smith, R. C., & Sperber, E. (2014). Democracy in crisis: Toward a foundational, alternative theory of participatory democracy. Retrieved from http://www.heathwoodpress.com/wp-content/uploads/2014/05/Democracy-in-Crisis-Toward-a-Foundational-Alternative-Theory-of-Participatory-Democracy_HEATHWOOD_RCSMITH_ELLIOTSPERBER.pdf.

Street, P. (2014). *They rule: The 1% v. democracy*. Boulder, CO: Paradigm.

———. (2015). Democracy wrecked again. ZNet. Retrieved from http://zcomm.org/sendpress/eyJpZCI6OTc1Mjc5LCJ2aWV3IjoiZW1haWwifQ/?utm_medium=email&utm_source=sendpress&utm_campaign.

Stewart, J. (2004). *America (the book): A citizen's guide to democracy inaction*. New York: Warner.

Szymanski, A. (1978). *The capitalist state and the politics of class*. Cambridge, MA: Winthrop.

Tanielian, T., & Jaycox, L. H. (Eds.). (2008). *Invisible wounds of war psychological and cognitive injuries, their consequences, and services to assist recovery*. Santa Monica, CA: Rand Center for Military Health Policy Research. Retrieved from http://www.rand.org/content/dam/rand/pubs/monographs/2008/RAND_MG720.pdf.

Thompson, N., & Sholette, G. (2004). *The interventionists: User's manual for the creative disruption of everyday life*. North Adams, MA: MASS MoCA.

Trier, J. (Ed.). (2014). *Detournement as pedagogical praxis*. Rotterdam, Netherlands: Sense Publishers.

U.S. Senate Select Committee on Intelligence. (2014). Committee study of the Central Intelligence Agency's Detention and Interrogation Program. Washington, DC: U.S. Senate Select Committee on Intelligence. Retrieved from http://www.nytimes.com/interactive/2014/12/09/world/cia-torture-report-document.html.

Vinson, K. D., & Ross, E. W. (2001). What can we know and when can we know it?. *Z Magazine, 14*(3), 34–38. Retrieved from https://zcomm.org/zmagazine/what-we-can-know-and-when-we-can-know-it-by-kevin-d-vinson/.

———. (2003). *Image and education: Teaching in the face of the new disciplinarity*. New York: Peter Lang.

Whitney, M. (2015, August 7). Trump's triumph: Billionaire blowhard exposes fake political system. *CounterPunch*. Retrieved from http://www.counterpunch.org/2015/08/07/trumps-triumph-billionaire-blowhard-exposes-fake-political-system/.

Zinn, H. (1970). The problem of civil obedience. Retrieved from http://www.thirdworldtraveler.com/Zinn/CivilObedience_ZR.html.

———. (2006). *A power governments cannot suppress*. San Francisco, CA: City Lights.

Chapter Seven

Civil Liberties, Media Literacy, and Civic Education in the Post-9/11 Era

Helping Students Think Conceptually in Order to Act Civically

Stephen S. Masyada and Elizabeth Yeager Washington

Civic education in the twenty-first century is at a crossroads. Political leaders and citizens advocate for improved civic knowledge, lamenting the lack of both engagement and knowledge across a broad spectrum of American society (e.g., Galston, 2001, 2004; Quigley, 2004). Despite these lamentations, civics, like much of the rest of the social studies, remains a struggling element of the public school curriculum in many states.

In this era following the events of September 11, 2001, when an understanding of what it means to be a citizen, and to be engaged as a citizen, is so important, civics educators must figure out how to best prepare the next generation while acknowledging the current limitations faced by social studies teachers. In this chapter, we will explore what dedicated civics teachers should do to prepare students for this post-9/11 United States, an era of increased focus on how we balance the needs of national security with individual liberty.

In considering the role of schools as the carriers of the civic mission, and what that role must look like in a post-9/11 society, we should also consider that there is no one correct vision of what sort of "good citizen" we are seeking to create. Westheimer and Kahne (2004) have argued that our schools tend to focus on one of three civic models: the citizen as personally responsible, the citizen as participatory, or the citizen as oriented toward social justice.

A personally responsible citizen sees good citizenship as connected to good character and traditional understandings of citizenship (honesty, responsibility, obedience, etc.). A participatory citizen sees good citizenship as necessarily focused on solving social problems through engagement and leadership. A citizen with a social justice orientation seeks to get to the root causes of those problems, even if it means challenging stability and traditional community.

Each of these civic models has its own strengths and weaknesses, and while the ideal orientation may depend on particular political or social goals, most schools tend toward Westheimer and Kahne's (2004) personally responsible or participatory citizen. Because of this diversity in approaches, we focus on instruction that is applicable no matter which type citizen our schools strive to mold.

This is an era in which so-called old media, in the form of traditional newspapers, magazines, and television productions, is in decline, being replaced with new forms of information sharing, perception shaping, and engagement (Gerhards & Schafer, 2010; Wei & Hindman, 2011). The rise of social media, Internet-based news sites and blogs, and even the increasingly partisan cast of the old media, however, does not negate an old question: How do we develop within students a conception of media literacy that protects them from the slings and arrows of political and economic propaganda and media bias while still encouraging engagement with the current trends of civic culture?

In the post-9/11 era of civic education, it has become more necessary than ever to ensure that students understand how to integrate multiple perspectives in their own perception of the world. Exposure to different ways of thinking, opportunities to interact with those of different backgrounds, and learning how different political, social, and economic views can shape collaborations within a democratic republic are important components within an effective and well-rounded post-9/11 K–12 civic education. At the same time, if we want to encourage students to engage civically and to make good decisions, we must revisit how we teach these future citizens about civil liberties, the rule of law, and limited government.

In this chapter, we propose a framework for civic education that emphasizes a conceptual approach, integrating elements of media literacy and being driven by effective use of the *College, Career, and Civic Life (C3) Framework* (National Council for the Social Studies, 2013). This framework will encourage students to think conceptually, across time and place, in order to make connections between civic life and issues that have occurred in the past and those yet to happen.

In doing so, students will gain and practice the skills necessary for addressing significant questions of civic life and find ways to both communicate their ideas and take action that can help answer those significant questions. But first, we must consider what we mean by *conceptual thinking*.

CRITICAL THINKING AS CONCEPTUAL THINKING

"Teach them critical thinking" is often the common response when one asks how to help children follow a path toward good citizenship. Just what, however, is meant by the term "critical thinking"? Perhaps not surprisingly, this has been somewhat of a difficult question to answer. Vague and varied definitions of what critical thinking actually means make it more difficult to decide on appropriate content, necessary pedagogy, and measures of success in instruction and make the path toward developing a consistent and effective definition difficult, with both students and society facing the consequences (Sanders & Moulenbelt, 2011).

At the same time, the term itself has gotten somewhat of a negative reputation. For example, the 2012 platform of the Texas Republican Party opposed the teaching of Higher Order Thinking Skills (HOTS) (values clarification), critical thinking skills, and similar programs that are simply a relabeling of outcome-based education (OBE) (mastery learning), which focuses on behavior modification and has the purpose of challenging the student's fixed beliefs and undermining parental authority (Republican Party of Texas, 2012, p. 12).

We do not try to grapple with the definition of critical thinking within the scope of this chapter; critical thinking is too broad a concept with too many avenues for consideration to address in this space. However, we may at least provide some context to guide our discussion of what civic education might look like in the twenty-first century, through a focus on *conceptual* thinking. To provide this context, we hearken back to ideas from the early twentieth century.

Indeed, it seems almost a consistent trend that when people write about civic education, they make some sort of reference to John Dewey. In this chapter, we refer to Dewey only to provide a foundation for what comes later. For the purpose of this discussion, let's consider that critical conceptual thinking is informed by curiosity, knowledge building, reflection, an openness to others' ideas and viewpoints, and ultimately a desire to answer a pressing question honestly and accurately (Dewey, 1916). This idea of questioning is at the heart of how we choose to define critical conceptual thinking through a civics lens.

A civics education geared toward twenty-first-century American life recalls Dewey's call for a democratic education that prepares today's children to address the problems of civil society tomorrow (Dewey, 1916, 1938). A conceptually rich inquiry model of civic education, then, centered around exploring difficult, conceptually oriented questions without one correct answer, could serve as a means of stimulating student thinking and developing the engagement skills and media literacy necessary for civic life.

We will be referring to a conceptual way of approaching civic education throughout this chapter. By *conceptual*, we mean a focus on the foundational ideas of civics that are transferable across time, place, and situation—no matter the content that is being studied—moving beyond rote vocabulary and facts. These ideas are varied and might include such concepts as liberty, equality, security, collaboration, and conflict, among others.

Students can draw on these big ideas in order to reinforce instruction and make connections between the content they are learning (Erickson, 2007; Harris & Shreiner, 2014; Obenchain & Pennington, 2015). We explore this approach by focusing on areas of concern important to civic educators: civil liberties and media literacy.

CONCEPTUAL CIVIC INSTRUCTION AND CIVIL LIBERTIES

In the post-9/11 era, while the issue of government surveillance and overreach fills our civic conversations, we must encourage our students to explore significant questions. How have our civil liberties been challenged since the turn of the century, and how do we teach our students about the relationship between citizen and government? Going deeper, how do we do so when the very idea of what it means to be a good citizen is often up for debate (Galston, 2001, 2004; Westheimer & Kahne, 2004)? These are complex questions, for sure, but as civic educators we must confront them if we are to prepare our students for the realities of twenty-first-century civic life in the United States.

The questions we pose are not easy to answer, and if we are honest with ourselves as a nation, we must admit that they never have been. The incidents over our history are many, and those listed here are just some of the examples from our nation's civic history that illustrate the fragile nature of civil rights and liberties:

- the Alien and Sedition Acts of 1798
- Lincoln's attempts to restrict anti-war newspapers from the mail, arrests of editors, and suspension of habeas corpus during the Civil War (though such action was essentially retroactively approved by the Habeas Corpus Act of 1863)
- the creation and implementation of Jim Crow laws throughout the southern United States
- the Sedition Act of 1918
- Japanese American internment during World War II
- the actions of the National Security Agency over the past decade concerning private communications among American citizens

So how are we to teach about civil rights and liberties, the rule of law, and limited government in the twenty-first century without allowing our students or ourselves to give in to cynicism?

It's the Big Ideas that Matter

"Teach the controversy" has been a common refrain for those challenging instruction in evolution in schools, so much so that it is often a running joke among defenders of science education (Johnson, 2015). Yet this idea provides us with a starting point for our approach to civic education grounded in the idea of rule of law and the maintenance of civil liberties. When we suggest that civics educators "teach the controversy," we propose that both the content and the pedagogy of civic education focus on questions and big ideas concerning the challenges and the controversies involving civil liberties and the role of government in the post-9/11 era.

We must first recognize that content-oriented, objective-driven standards currently drive much of both social studies and general instruction in the United States. This has been the situation since at least the release of the Ronald Reagan administration's 1983 *A Nation at Risk* report, which decried the supposed lack of standards and success on the part of schools in the United States.

Moreover, it has only increased over time with the growth of the school reform movement and the increased emphasis on using very specific content-oriented standards to assess a narrow test-oriented definition of student achievement. Curriculum and instruction have narrowed, often focusing only on the specific content in the standards, rarely encouraging more than rote and forgettable learning and preventing any sort of deeper reflection or critical thinking in social studies (Vogler & Virtue, 2007).

The teaching of civics has not been spared in the pursuit of curricular and school reform, especially as Common Core Standards (National Governors Association, 2010) have been implemented across the country. These Common Core Standards, with an emphasis on English-language arts (ELA) and math, mention history and the social studies only as appendices connected in context to the ELA standards. Civics is rolled into those particular social studies standards, with all of the attention that may imply (F. Hess, 2009).

At the same time, while a majority of states require some form of civic instruction in schools, the standards in these states are quite often very narrowly focused on facts above skills and dispositions and provide little context or opportunity for students to practice citizenship or make connections across their learning (Godsay, Henderson, Levine, & Littenberg-Tobias, 2012). The result of this approach to standards, curriculum, and instruction is evident in the most recent National Assessment of Educational Progress (NAEP; U.S. Department of Education, 2014) data connected to civics instruction.

According to NAEP data, despite the emphasis on content-driven standards in social studies classrooms across the country, only 23 percent of American students scored proficient on the civics portion of the assessment. Even now, however, there remains an effort to require a recall-driven assessment as a measure of civic learning, despite little evidence that the federal naturalization test results in improved civic proficiency or is even an adequate measure of civic knowledge as constructed (Levine, 2015; Winke, 2011).

What does this mean for civic education as it is approached today? Students rarely retain an adequate knowledge of events that limited their civil liberties, of legislation that challenged ideas of limited government, or actions that paid scant heed to the rule of law. The long-term impact of this sort of objective-focused, content-oriented education is, ultimately, null; it is as if it were never learned at all.

Students often fail to make connections beyond the surface level, and the material is often approached as a series of isolated facts without obviously transferable conceptual elements or skills. Students may come away with surface *knowledge*, but are they honestly coming away with the deeper *understandings* and *skills* necessary to make conceptual connections concerning the content they have learned?

A move away from objective-driven instruction and standards based on content knowledge, however, does not mean a complete abandonment of content. What we suggest is a move toward a conceptual approach to education for citizenship. With this approach, content remains significant, but the concepts and generalizations underlying the content are the target (Erickson, 2007; Erickson & Lanning, 2014; Obenchain & Pennington, 2015). It is these concepts and generalizations, perhaps developed around conceptions of civic virtue, civil discourse, and civic engagement, that we want students to be able to explain, remember, and ultimately recognize as important in the protection of our civil liberties.

A conceptual approach moves beyond the traditional approach to both civics and social studies education, with its "fire and forget"/"teach it and move on" model. Instead, it would encourage students to make connections across time, places, and situations. As they learn about the Alien and Sedition Acts, for example, they also learn about big ideas connected to civil liberties and limited government.

By beginning with the underlying concept and teaching the concept first, the content fills in the blanks and acts as a support for further instruction and connection building across content. The Alien and Sedition Acts would be connected to Lincoln's suspension of habeas corpus in the Civil War, to the Sedition Act of 1918, to Japanese American internment in World War II, to the actions of the National Security Agency in the post-9/11 era, and so on.

Of course, we know that concepts have always played a significant role in social studies instruction, so in some ways this is not a completely new approach. The conceptual model of standards-based civics instruction we are advocating goes beyond concepts, however. In this model, concepts are developed into generalizations that give meaning and structure to those concepts (Erickson, 2007; Erickson & Lanning, 2014).

A generalization taught through the content we have described might be "Challenges to civil liberties and limited government may be driven by political, social, or military conflict" or perhaps "The needs of national security might promote restrictions on individual liberty." Significantly, in this model, it is not important that students are able to give every example of or simply regurgitate facts about these controversies or challenges to civil liberties, rule of law, or limited government. Rather, they should be able to explain the generalization (and its associated concepts) and draw on the content to support that explanation.

Students are not just demonstrating knowledge; they are also demonstrating both the deeper understanding and the actual skills necessary to address the civic issue. The final performance task, aligned to the conceptual standards, curriculum, and skills, would measure not just specific content knowledge but rather an understanding of the generalization they have learned. We need not specify what that content must be; rather, students will draw on the connections between content in order to support the generalization (Erickson, 2007; Erickson & Lanning, 2014). Textbox 7.1 illustrates a sample performance task for our generalization "The needs of national security might promote restrictions on individual liberty."

What: As a member of a civil liberties organization, argue for or against legislation that will restrict free speech on the Internet in order to fight the threat of terrorism.

Why: In order to understand that: The needs of national security might promote restrictions on individual liberty.

How: Research examples of ways in which the U.S. government has approached restrictions on civil liberties in times of foreign or domestic conflict. Drawing from your research, write a case study for your organization describing the positive and negative impact of the ways in which the U.S. government has balanced national security with civil liberties. Present the highlights of your case study in a briefing for your local congressperson, using visuals or multimedia, detailing the lessons that may be learned from past actions.

Note that in this performance task, students have to demonstrate an understanding of the explicit and implicit concepts we find in the generalization: national security, national needs, and individual liberty. They must be able to connect these to content that they have learned, but are given the freedom to determine which content will support the generalization. This performance task also expects that students will use a specific disciplinary lens to demonstrate their understanding and to practice social studies and civics-oriented skills for successful completion.

A Framework for Conceptual Critical Thinking and Media Literacy

The skills that are implied as necessary to complete the performance task, as we have described, can connect to media literacy within a civic context as well. These might include the selection of valid sources, being able to identify bias within even a government-created text, and the creation of media in order to share information and persuade an audience. Why should these skills matter?

Increasingly, we are in a media sound bite world, with political decisions most often coming down to which ads turn people off of a candidate the least. The recent 2014 midterm election was in many ways the most expensive in history. In Florida, for example, combined spending in the governor's contest between Democrat Charlie Crist and Republican Rick Scott exceeded $150 million (March, 2014). Overall, ad buys nationally in the 2014 midterm election were more than $1 billion (Wesleyan Media Project, 2014). How do we teach students to sort the wheat from the chaff and to develop the skills necessary to become media literate?

Almost from the time they can walk, children are involved with media of some form or another. Electronic media exposure, for example, has become ubiquitous, and these young people live in an increasingly connected and interactive world that shapes their lived experience (Bennett, Wells, & Rank, 2009). Whether it is the 2.4 televisions per American household, the 75 percent of U.S. homes with children between the ages of three and seventeen that start up a computer, or the more than 60 percent of those same homes that connect to the broader world online (Roberts & Foehr, 2008), these data indicate that the digital generation exists.

Our question, then, is how does this generation civically engage with those same media? We must, after all, recognize that how students interact with media and the digital world in their personal lives does not always translate to what is done in the classroom (Bennett & Maton, 2010). How do we help these future citizens make sense of the demands of citizenship as expressed through media?

In order to prepare our youngest citizens, we need a conceptually oriented framework that engages them with media as well as with civics. First, we want to clarify our definition of "media." For our purposes, it is the means by which information is shaped and delivered between relevant stakeholders within a community.

This definition, then, would include the traditional media such as television, movies, radio, and print, as well as newer media such as Internet sources, social media, and web-based forums. We should also include within this definition all of the tools involved in the crafting of the message, the construction of the medium, and the interplay between those crafting the message and those responding to it (Hobbs & Jensen, 2009; Koltay, 2011; Livingstone, 2004; Potter, 2013).

This framework for considering media literacy within a civics context necessarily integrates elements of the National Association for Media Literacy's core principles (Bergsma et al., 2007). Indeed, each of the six core principles seems designed for a civics lens, as shown in textbox 7.2.

> Principle 1: Students must be given opportunities to engage in inquiry and to think critically about how media both old and new influence and shape their lives.
>
> Principle 2: Students must understand that media encompass both traditional forms, such as newspapers, television, and film, and new forms, such as interactive games, search algorithms, weblogs, and social media.
>
> Principle 3: Students must be given ongoing opportunities to engage with media throughout their schooling in order to develop and reinforce their understanding and use of media.
>
> Principle 4: Students must prepared to become active, informed, and engaged citizens in a democracy.
>
> Principle 5: Students must be given the opportunity to understand that media serve as a means of socialization and shape politics, culture, and other elements of society.
>
> Principle 6: Students must recognize that each individual interacts with media differently, and as a result each individual constructs his or her own meaning based on those interactions.

We thus consider media broadly. Our citizens are as diverse in their media preferences and engagement as they are in their demographics, and the rise of the "new media" has not necessarily lessened the impact of the "old media" (Bennett & Maton, 2010; Bergsma et al., 2007; Wei & Hindman, 2011). As we consider, then, the role of media in the civic education of our children, we must develop an adequate framework for teaching them the importance of thinking conceptually about media and how to engage civically with and through various forms of media. For our purposes, let's consider one particular means of standards development, instruction, and learning: the *College, Career, and Civic Life (C3) Framework*.

THE *C3 FRAMEWORK*, MEDIA LITERACY, AND CONCEPTUAL THINKING

The recently released *C3 Framework* from the National Council for the Social Studies (NCSS; 2013) reflects the idea that students, in preparation for the responsibilities and obligations of citizenship, should be encouraged to question, research, communicate, and act. It is, for our purposes, an ideal framework for pursuing a conceptual model of civics instruction. It contains four key dimensions that are intended to guide standards and curriculum development:

- Dimension One: Students collaboratively develop both *compelling* and *supporting* questions in order to plan extended inquiries into important topics.

- Dimension Two: The framework itself provides an overview and K–12 pathways for what students should be able to do using four specific disciplinary domains: history, geography, economics, and, of course, civics.
- Dimension Three: Students gather and evaluate sources of information that can be used to address their inquiry.
- Dimension Four: Once they have completed their research and addressed their questions, students communicate their findings and take informed action. Both the communication of their findings and the taking of informed action may vary based on the question, the findings, the target audience, and the goals.

The emphasis within the *C3 Framework* is on inquiry as a means of learning, hearkening back to Dewey and perhaps in some degree to the New Social Studies of the 1960s and 1970s, as embodied by Kownslar's inquiry-based approach to history education (Washington & Dahlgren, 2010).

Unlike Kownslar's approach, the Inquiry Arc in the *C3 Framework* avoids any specific focus on content; instead, it emphasizes the skills and dispositions necessary for exploring issues of relevance. At the same time, each dimension of the framework lends itself well to integrating a conceptual instructional model, encouraging a conceptual and collaborative exploration of controversial issues, and developing student media literacy.

Dimension One: Developing Questions and Planning Inquiries

One of the most significant considerations of a Deweyan model of social studies education is that students should be given the tools necessary to solve the problems of American life, even before they know what those problems may be. The *C3 Framework*, then, engages students in collaboratively developing both *compelling* and *supporting* questions.

Compelling questions are ones in which there is not necessarily one clear answer and which require some level of both research and argument, while supporting questions guide the exploration of the compelling question. If we are to use a conceptually oriented approach here, the inquiry model that begins with these compelling questions would have students explore "big idea" questions that can be derived from a generalization.

Within a unit on the Patriot Act of 2001, for example, one of the generalizations might be "The needs of national security may promote limitations on individual liberty." This would not necessarily have been the first time that students encountered this generalization; they may have come across it in an earlier unit on Lincoln and the Civil War and in studying the actions of the Woodrow Wilson administration during World War I. A generalization is not intended to be a value statement; it simply integrates concepts that are evident in the content. It is the questions that are connected to the generalization that can help draw out its positive and negative elements.

Using an inquiry model, students can be encouraged to develop a compelling question for this generalization, such as "How might I work to preserve my rights and liberties as an American citizen?" It is the student who most often develops the questions within this framework, though certainly the teacher can provide guidance, especially when it comes to crafting the supporting questions. These supporting questions may begin to integrate connections to media literacy as well.

For example, students might consider how popular literature, films, and other media portray the effort to protect American liberties. Our goal, in this case, in addition to guidance in crafting supporting questions that can contribute to addressing the compelling question, is to assist students in seeing that the information we get from the media is socially constructed and reflective of the time, place, and purpose of production (Koltay, 2011; Livingstone, 2004; Potter, 2013).

Our supporting question then might be, "How have efforts to protect civil liberties been portrayed over time?" Working collaboratively, the teacher and the students use the content foundation taught within this unit and additional units, as well as various media, to create these questions and guide their thinking throughout the rest of the framework. This would be the first step toward completing a performance task in Erickson's (2007) concept-based approach.

Dimension Two: Applying Disciplinary Concepts and Tools

The second dimension of this framework encourages the use of field-specific lens in order to develop and explore both compelling and supporting questions. Consider our previous generalization: "The needs of national security may promote limitations on individual liberty." The compelling question that students develop and the tools they use to explore that question are shaped by the specific lens they use, as indicated by table 7.1.

The answers to all of these questions may be different, but they can be connected back to the generalization, and all are valid and relevant questions that cannot simply be answered via Google.

Dimension Three: Evaluating Sources and Using Evidence

This third dimension of the *C3 Framework* is incredibly important and connects to our discussion concerning media literacy. Indeed, we can integrate work on student media literacy skills directly into this dimension. Our development of media-oriented supporting questions could come into play here, but this also would be where students must take into account different types of media and how they can be used to gather information.

Students must be able to gather and, more importantly, evaluate sources and information that can be used to answer their question concerning the protection of rights and liberties accurately. They must ask themselves questions such as:

- Is the source credible?
- Does it present as fact something that is opinion?
- Do the sources provide multiple perspectives?
- How do the sources frame their arguments?

These are all questions that should come naturally to students as they develop an understanding of media literacy and are important in breaking down and properly using sources to help

Table 7.1. Using a Disciplinary Lens to Craft Compelling Questions

Social Studies Disciplinary Lens	Potential Discipline Oriented Question
History	How have our rights been limited in times of war?
Geography	How have our liberties been impacted by where we live?
Economics	How have restrictions on liberty impacted economic development?
Civics	How might I work to preserve my rights and liberties as an American citizen?

answer their compelling question (Livingstone, 2004). This dimension requires students to develop their arguments connected to the question by considering both sides and building a foundation that can ultimately support their conclusion.

Dimension Four: Communicating Conclusions and Taking Informed Action

An ongoing debate within the media literacy realm concerns the role that the production of media by students should play within broader media literacy education. Does the production of media on the part of students actually contribute to a more critical conceptual analysis of this media or does it simply encourage students to copy the professional developers without really thinking more deeply about contexts and critiques? This is a question concerning media literacy education that is an element of the *C3 Framework* itself, which emphasizes the importance of students both understanding and being able to use media as a means to both address compelling questions and take informed action in order to get them to that deeper thinking.

Once students have answered their questions, they must be able to communicate their findings through a variety of tools. At the same time, this fourth dimension expects that students will, after answering their questions and communicating their findings, take some sort of informed action to address the issues raised in the inquiry. This action would draw on what they learned conceptually and collaboratively within their inquiry and in the final reflection on and critique of their conclusion, and should be a "purposeful, informed, and reflective experience" (NCSS, 2013, p. 62).

For our question, "How might I work to preserve my rights and liberties as an American citizen?," students may take a variety of routes for both communicating their findings and taking informed action, and it may be that the communication is connected to the action itself. Table 7.2 illustrates some possibilities.

Ultimately, the goal for these students is to communicate their findings in such a way that their argument is clear and their use of media tools is effective, while also allowing for honest reflection and critique of those conclusions. However, as Dewey (1938) argued, citizens must be given the opportunity to make their own decisions and learn from their own experiences,

Table 7.2. Communicating Findings and Taking Informed Action to Address a Compelling Question

Communicating Findings	Taking Informed Action
Present their conclusions through a presentation to a community group (League of Women Voters, American Legion, or something similar).	Students get involved with a civic-minded organization (American Civil Liberties Union or American Center for Law and Justice, for example) that allows them to convince a broader audience to address the issue while taking concrete steps to address the compelling question.
Draft a blog post that shares the most important elements of their findings.	Students create a website and social media tool that tracks challenges to civil liberties, is open to the public, and available as a center of information and discussion around the compelling question.
Create and distribute a video series that highlights why the compelling question matters and what can be done about it.	The communication in this case *is* the informed action, as long as students are ensuring it is distributed and follow up with a reconsideration of the question at a later point.
Craft an essay that can be published in the school or local newspaper.	Students host a discussion forum based on the editorial for a broader community discussion of the compelling question, in order to develop and implement a concrete plan to protect civil liberties in the community.

and whether we are considering the questions students explore, the sources they use, or the informed actions they take, they must be allowed to do it for themselves whenever possible, with the teacher as facilitator.

EDUCATION FOR CITIZENSHIP, NOT ABOUT CITIZENSHIP

Civic educators only have so many opportunities to contribute to the development of the next generation of citizens. As such, it is important that when we consider how to approach such big ideas as the protection of civil liberties, we provide students a framework that encourages the ability to think conceptually, analyze and use media, and transfer their understanding of big ideas in such a way that they are capable of addressing multiple situations they may encounter in this post-9/11 world.

The content of civic education remains important, and we do not advocate an abandonment of that content. It is the content, after all, that provides students a foundation to help drive their understanding of the concepts and generalizations that recur throughout American history and civic life. An inquiry model that offers opportunities for media literacy integration, such as we find in the *C3 Framework*, combined with conceptually oriented instruction, could offer an approach that provides students with the tools they need for an era of challenges to the maintenance of our civil liberties, the rule of law, and limited government.

Within standards-based instruction that is conceptually driven and based on the *C3 Framework*, teaching the controversy becomes a viable way to organize material, and this model could address the significant concerns that teachers have about teaching controversial topics (Dahlgren, 2009; D. Hess, 2009). Generalizations may be crafted in such a way that both examples and nonexamples cross partisan lines and encourage students to engage outside their comfort zones, while also encouraging the development of skills that can be connected to media literacy.

Our proposed conceptual model is a return to the Deweyan idea of "education for citizenship," rather than simply "education about citizenship." This model, with the *C3 Framework* providing the foundation, emphasizes providing students with experiences that build and connect conceptual knowledge and understandings and encourages them to consider and solve the problems relevant in a modern democracy through discourse and discovery (Dewey, 1916).

To paraphrase Dewey, only by wrestling with the big ideas and concepts within civics, making connections between what has come before in our civic life and what is yet to come, engaging in inquiry concerning compelling questions, and learning to actively engage with and address the problems of American democratic life in the post-9/11 era does a citizen think. Isn't that, ultimately, what we want our students and our citizenry to do?

REFERENCES

Bennett, S. J., & Maton, K. (2010). Beyond the "digital natives" debate: Towards a more nuanced understanding of students' technology experiences. *Journal of Computer Assisted Learning, 26*, 321–331.

Bennett, W. L., Wells, C., & Rank, A. (2009). Young citizens and civic learning: Two paradigms of citizenship in the digital age. *Citizenship Studies, 13*, 105–120.

Bergsma, L., Considine, D., Culver, S. H., Hobbs, R., Jensen, A., Rogow, F., . . . Thoman, E. (2007). *Core principles of media literacy education in the United States.* Cherry Hill, NJ: National Association for Media Literacy Education.

Dahlgren, R. (2009). "Fahrenheit 9/11" in the classroom. *Teacher Education Quarterly, 36*, 25–42.

Dewey, J. (1916). *Democracy and education: An introduction to the philosophy of education.* New York: Macmillan.

———. (1938). *Experience and education.* New York: Macmillan.

Erickson, H. L. (2007). *Concept based curriculum and instruction for the thinking classroom.* Thousand Oaks, CA: Corwin.

Erickson, H. L., & Lanning, L. (2014). *Transitioning to concept-based curriculum and instruction: How to bring content and process together.* Thousand Oaks, CA: Corwin.

Galston, W. (2001). Political knowledge, political engagement, and civic education. *Annual Review of Political Science, 4,* 217–234.

———. (2004). Civic education and political participation. *PS: Political Science and Politics, 37,* 233–266.

Gerhards, J., & Schafer, M. (2010). Is the internet a better public sphere? Comparing old and new media in the USA and Germany. *New Media and Society, 12,* 143–160.

Godsay, S., Henderson, W., Levine, P., & Littenberg-Tobias, J. (2012). *State civic education requirements fact sheet.* Retrieved from http://www.civicyouth.org/wp-content/uploads/2012/10/State-Civic-Ed-Requirements-Fact-Sheet-2012-Oct-19.pdf.

Harris, L., & Shreiner, T. (2014). Why can't we just look it up? Using concept formation lessons to teach global connections and local cases in world history. *World History Connected, 11*(2). Retrieved from http://worldhistoryconnected.press.illinois.edu/11.2/harris.html.

Hess, D. (2009). *Controversy in the classroom. The democratic power of discussion.* New York: Routledge.

Hess, F. (2009). Still at risk: What students don't know, even now: A report from the Common Core. *Arts Education Policy Review, 110,* 5–21.

Hobbs, R., & Jensen, A. (2009). The past, present, and future of media literacy education. *Journal of Media Literacy Education, 1,* 1–11.

Johnson, S. (2015, March 3). Teach the controversy: Education bills contain a revealing confusion. *Ars Technica.* Retrieved from http://arstechnica.com/staff/2015/03/teach-the-controversy-education-bills-contain-a-revealing-confusion/.

Koltay, T. (2011). The media and the literacies: media literacy, information literacy, digital literacy. *Media, Culture, and Society, 33,* 211–221.

Levine, P. (2015, February 8). Good citizenship transcends a test: Opposing view. *USA Today.* Retrieved from http://www.usatoday.com/story/opinion/2015/02/08/citizenship-civics-social-studies-editorials-debates/23088621/.

Livingstone, S. (2004). Media literacy and the challenge of new information and communication technologies. *Communication Review, 7,* 3–14

March, W. (2014, November 1). Fla. governor's race will top $150 million, costliest in U.S. *Tampa Tribune.* Retrieved from http://tbo.com/news/politics/fla-governors-race-will-top-150-million-costliest-in-us-20141101/.

National Council for the Social Studies (NCSS). (2013). *The college, career, and civic life (C3) framework for social studies state standards.* Silver Spring, MD: National Council for the Social Studies.

National Governors Association Center for Best Practices & Council of Chief State School Officers. (2010). *Common Core State Standards for English language arts and literacy in history/social studies, science, and technical subjects.* Washington, DC: National Governors Association Center for Best Practices & Council of Chief State School Officers.

Obenchain, K., & Pennington, J. (2015). *Educating for critical democratic literacy: Integrating social studies and literacy in the elementary classroom.* New York: Routledge.

Potter, W. J. (2013). *Media literacy.* Thousand Oaks, CA: Sage.

Quigley, C. (2004, December). *The status of civic education: Making the case for a national movement.* Paper presented at the Second Annual Congressional Conference on Civic Education, Washington, DC.

Republican Party of Texas. (2012). *Report of the platform committee.* Austin, TX: Republican Party of Texas. Retrieved from http://www.texasgop.org/wp-content/themes/rpt/images/2012Platform_Final.pdf.

Roberts, D. F., & Foehr, U. G. (2008). Trends in media use. *The Future of Children, 18*(1), 11–37.

Sanders, M., & Moulenbelt, J. (2011). Defining critical thinking: How far have we come? *Inquiry: Critical Thinking Across the Disciplines, 26,* 38–46.

U.S. Department of Education. (2014). National Assessment of Educational Progress, 2014 Civics Assessment. Retrieved from http://www.nationsreportcard.gov/hgc_2014/#civics/achievement.

Vogler, K., & Virtue, D. (2007). "Just the facts, ma'am": Teaching social studies in the era of high stakes standards and testing. *Social Studies, 98,* 54–58.

Washington, E. Y., & Dahlgren, R. (2010). "The Quest for relevancy": Allan Kownslar and historical inquiry in the new social studies movement. In B. S. Stern (Ed.), *The new social studies: People, projects & perspectives* (pp. 95–110). Charlotte, NC: Information Age.

Wei, L., & Hindman, D. B. (2011). Does the digital divide matter more? Comparing the effects of new media and old media use on the education-based knowledge gap. *Mass Communication and Society, 14,* 216–235.

Wesleyan Media Project. (2014). *Ad spending tops $1 billion.* Retrieved from http://mediaproject.wesleyan.edu/releases/ad-spending-tops-1-billion/.

Westheimer, J., & Kahne, J. (2004). Educating the good citizen. Political choices and pedagogical goals. *PS: Political Science and Politics, 37,* 241–247.

Winke, P. (2011). Investigating the reliability of the civics component of the U.S. Naturalization Test. *Language Assessment Quarterly, 8,* 317–341.

Chapter Eight

Role-Playing and Role-Dropping

Political Simulations as Portals to Pluralism in a Contentious Era

Jane C. Lo and Walter C. Parker

In the months immediately following September 11, 2001, Singleton's (2001) article in *Social Education* applauded teachers for conducting activities that allowed students to process their fears and feelings following the event. She argued, however, that teaching about tragic events should allow for candid discussions of alternative perspectives. Simply helping students dispel feelings of fear is not enough.

Rather, teachers "must help students realize that, while we are united in grief, we can be just as united when we passionately disagree about how to respond to a tragic event because we share a common commitment to inquiry and self-government" (Singleton, 2001, p. 413). Fifteen years later, the landscape of American politics hardly reflects this common commitment, and Singleton's hopes for civil deliberation seem to have been forgotten.

Instead of a diverse yet cohesive front, public discourse is splintered by increasing partisanship (Fiorina & Abrams, 2008; Hess & McAvoy, 2015). The persistent resegregation of American society further divides us (Bishop & Cushing, 2008), and the media continue to exacerbate the "othering" of marginalized populations (Mutz, 2006).

Social studies is proceeding in what appears to be an increasingly polarized, frightened, and militarized world (Ignatieff, 2014). Pluralism, which we define, after Berlin (1997), as peaceful coexistence of diverse and competing ideological systems, is under attack in some quarters, and the social contract itself may be at question. What, then, are some sensible ways forward in social studies classrooms?

This chapter presents a project-based learning (PBL) approach to social studies in a post-9/11 world. The approach aims to engage students in meaningful learning about government, politics, and democracy through a sequence of rigorous simulations. Following Mehlinger's (2002) suggestion, our approach asks students not only to *know* issues or to know *how* political processes can help resolve them, but also to understand the conflicts and concepts from which contentious issues arise.

By engaging students in conflicting perspectives through role-play and simulations, our curriculum offers a way to bring pluralism into the classroom by design. Specifically, we hope students may develop *enlightened political engagement* (Parker, 2003; Nie, Junn, & Stehlik-Barry, 1996) through the course. The term means "knowledgeable civic action." The two dimensions of the term, while distinct, are interdependent.

Enlightened suggests an "understanding of democratic rule through knowledge and acceptance of the norms and procedures of democracy." Meanwhile, *political engagement* signifies the "capability of citizens to engage in self-rule and encompasses behaviors and cognitions necessary for identifying political preferences, understanding politics, and pursuing interests" (Nie et al., 1996, p.11). This is our ultimate goal: for students to possess an understanding of democracy in order to engage in self-rule. We contend that a curriculum focused on rigorous, authentic, political simulations can help prepare students for enlightened political engagement in a world rife with political conflict.

PLURALISM AND ENLIGHTENED POLITICAL ENGAGEMENT

Pluralism is a fact of modern democratic states, where individuals and groups have multiple and often conflicting conceptions of the good life (Levinson, 1999). The events of 9/11 highlighted many of these differences, even if some of the conflicts were temporarily set aside. While the nation seemed more united immediately following the tragedy, visions of the future began to splinter as the nation responded with military force. Ideological rifts about warfare, terrorism, and extremism became points of contention.

Singleton (2001) feared that 9/11 could lull the nation into a placid state of blind patriotism, but the fallout of the Iraq war and subsequent military action has led to an era of mistrust, skepticism, and discontent. Further, conflicts about conceptions of the good life continue to play out in the political arena, as politicians entrench themselves along party lines. This conundrum between unity and diversity can be described as a part of the "problem of diversity" (Parker, 2003), where diverse interpretations of what it means to live a good life come into conflict, inevitably, within diverse societies that are trying to be liberal, plural democracies.

Especially in a time of increasing polarization, an "us versus them" attitude can be detrimental to the health of democratic processes (Binder, 2014). At the same time, political theorists from Rawls (2005) to Mouffe (2000) have argued that pluralism is not only a fact of liberal democracies, but also desirable, and that these different perspectives should be preserved in the name of liberty, equality, and justice.

One of the main challenges for social studies educators in a post-9/11 era, then, is to help students recognize the importance of pluralism in a vibrant democracy, while teaching them how to navigate diversity in a democratic way. We believe an assemblage of pedagogies is needed; accordingly, we feature three of the six promising practices that are featured in the report, *The Civic Mission of Schools* (Gibson & Levine, 2003):

- Simulations
- Discussion
- Direct instruction on government and politics

The PBL approach to social studies that we present in this chapter aims to help students develop enlightened political engagement by providing them with opportunities to participate *now* in the political system through simulations, deliberating controversial public issues (historical and contemporary), and forming their own views about what government should and shouldn't do. Although this approach may be applicable to social studies in general, the curriculum presented in this chapter was developed for the purpose of improving the high school U.S. government course.

THE GOVERNMENT COURSE

The government course remains a staple of the high school curriculum.[1] The course is intriguing on the landscape of civic education because it is both prevalent and humdrum. Most high school students take the course before they graduate, and yet people often provide anecdotes of it being a boring, facts-driven class (Kahne & Middaugh, 2008b). Students' exposure to the course is enormous, but it almost escapes the attention of political critics and also, curiously, of educational researchers and civic education scholars.

The subject matter of the government course has been settled for decades, and it escapes the partisan wrangling that routinely besets the U.S. history curriculum. Unlike the tumultuous discussions most recently seen around the advanced placement (AP) U.S. History curriculum (2015), the government course is typically presented as a process and procedures course: outlining how a bill becomes a law, how elections are conducted, and how public policies are made. There are seldom disagreements about the importance and procedures of these processes even in a post-9/11 world. However, as the partisan divide widens in the United States, one begins to wonder if the government course should continue to be so humdrum.

With a focus on current political issues, the high school government course has the potential to help students understand pluralism, partisanship, and older controversies that have (re)arisen in the post-9/11 era, such as the proper role of government in a democracy. In this chapter, we focus specifically on an increasingly popular "advanced" version of this course: Advanced Placement U.S. Government and Politics (APGOV).

Student enrollment in AP courses has skyrocketed since the late 1990s thanks to an "excellence for all" trend that has brought social-justice school reformers into an alliance with social-efficiency reformers. A historic union has been achieved between advocates of school tracking for "excellence" and advocates of detracking for "equity." The thrust of this reform movement is to give all students, in the name of equity, access to "America's best curriculum."

Given this push toward equity of access, we began to wonder if all students could actually navigate the APGOV curriculum. To help answer this inquiry, we worked to design a PBL-oriented version of the curriculum that could engage more students in the APGOV course.

The curriculum we present in this chapter is a form of PBL that is based on six annual iterations of implementation, analysis, and redesign. The work was conducted by a multidisciplinary team of teachers, researchers, and political scientists (Parker et al., 2011, 2013). Our methodology was *design-based implementation research* (Penuel, Fishman, Cheng, & Sabelli, 2011), where the objective was to improve practice while also developing theory—problem redefinition and refinement of central categories.

To develop an effective social studies curriculum that engages students in productive deliberative processes and deep political learning, the curriculum draws from contemporary research on how people learn and what learning is, building especially on the learning cycles research of Bransford and colleagues (2000, 2006). Designed to help students have authentic political experiences through simulations, this government curriculum asks students to consider plural perspectives, via role-playing in simulations, as a way to deliberate contentious political issues in an increasingly polarized polity.

CURRICULUM DESIGN

We worked with four design principles:

- Projects are, as Larmer and Mergendoller (2010) put it, "the main course, not dessert."
- Students are engaged in roles immediately (before new information has been learned).
- Students are then asked to drop those roles to form and assess their own opinions.
- Key concepts are revisited overtime through "quasi-repetitive activity cycles" (Bransford et al., 2006, p 233).

As the third principle suggests, the curriculum was designed to develop students' political voice—their autonomy to make uncoerced decisions about government and politics. Generally, these concern the fundamental political question: "How should we live together?" (Hess & McAvoy, 2015, p. 4).

Across five simulations, students role-play legislators, judges, executives, member of the media, agency and interest group leaders, and campaign managers, but they also abandon these roles at key junctures to articulate their own views on the issue at hand. These political autonomy moments (PAMs) give students a chance to express what they really think about polarizing political issues outside of their roles.

Before outlining the four design principles, we will foreshadow the argument made in this chapter: Since roles offer students a low-stakes opportunity to "try on" diverse opinions and perspectives (the pluralism of our title), the PAMs give them an open opportunity to (re)consider their own ideas about contentious issues. The roles also provide a diversity of opinions that may be lacking in a more homogenized classroom.

Projects as the Spine

In our PBL approach to social studies in a post-9/11 world, projects are political simulations in which students take roles as political actors (e.g., campaign managers, justices, and members of Congress) and work with classmates who take complementary political roles. Students are engaged in these political simulations throughout the entire course. Unlike many social studies courses, where the projects or simulations come at the end of the unit (after students have already learned the necessary information), our political simulations are themselves the vehicles through which students learn about politics and government.

Each simulation is divided into tasks that target specific processes of U.S. government and politics. Consequently, the projects are lengthy and provide students with multiple opportunities to try out, revisit, and reflect on their current level of understanding and opinions about contentious political issues. Instead of functioning like an end-of-unit capstone, our simulations are the spine of the course and they *drive* the learning of each unit.

Our projects are political simulations because simulations reflect reality in a structured and limited way, while illustrating important processes (Wright-Maley, 2015). Furthermore, as indicated above, simulations are considered to be a best practice of civic education (Gibson & Levine, 2003; Kahne & Middaugh, 2008a). Generally speaking, political simulations can give students opportunities to deliberate contentious issues so as to analyze and evaluate conflicting value systems while formulating their own views.

Traditionally, standalone legislative simulations in government courses are a popular way for students to learn about different political perspectives (e.g., Baranowski, 2006; Pearcy, 2015), as are moot courts (Bell, 2002; Pagnotti & Russell, 2015). Our course extends these tried-and-true classroom projects and involves other simulations (e.g., ratification of the Constitution, elections, and public policy making).

Engagement First

Our PBL approach hinges on engaging students first in roles *before* they interact with new content information. In "A Time for Telling," Schwartz and Bransford (1998) concluded that there is a "readiness" for learning from textbook readings or lectures when students have had an opportunity to generate some understanding in other ways. This means that students tend to understand information better when there is a *need to know* it. In this way the "telling" of information has someplace to go because the classroom activity is already occurring and students have a reason to attend to the information as well as a context for interpreting it (Parker et al., 2011).

Typically in social studies classrooms, background information is laid down first as a foundation (e.g., a lecture or reading on how a bill becomes a law) before students are allowed to engage in an activity (e.g., mock congress). Our PBL approach inverts this traditional sequence—engaging students first in the activity (e.g., assigning them roles and tasks) so that they will have a reason to find out how they will accomplish their tasks (through lectures and readings).

By assigning students to roles in politically contentious simulations or tasks, the teacher can help engage students in learning about political issues and processes that can seem mundane or boring. These emotional connections that students might make (favorable or not) about the role to which they are assigned can help focus their attention and bring awareness to the task at hand (Medina, 2008). Also, because each simulation consists of multiple tasks, students have a way to try out different political stances over a period of time, thereby *experiencing* pluralism in their own skin and discovering for themselves the conflicting nature of certain political positions.

Role-Playing and Role-Dropping

The role assignments thrust students into the middle of the simulations, often before they have a good grasp of what the simulations are about, which is part of the engagement-first principle mentioned above. At the same time, roles provide students with opportunities to take on perspectives that may be different from their own, or to try on different positions if they do not already have one. This approach helps students get a sense of how different political parties (or value systems) perceive and value the democratic virtues of liberty, equality, and justice.

Because students are interacting with other students who also are in roles, the simulations become spaces where students can deliberate contentious political issues in authentic ways. For example, in the presidential election simulation detailed below, students who play candidates of the two major parties must learn how to debate various policies (such as climate change, the threat of Islamic State of Iraq and al-Sham [ISIS], education reform, or health care) from their respective positions. Meanwhile, students who role-play members of the media (e.g., Fox News, MSNBC, and CNN) must be able to "spin" the information they collect from the candidates in order to cater to their viewership.

While these authentic roles give students opportunities to become more enlightened about political issues, our PBL approach also asks students to drop their roles at various times in each simulation. These intentional breaks from roles were created to facilitate students' development of *political autonomy* and assess their own opinions and ideas about an issue (Brighouse, 1998). These strategically placed PAMs give students opportunities to reflect on their roles, formulate their own political opinions, and analyze their experiences in the simulations.

Much like the "feel free to drop your role" moment in a structured academic controversy (Parker, 2011), PAMs free students from the constraints of their roles and the simulation momentarily so that they can consider what their own stance might be on the contentious issue at hand (e.g., immigration policy, race relations, legalization of gay marriage, or income inequality). The role-playing and role-dropping combination gives students a way to consider different sides of an issue, recognize there may be more than one legitimate perspective, and determine their own political stance (Lo, 2015).

Looping

The curriculum also features a fourth design principle: "quasi-repetitive activity cycles" (Bransford et al., 2006, p. 233), or what our teachers dubbed "looping." Looping means to revisit information, skills, and concepts so that students can revise and deepen their evolving understandings of the course subject matter. In *Brain Rules*, the molecular biologist John Medina (2008) points out that revisiting information can help lead to short-term and long-term memory building.

In our curriculum, looping gives students multiple opportunities to reflect on their learning, revisit earlier subject matter, and reconsider their own understandings. However, because the AP version of the course requires students to be familiar with such a broad array of concept labels, our team had to distill a set of core concepts that were worthy of looping; that is, they could serve as anchors for other concepts.

We envision these central concepts as stars around which lesser concepts orbit, like planets (Parker & Lo, at press). For example, federalism as a key concept brings with it lesser concepts like states' rights, devolution, block grants, and selective incorporation. As students learn about the lesser concepts, they refine their understanding of the core concept and vice versa. Subject matter that is looped throughout the course includes concepts (e.g., federalism, political parties, interest groups, civil rights, and balance of powers) as well as skills (e.g., deliberation, perspective taking, constitutional reasoning, and learning information from texts).

As students move through the political simulations, they also repeatedly respond to (loop back on) a master course question: What is the proper role of government in a democracy? By generating and revising their responses to this question throughout the course, students formulate political opinions about how we might live together despite our differences. Having these candid conversations throughout the simulations may help students understand the political conflicts that face our society in a post-9/11 era.

THE SIMULATIONS

The curriculum has five political simulations. Table 8.1 shows the simulations and their tasks in order. Each simulation takes four to six weeks to complete. Students are assigned to roles at the beginning of each simulation (per the engagement first design principle). The assigning of roles is important to the goal of helping students take on, evaluate, and analyze various conflicting value systems. It is not uncommon for students to take on a role that does not align with their own beliefs.

Table 8.1. The Five Political Simulations, Their Duration, Tasks, and Purposes

	Founders' Intent	Elections	SCOTUS	Congress	Government in Action
Number of Weeks	4 Weeks	6 Weeks	3–4 Weeks	5 Weeks	5–6 Weeks
Tasks	1. Ratification Debate 2. Historical SAC 3. Modern SAC	1. Warming up to the race 2. Navigating the campaign trail 3. Primary elections 4. Preparing for the general election 5. General election	1. Trial court 2. Appellate circuit court 3. Appellate circuit court (optional) 4. Appellate Supreme Court	1. Constituency research 2. Write and submit bills 3. Committee work 4. Floor session	1. Meet the clients 2. Press conference 3. Litigation 4. Letter to the president 5. Congressional testimony 6. Create political action plans
Purpose of Simulation	Help students establish a beginning understanding of federalism and politics in the United States	Help students understand the relationships between interest groups, political parties, and the media	Help students understand the role of the courts in checks and balances	Help students understand how politics connects to legislation and policy	Help students understand the relationship between the three branches of government and interest groups

For example, a student who lives in a politically liberal community, whose parents consistently vote for the Democratic Party candidate, may be assigned to play a staunch Tea Party presidential candidate. Or a student who was raised in a conservative community may be assigned to play a liberal Democratic member of Congress. In both cases, the student has to enact the political opinions and perspectives of the role he or she is assigned.

While students may bemoan this misalignment, our research shows that this political dissonance actually proves to be enlightening for students (Lo, 2015). Ultimately, the actions students take in these roles are bound by the simulation and their roles, but unscripted so that they can learn from dynamic and veritable interactions with their peers through the simulations. Before explaining why this is so, we will briefly introduce each of the simulations.

Founders' Intent

The course opens with Founders' Intent, an introductory simulation. Students become delegates to the Constitutional Convention of 1787 and are introduced to role-playing and to the system of limited government and divided powers that the Constitution creates. In these roles, they engage in three deliberations on controversial constitutional issues. First, and quickly (it is a review for many students), they decide whether to approve the Constitution and thereby bring to life the federalist and anti-federalist arguments over the division of power between the national and state governments, representation, among others. Second, still in these roles, but now in Structured Academic Controversy (SAC) (Johnson, 1988) teams, they deliberate on a federalism controversy from the past (e.g., the argument over the national bank).

SAC is a form of deliberation that asks students to consider both sides of an argument in an effort to come to a consensus about a contentious issue. In our adaptation (Parker, 2011), however, students are asked to drop the roles. This is the PAM discussed earlier. Third, again in SAC teams, they deliberate a contemporary federalism controversy (e.g., the argument over immigration). This final task revisits federalism in a modern conflict and introduces political parties, which launches students into the purpose of political parties: winning elections.

Founders' Intent is designed to help students get used to playing a role in a simulation. Because the roles are historical figures (i.e., students perform the roles of delegates to the constitutional convention), a robust set of information is available to help students figure out how they are supposed to think and act in their roles. This simulation also gives teachers an opportunity to help students remember the boundaries of the simulation.

Since Founders' Intent mirrors real-world debates that had "real" end results (e.g., the Constitution was *actually* ratified), teachers can help students stay true to historical authenticity (and eventually the authentic boundaries of simulations) as they navigate the dynamic verisimilitude of simulations. This is a way to hold students responsible to how *real* complex political processes occur even as they dynamically perform their roles. Through this first historical simulation, students begin to see that some of the current polarizing political issues are imbedded in our historical past. They can also begin to see how these polarizing issues are exacerbated in current times.

Elections

This is a simulation of a U.S. presidential election and the second scenario in which students wrestle with complex polarizing issues in our society. Students take roles as candidates, campaign managers, media journalists, leaders of interest groups, and political party leaders. As with Founders' Intent, students are held accountable to the rules of the electoral process, albeit a simplified and truncated one.

For example, students (in their roles) follow the entire electoral process from announcing their candidacy to the general election, but instead of spending months on the campaign trail, students conduct the simulation in a matter of weeks. Even so, students are required to follow campaign finance rules and to staunchly adhere to the actions and beliefs of their roles (e.g., typically, Fox News better not print a positive story about the Democratic candidate).

In many ways, the authenticity of the simulation is bound by the polarization of political issues we see in Congress today. However, rather than focusing myopically on the conflicts, the simulation is designed to help students think about these gridlocks and how to overcome them through grassroots efforts.

Through the simulation, students learn about public opinion, political ideology, polls, and the voting characteristics of the electorate. They also learn about the relationships between interest groups, political parties, and the media as they attempt to navigate and influence the campaigning process. Most important, students analyze and consider the polarizing rifts that currently exist between the two major political parties.

Students often note that the Elections simulation is where they learn to see that "the other side isn't crazy." Even though many students still adhere to their own original political opinions, they begin to see that other opinions have merit. This is one example of the simulations helping students become more enlightened about the polarizing issues that plague our national politics today. Eventually, after scandals, campaign struggles, and media blitzes, students vote to elect the next president of the United States at the end of the simulation. Once the president is elected and sworn in, students witness how the election can influence the eventual appointment of justices to the Supreme Court.

Supreme Court of the United States

In the third simulation, Supreme Court of the United States (SCOTUS), students take on roles in the judicial branch of government. Students become lawyers and judges, first in a trial court and then in appellate courts: a circuit court of appeals and then the Supreme Court. The trial court activity allows students to role-play their understandings (or misunderstandings) about trial courts (i.e., often what they see on court television). By conducting the trial court activity first, students can see the differences between trial and appellate courts.

In the moot court simulations, students practice judicial argumentation and constitutional reasoning as they experience how courts define and implement public policy that deal with civil rights and civil liberties. Again, the polarization of political issues that students experienced first in the Founders' Intent simulation and then through Elections is looped here in the SCOTUS simulation.

However, this time students see how the judicial branch attempts to navigate these conflicts in order to render decisions that are true to the Constitution and changing social dynamics. Students also learn how justices and lawyers navigate the political pressures of public opinion, media, and interest groups. Throughout the project, students experience the interdependence of the three branches, such as judicial review and the impact of the presidential election on appointments to the Supreme Court.

Congress

The fourth simulation is probably the most widely used simulation in government courses: A mock Congress. Unlike most legislative simulations that show students how a bill becomes a law, in this simulation students become legislators to learn not only the process of passing a bill but also how interest groups and the media influence public policy. In committee compromises and floor debates, students navigate political pressures—from constituency, political party, and interest groups—for and against particular legislation. Again, students are faced with the contentious issues that are polarizing the two major political parties.

Because students are bound to their roles, they must make legislative decisions (and write bills) that are consistent with their roles. Students often find this process frustrating, because they may be pushing for legislation that they may not actually believe in; however, they also begin to see the importance of making compromises on the right issues to satisfy their constituencies. It is often in this simulation that students learn just how difficult the political process can be. Many students learn to empathize with members of Congress through this simulation.

In short, the simulation revisits the party platform promises that presidential candidates made in the Elections project and the bicameral system set up by the Constitution in Founders' Intent. Rather than sidestep the conflict and gridlock that exist in politics, all of these reminders help students navigate the contentious issues that exist in our political process today.

Government in Action

In this final simulation, students become consultants to interest groups that have strong positions on immigration policy. Because each client has a different agenda (e.g., some wish to build a fence along the border to Mexico, others wish to help create a path toward citizenship for undocumented immigrants), students have to determine the best way to help their clients achieve their goals. Applying knowledge from previous simulations, students study their client's position and what makes the group a serious contender in the public policy arena.

The students' job is to draw up a smart political action plan that will help their client advance its agenda through the political system—through the branches of government and the bureaucratic agencies—thereby learning how interest groups work with government to create, implement, and evaluate public policies. The idea is for students to rely on their (simulated) experiences with party politics, elections, courts, and Congress to come up with sound political strategies for their clients.

As it is with the other simulations, students' actions are bound by the rules of simulation—in this case, the client they wish to please. While students have autonomy in deciding what political actions to take, the success of their plan is ultimately determined by the resources of their client and how likely it is that their client can carry out their plan.

The five simulations described above are designed to showcase the governmental and political processes in the United States. In each case, students' roles in the simulations give them reasons to learn about the content and to understand how political processes work. At the same time, the roles and tasks are designed to expose students to conflicting values from diverse perspectives.

While these clashes may bring discomfort to the student, the role and PAM combination can help students negotiate this discomfort. Role-*playing* presents multiple perspectives to students, while role-*dropping* gives them opportunities to formulate their own political ideas about issues around pluralism, diversity, justice, and equality. The following section discusses how role-playing and role-dropping can serve as a portal to plurality in a contentious era by helping students consider conflicting perspectives and develop their own opinions in the process.

ROLES AS PORTALS TO PLURALITY

In social studies classrooms that feature controversies, students may find it difficult to engage with an issue because they do not want to be judged for their opinions on it but also because they may not yet have an opinion about it. Moreover, Hess (2009) suggests that teachers may avoid teaching controversial issues because they wish to shield students from the discomfort and awkwardness that may arise in these discussions or to protect themselves from negative parental reaction. In a time where differences seem to further the "othering" of marginalized populations, skirting controversial issues in social studies may seem a safe and sensible route to take.

However, the banality of an uncontroversial social studies classroom may mask intolerance at best and become an avenue for entrenched bigotry at worst. In turn, "if we want democratic education to be both democratic and educational, then we have to teach young people about controversial political issues" (Hess, 2009, p. 162). This is especially true in a post-9/11 era where polarization has rendered a perpetual stalemate on more than a few contentious issues. So, how might simulations help students engage in these discussions in productive ways?

Findings from our research suggest that assigning roles offers a low-stakes entry point for students to engage with contentious issues (Lo, 2015). These roles also give students reasons to learn about the political processes through the rules of the simulation. In a sense, the role acts as a *portal to plurality*—a gateway into the issues and processes around definitions of "the good life" in a pluralistic liberal democracy. The stakes are low because everyone in the class is assigned a role, and students feel as if they can try on an opinion behind the safety of their roles without needing to "out" their own opinions (or lack thereof) about the issue.

At the same time, students who already have strong political opinions find they can voice an opposing opinion just for fun—to see what it is like to be on the other side. Through this portal, students can learn to consider varying political perspectives. The assigned roles give students a way to enter into the conversation—as if they were given access to a script on how to behave in a given situation. The simulations provide the setting and context (or norms and rules) of the play-acting, while the roles function like characters students can lean on when they are unsure of what to say, what stance to take, or how to express an opinion (Lo, 2015).

This play-acting allows students to experience controversial issues, with their differing opinions and complexities, along with political processes. Afterward, teachers ask students to drop their roles so that students have an additional opportunity to reflect on the issue and to assess their own opinions on the matter. This political autonomy moment is crucial to the success of role-playing to serve not only as a *portal* to plurality, but also for students to actually experience the complexities of a pluralistic democratic society.

Without the reflexivity offered by PAMs, roles would only provide portals into an imaginary plurality, where students could easily disregard the "fake," simulated deliberation and not genuinely (re)consider their own political perspectives. Similarly, without this inner dissonance, students could disregard the views presented by another member of the class or even ignore a classmate with a different perspective altogether.

Because students need to assess their own *actual* opinions on a topic in the PAMs, they have the opportunity to reconcile their own beliefs with the realities of pluralistic thinking that their roles present. This reflective and metacognitive process completes the role's purpose as a portal into the conflicts of a pluralistic society—offering students a way to see past polarized perspectives.

Given that the roles provide a set of boundaries within which students can freely act, the simulations include a dynamism that allows students to influence the outcome of the simulation. The simulations also provide a verisimilitude that requires students to learn about politics and government. Sure, the election simulation always ends with someone being elected president, but the outcome of who gets elected is determined by the process of the simulation.

In this way, the roles bind students to a particular way of thinking, but also provide them with some autonomy in the process. At the same time, the roles give students a unique opportunity to think differently—not necessarily to walk in someone else's shoes, but at least for students to be in shoes that they would not typically choose to wear.

Role-playing experiences can serve as distinct experiences of their own, where students' perspectives can potentially be broadened through "being pulled up short" (Kerdeman, 2003) by unexpected encounters with or in their roles, encounters that cause them to reassess their understandings and opinions. Each journey that students take in a role becomes an opportunity for them to broaden their horizon.

Even in classrooms where the student population is not particularly diverse, teachers can use authentic roles to introduce legitimate opinions that are different from the norms of the class and the community. These varying positions in the world complicate and enrich democratic life, and it is by being exposed to them (and perhaps learning to sympathize with them) that students can better understand the responsibilities of citizens in a pluralistic democratic society.

To summarize, we believe role-playing in political simulations has the potential to help students engage in pluralistic democratic deliberations and decision making. It may elicit questions about democratic values that cause students to think critically about political issues and their own political involvement. At the very least, it exposes students to perspectives that they may never have considered.

CONCLUSION

In the months after 9/11, Singleton (2001) urged civic educators to "help students think critically about such events as the September 11 terrorists attacks, particularly when much of the media to which students are exposed fail to provide multiple perspectives on the issues" (p. 413). Singleton suggested that teachers choose a model for facilitating good discussion of issues in the classroom, not as a way to promote dissent, but rather as a way to make room for dissent and critical perspective taking.

Even though 9/11 is no longer a current event, our nation's response to it begot many current events: ongoing military conflict, the "othering" of Muslims in America, unsanctioned use of torture, surveillance, and increased uncertainty about how we should live alongside those who are different from us. All these years later, civic educators still have a responsibility to engage students in productive public discussions about these issues. We have presented one strategy centered on political simulations and role-play.

In a context of bifurcating polarization along party, racial, and economic divides, strategies like PAM and role-play can help students reclaim the promise of a social contract that includes the plural voices of all, not just some or most. The roles help students gain entry to issues and stances that may otherwise elude them, while the PAM gives students the space to formulate their own views about the issues. This role-playing and role-dropping format may encourage student to participate in discussions of controversial issues, all the while providing teachers a way to facilitate deeply engaging deliberations.

By playing and dropping roles in social studies simulations, students have the opportunity not only to learn essential knowledge (enlightened), but also to be prompted and empowered to act (political engagement). Furthermore, the roles can help students broaden their horizons and allow for deep, critical, yet productive ways of disagreeing and agreeing with one another.

Even though simulations and role-play may not be able to resolve the problem of diversity, it is our belief that the curriculum presented in this chapter gives teachers a way to help students deliberate important social studies issues.

NOTE

1. According to the most recent high school transcript study, four-fifths of graduates have taken a government course (National Assessment of Educational Progress, 2009).

REFERENCES

Baranowski, M. (2006). Single session simulations: The effectiveness of cohort congressional simulations in introductory American government classes. *Journal of Political Science Education, 2*, 33–49.

Bell, K. (2002). Using moot courts in the classroom. (Cases, controversy, and the court). *Social Education, 66*, 42.

Berlin, I. (1997). The pursuit of the ideal. In H. Hardy & R. Hausheer (Eds.), *The proper study of mankind: An anthology of essays* (pp. 1–16). London: Chatto & Windus.

Binder, S. A. (2014). *Polarized we govern?* Center for Effective Public Management at Brookings. Retrieved from http://www.brookings.edu/research/papers/2014/05/27-polarized-we-govern-congress-legislative-gridlock-polarized-binder.

Bishop, B., & Cushing, R. G. (2008). *The big sort: Why the clustering of like-minded America is tearing us apart.* Boston: Houghton Mifflin Harcourt.

Bransford, J., Brown, A. L., & Cocking, R. R. (2000). *How people learn: Brain, mind, experience, and school.* Washington, DC: National Academies Press.

Bransford, J., Vye, N. J., Stevens, R., Kuhl, P., Schwartz, D. L., Bell, P., . . . Sabelli, N. (2006). Learning theories and education: Toward a decade of synergy. In P. A. Alexander & P. H. Winne (Eds.), *Handbook of educational psychology* (2nd ed., pp. 209–244). Mahwah, NJ: Erlbaum.

Brighouse, H. (1998). Civic education and liberal legitimacy. *Ethics, 108*, 719–745.

Fiorina, M. P., & Abrams, S. J. (2008). Political polarization in the American public. *Annual Review of Political Science, 11*, 563–588.

Gibson, C., & Levine, P. (2003). *The civic mission of schools.* New York: Carnegie Corporation of New York and the Center for Information and Research on Civic Learning and Engagement. Retrieved from http://civicyouth.org/PopUps/CivicMissionofSchools.pdf.

Hess, D. E. (2009). *Controversy in the classroom: The democratic power of discussion.* New York: Routledge.

Hess, D. E., & McAvoy, P. (2015). *The political classroom: Evidence and ethics in democratic education.* New York: Routledge.

Ignatieff, M. (2014, September 25). The new world disorder. *New York Review of Books.* Retrieved from http://www.nybooks.com/articles/archives/2014/sep/25/new-world-disorder/.

Johnson, D. W. J. (1988). Critical thinking through structured controversy. *Educational Leadership, 45*, 58.

Kahne, J., & Middaugh, E. (2008a). *Democracy for some: The civic opportunity gap in high school* (No. 59). Washington, DC: Center for Information and Research on Civic Learning (CIRCLE). Retrieved from www.civicyouth.org/?p=278.

———. (2008b). High quality civic education: What is it and who gets it? *Social Education, 72*, 34–39.

Kerdeman, D. (2003). Pulled up short: Challenging self-understanding as a focus of teaching and learning. *Journal of Philosophy of Education, 37*, 293–308.

Larmer, J., & Mergendoller, J. R. (2010). The main course, not dessert. Buck Institute for Education. Retrieved from http://www.bie.org/tools/freebies/main_course_not_dessert/.

Levinson, M. (1999). Liberalism, pluralism, and political education: Paradox or paradigm? *Oxford Review of Education, 25*, 39–58.

Lo, J. C. (2015). *Learning to participate through role-play: Understanding political simulations in the high school government course.* (Unpublished doctoral dissertation). University of Washington, Seattle, WA.

Medina, J. (2008). *Brain rules: 12 principles for surviving and thriving at work, home, and school.* Seattle, WA: Pear Press.

Mehlinger, H. D. (2002). Teaching about September 11 and its aftermath. *Social Education, 66*, 303–306.

Mouffe, C. (2000). *The democratic paradox.* London: Verso.

Mutz, D. C. (2006). How the mass media divide us. In P. S. Nivola & D. W. Brady (Eds.), *Red and blue nation?: Characteristics and causes of America's polarized politics* (pp. 223–248). Washington, DC: Hoover Institution on War, Revolution, and Peace, Stanford University; Brookings Institution Press.

National Assessment of Educational Progress. (2009). U.S. Department of Education, Institute of Education Sciences, National Center for Education Statistics, National Assessment of Educational Progress (NAEP), 2009 High School Transcript Study (HSTS).

New AP U.S. History standards from College Board—CNN.com. (2015). Retrieved from http://www.cnn.com/2015/07/31/living/ap-history-united-states-curriculum-change/index.html.

Nie, N. H., Junn, J., & Stehlik-Barry, K. (1996). *Education and democratic citizenship in America*. Chicago: University Of Chicago Press.

Pagnotti, J., & Russell, W. B. (2015). A problem-based learning approach to civics education: Exploring the free exercise clause with supreme court simulations. *Social Studies, 106*, 281–292.

Parker, W. (2011). Feel free to change your mind. A response to "The Potential for Deliberative Democratic Civic Education." *Democracy and Education, 19*. Retrieved from http://democracyeducationjournal.org/home/vol19/iss2/9.

Parker, W. C. (2003). *Teaching democracy: Unity and diversity in public life*. New York: Teachers College Press.

Parker, W. C., & Lo, J. (at press). Content selection in advanced courses: Deep learning amid the "hundred million things." *Curriculum Inquiry*.

Parker, W. C., Mosborg, S., Bransford, J. D., Vye, N. J., Wilkerson, J., & Abbott, R. (2011). Rethinking advanced high school coursework: Tackling the depth/breadth tension in the AP US Government and Politics course. *Journal of Curriculum Studies, 43*, 533–559.

Parker, W., Lo, J., Yeo, A. J., Valencia, S. W., Nguyen, D., Abbott, R. D., . . . Vye, N. J. (2013). Beyond breadth-speed-test: Toward deeper knowing and engagement in an Advanced Placement course. *American Educational Research Journal, 50*, 1424–1459.

Pearcy, M. (2015). "Playing the President": The value of simulations in promoting civic literacy. *Ohio Social Studies Review, 52*(1). Retrieved from http://edhd.bgsu.edu/ossr/journal/index.php/ossr/article/view/173.

Penuel, W. R., Fishman, B. J., Cheng, B. H., & Sabelli, N. (2011). Organizing research and development at the intersection of learning, implementation, and design. *Educational Researcher, 40*, 331–337.

Rawls, J. (2005). *Political liberalism: Expanded edition* (2nd ed.). New York: Columbia University Press.

Schwartz, D. L., & Bransford, J. D. (1998). A time for telling. *Cognition and Instruction, 16*, 475–522.

Singleton, L. R. (2001). Following a tragic event: A necessary challenge for civic educators. *Social Education, 65*, 413–418.

Wright-Maley, C. (2015). Beyond the "Babel problem": Defining simulations for the social studies. *Journal of Social Studies Research, 39*, 63–77.

Chapter Nine

The Psychology of Controversial Issues' Discussions

Challenges and Opportunities in a Polarized, Post-9/11 Society

Christopher H. Clark and Patricia G. Avery

Controversial issues' discussions have long been considered a cornerstone of high-quality social studies education. One of the six "proven practices" identified by the Campaign for the Civic Mission of Schools (2011), student participation in issues' discussions has been associated with greater political knowledge, efficacy, interest, tolerance, trust, and participation; expected and actual electoral participation; and perspective taking (e.g., Avery, Levy, & Simmons, 2014; Barr et al., 2015; Torney-Purta, Lehmann, Oswald, & Schulz, 2001).

Over the past fifteen years, there has been an increased focus on various aspects of classroom discussions, including:

- the practices of exemplary teachers (Hess, 2009)
- the likes and dislikes of students with regard to discussions (Hess & Posselt, 2002)
- the political and cultural contexts of discussions, both inside and outside the classroom (Journell, 2011; Kawashima-Ginsberg & Levine, 2014; McAvoy & Hess, 2013)
- the disparity between dominant and marginalized groups in opportunities to engage in discussions (Kahne & Middaugh, 2008)
- the nature of students' identities during discussions, particularly when issues have a direct bearing on those identities (Beck, 2013; Goldberg, 2013)

These studies have deepened our understanding of the complexities of classroom discussions and are predicated on assumptions we share: Conflicting perspectives can be a democratic resource, societies benefit from consideration of a range of perspectives, and citizens need to be able to engage in constructive deliberations about controversial public issues.

Over the past several decades, scholars of political psychology have studied various aspects of political disagreement, polarization, and opinion change in the United States (e.g., Abramowitz, 2010; Haidt, 2012; Levendusky, 2009; Lodge & Taber, 2013) that have implications for discussions of controversial issues in K–12 classrooms. Insights from this area have received little attention in social studies in part because most of the research was conducted with adults. However, some of the theories and concepts from political psychology, such as motivated reasoning, biased information seeking, and homophily, may be useful in understanding the difficulties in engaging students in the deliberation of complex issues.

The goal of this chapter is to provide an accessible introduction to several key psychological factors that can shape how people engage with controversial issues. We begin with a description of the current divided political climate in the United States and argue that these divisions often manifest themselves in the classroom. We then identify important concepts and theories that help explain the impacts of divisiveness on civic discourse inside and outside classrooms. Our concluding section focuses on recommendations for educators, such as student affirmations, classroom community building, strategic grouping, and values-based persuasion, which may address some of the factors that constrain productive civic deliberation.

ANGER, ANXIETY, AND POLARIZATION POST-9/11

In the immediate aftermath of the events of September 11, 2001, U.S. public trust in the government to do the right thing "all or most of the time" increased to the highest level since before Watergate. Hahn (2002) cited a national survey indicating that "79% of college students said they trusted the military, 69% said they trusted the president, and 62% said they trusted Congress" (p. 159). Displays of patriotism were abundant, and support for cultural pluralism increased under the banner of national unity (Davies, Steele, & Markus, 2008).

Although 9/11 prompted demonstrations of national solidarity, the George W. Bush administration's *response* to 9/11 ushered in a period of intense political polarization, perhaps in part due to the tendency of individuals to react to terroristic threats with one of two emotions—anger or anxiety (Huddy & Feldman, 2011). People who displayed anger were more supportive of military action, while those who felt anxiety were more risk averse.

Further, for individuals who tend to see the world as a threatening place, a characteristic of right-wing authoritarianism, acts of terrorism increase their perception of threat, support for limits on civil liberties, and intolerance for dissenting views.[1] Hetherington and Weiler's (2009) research suggests that threatening circumstances may actually drive individuals with nonauthoritarian dispositions to behave more like authoritarians, thus leading to a convergence of support for policies such as warrantless wiretapping.

Although some researchers have suggested a general shift toward political conservatism following 9/11 (Jost, Glaser, Kruglanski, & Sulloway, 2003), others cite evidence indicating heightened ideological commitments, with conservatives becoming more conservative and liberals becoming more liberal (Pyszczynski, Solomon, & Greenberg, 2003). This *ideological intensification hypothesis* is consistent with the current level of political polarization in the United States (Huddy & Feldman, 2011).

A 2014 Pew Research Center report shows that the percentage of Americans whose positions on policy issues are neither consistently liberal nor conservative ("middle-of-the-road") decreased from 49 percent in 1994 to 39 percent in 2014, while those who hold consistently conservative or liberal policy preferences increased from 10 percent to 21 percent over the same time period. Unfavorable opinions of the other political party have more than doubled: 27 percent of Democrats and 36 percent of Republicans believe the other party's policies "threaten the nation's well-being" (p. 7).

IS POLARIZATION PROBLEMATIC?

The question of whether political polarization is problematic for democracies depends on how it is defined. Abramowitz (2010) defines polarization as increasing alignment between political beliefs and partisan identities, resulting in fewer individuals whose issue opinions cross partisan lines. In other words, a person's degree of polarization can be measured by counting the number of times her or his issue opinions align with those of one political party. Some researchers (e.g., Levendusky, 2009) argue that alignment between issue stances and choice of party is not necessarily problematic because alignment simply reflects ideological consistency.

From the perspective of social studies educators, partisan alignment may even be desirable, as partisans usually show higher levels of political engagement and issue knowledge (Hess & McAvoy, 2015). The problem arises when partisan polarization involves a tendency to mistrust and demonize the other party and to avoid compromise. Iyengar, Sood, and Lelkes (2012) suggest that it is *affective polarization*, or the degree to which individuals evaluate their own party positively and the opposition negatively, that is particularly problematic.

Affective polarization, however, still does not capture all of the normatively problematic elements of divisive partisanship in U.S. political discourse. In addition to disparaging the other side of the aisle, some partisans allow their political party to dictate their beliefs (Lenz, 2012). A vocal advocate of a given position will criticize the same position later if the party line has shifted or if opposing partisans have adopted a similar belief. While political elites such as politicians may switch positions for political advantage, the same change in a nonelite partisan may be more indicative of greater trust in the party than in one's judgment.

From an educational perspective, it is the affective and intellectual consequences of polarized partisanship that are concerning. Partisan identity in conjunction with enmity toward other parties or an abdication of personal judgment (whether due to incompetence or social influence) is antithetical to engaged and enlightened citizenship. This type of political polarization can have important real-world consequences.

For example, Iyengar and Westwood (2014) found people discriminated more on the basis of party identification than either gender or race when given fictional résumés and asked to make hiring decisions. In college classrooms, differences in political affiliation between students and professors are predictive of less student learning and lower course evaluations (Kelly-Woessner & Woessner, 2008). Further, strong opinions and partisan identifications can inhibit meaningful discussion among members of ideologically diverse groups.

YOUTH AND POLARIZATION

The Commission on Youth Voting and Civic Knowledge (2013) named political polarization as a challenge to youth civic engagement, noting that the polarized environment of contemporary politics serves to frustrate and disengage young voters. There is little research on whether secondary students themselves are politically polarized. However, young adult voters (ages eighteen to twenty-four) are more aligned with political parties in their issue opinions and voting choices than previous generations (Stoker & Jennings, 2008).

There are also distinct trends in party allegiances among young adults. For example, African American and Latino youth ages eighteen to twenty-nine were much more likely to vote for Democratic House candidates in the 2010 and 2014 elections than white youth (Center for Information and Research on Civic Learning and Engagement [CIRCLE], 2014). In the 2014 midterm elections, 88 percent of African American and 68 percent of Latino youth voted for Democratic House candidates in comparison to only 43 percent of white youth; the 2010 elections mirrored these results.

Teachers may find it more difficult to facilitate discussions in racially diverse classrooms in part because racial identity is increasingly an indicator of political identity. Young adults tend to view the importance of public policy issues differently depending on their racial/ethnic identity; for example, African Americans and Latinos cite unemployment and immigration, respectively, at higher rates than other groups (Kawashima-Ginsberg & Levine, 2015). Issues that have significant identity connections are also likely to generate greater passion and emotion in classroom discussions, a factor that leads some teachers to avoid these discussions.

It should not be surprising, then, that researchers find low levels of civic discussion in racially pluralistic schools. Two paradoxes are associated with controversial issues discussions and racial diversity in U.S. schools: First, the classrooms with the richest resources for civic dialogue (i.e., range of viewpoints and experiences) are also those that present the greatest challenges for teachers; and second, it is students of color, low-income students, and immigrants who are *least* likely to experience political discussions at home and school, but *most* likely to benefit from them at school when they do experience discussions (Kawashima-Ginsberg & Levine, 2014).

The polarized political climate will, as McAvoy and Hess (2013) argue, intrude upon the social studies classroom. Such a climate exacerbates many psychological processes, such as motivated reasoning, that work against the democratic habits civic educators seek to develop. Although not as recognizable as the partisan bickering prevalent in the news, these processes can be just as influential in shaping classroom discussions.

MOTIVATED REASONING, BIASED INFORMATION SEEKING, AND HOMOPHILY

In order to participate effectively in the public square, citizens in a democracy need to be able to make judgments about information relevant to the issues of the day. Yet in contemporary society the amount of information publically available on matters of import is simultaneously voluminous and incomplete. A key task in developing engaged and enlightened citizens is cultivating their capacity to wade through a mire of information and make critical judgments about conflicting evidence.

Such a task carries with it inherent challenges. Rather than conduct dispassionate analysis, humans frequently engage in *motivated reasoning*, the broad name applied to the cognitive, emotional, and social factors that counter, and often override, rational decision-making processes. As the name implies, motivated reasoners engage in logical thought, but they are pushed toward a specific conclusion (usually a reinforcement of their existing values, beliefs, or ideas) by affective or emotional forces (Lodge & Taber, 2013).

Individuals tend to view information through a network of affect-laden mental associations based on their prior experiences. This process, known as *hot cognition*, makes it very difficult for people to achieve an objective, rational stance because many of their associations occur outside conscious awareness. Morris, Squires, Taber, and Lodge (2003) found neurological evidence for hot cognition related to political terms. That is, political terms (e.g., Republican, Democrat) were more affectively charged than nonpolitical terms.

Encountering information is both a cognitive and affective experience. Responses to information will vary depending on the type of emotional feeling it generates. People like to view themselves as good and rational, so information that challenges their preexisting values and beliefs is likely to generate an unpleasant affective response and lower their self-esteem. Chaiken, Giner-Sorolla, and Chen (1996) argue that these negative feelings drive people toward *ego-defense*, a response that protects their emotional state and self-esteem.

As part of this protective process, instead of weighing evidence to determine the strongest argument, people tend to evaluate evidence in light of its agreement or disagreement with their preexisting notions, a process called *biased assimilation*. Lord, Ross, and Lepper (1979), for example, found that people reading evidence both for and against the deterrent value of the death penalty tended to be far more critical of evidence that contradicted their prior opinions on the matter.

Kardash and Scholes (1996), in a similar experiment, found that strength of preexisting beliefs was inversely related to willingness to incorporate new evidence into one's thinking. In their study, after reading two articles presenting conflicting scientific evidence on HIV/AIDS (a subject of debate at the time), individuals with strong prior beliefs were less likely to note the inconclusive nature of the scientific evidence in their later conclusions. Kadash and Scholes's findings also indicated that people without strong beliefs were more willing to consider conflicting evidence and mention it in their conclusions.

Such evaluative biases are not unique to adults. Experiments conducted by Klaczynski and Narasimham (1998) and Klaczynski (2000) measured the preexisting beliefs of students as young as fifth grade and evaluated how those students responded to evidence both for and against those beliefs. In these studies, which involved beliefs about social class and religion, students' reasoning served to confirm their existing ideas.

Further, Goldberg (2013) found that when evaluating the impact of a historical government policy, high school seniors viewed sources supporting their beliefs more credible. The results of these studies also indicate that children and adolescents are likely to employ sophisticated reasoning when discounting evidence that challenges their existing beliefs, while being far less critical of evidence that supports their beliefs.

In addition to attacking information that provokes a negative affective response, people are often motivated by *confirmation bias* to select information that supports their existing views. Chaiken et al. (1996) noted that many individuals will ignore "inconvenient" information, preferring to focus on information that supports their conclusions. Baumeister (1996) also found that people ignore information that is likely to produce ego threat and seek to distract themselves from threatening information. The decision to ignore information that can potentially challenge our beliefs is usually made quickly. Greenwald (1997) likened the process to individuals sorting through junk mail, choosing which pieces to discard simply by looking at the envelope.

It is increasingly possible to construct our informational environments such that we rarely encounter information that challenges our beliefs. In the political realm, for example, as individuals become increasingly partisan, they seek out media that reinforce their views. In a study by Iyengar and Hahn (2009), participants tended to select news stories that were attributed to sources they perceived as friendly, even on nonpolitical issues. Conservatives gravitated toward news stories from Fox News while liberals leaned toward CNN and National Public Radio (NPR). The danger of selective sourcing in the political realm is that its continual reinforcement of a particular worldview tends to lead viewers to perceive "others" as foolish or ill-willed.

People also prefer to be with those who share their general outlook on the world, a tendency called *homophily*. Homophily among politically like-minded individuals is often tied to increased political polarization. When like-minded individuals talk with one another, they have their beliefs reinforced. Schkade, Sunstein, and Hastie (2007) found that when partisans engaged in like-minded deliberation exercises, they not only had their ideas validated, but they also became more extreme in their respective ideologies.

SOCIAL IDENTITY

Students' identification as a member of various social groups strongly influences how they engage with others in discussions. Tajfel (1981) defined social identity as an individual's emotionally salient identification as a member of a group or groups. Fraser-Burgess (2012) noted that most group identities, be they political, economic, religious, cultural, or otherwise, carry with them beliefs or values that are definitive of group membership. These beliefs are so central to the group's identity as to be considered beyond question by members of that group. James (2010), for example, found that some of her fundamentalist Christian students were unwilling to discuss ideas that threatened their particular worldview.

Group identity may also influence how individuals make sense of information. Interpretation of historical events, for example, is often done through group frames of reference. In a study of Jewish and Arab students' retelling what they had learned about a historical conflict, Porat (2004) found that students evaluated narratives from a textbook in light of their prior cultural understandings of the events. Similarly, Epstein (2009) found that black and white students interpret U.S. history differently, particularly when race was a prominent theme. In short, individuals will privilege information that supports their identity over information that contradicts it.

Haidt (2012) proposed an evolutionary explanation for the importance of some group identities. A strong sense of group cohesion increases the likelihood of success over opposing groups. That cohesion comes from a shared set of values, rituals, stories, and understandings. Challenges to these central tenets of group identity are not perceived as legitimate inquiries but as attacks on the group. In the case of political discussions, individuals' political identifications may cause them to root for their particular "team," regardless of their evaluations of particular policies (Groenendyk, 2013).

Up to this point we have painted a fairly bleak picture of the possibilities for robust democratic discussions. Indeed, in a society as divided as the United States has been in the past fifteen years, there is much that can stand in the way of democratic discussion. Many of the obstructions to such discussion stem from processes wired deeply into human consciousness.

At the societal level, distrust among political and social groups inhibits the willingness of discussants to listen to or work with one another. The presence of strong political identities and opinions activates mental processes that are designed to confirm our existing values and beliefs and avoid the discomfort of having them challenged. Further, identity shapes how people receive and react to information, meaning it is difficult to agree on the value and credibility of factual information, as well as the most basic of interpretations of such information.

Although democratic discussion in classrooms faces challenges rooted deeply in the human psyche, the psychological perspective on classroom discussions offers more than gloom and doom. Understanding the roots of discursive problems can lead to discursive solutions. Just as humans are prone to distrust, there exist mechanisms for developing trust. While we prefer cognitive shortcuts, we are capable of deep, reflective thinking. Although activating these more deliberative parts of the mind is often challenging, democratic discussion in classrooms is achievable.

WHAT TEACHERS CAN DO

Affirmation

One promising avenue for exploration is focusing on the root causes of motivated reasoning: identity and emotion. Motivated reasoning often stems, in part, from the feeling that one's beliefs or identity (individual or group) is coming under attack (e.g., Baumeister, 1996; Chaiken et al., 1996; Haidt, 2012). When presented with information that challenges one's beliefs, there usually follows a subsequent desire to protect one's self-concept from threat or damage.

Cohen et al. (2007) found that it is helpful to give individuals an opportunity to affirm their personal integrity or positive qualities prior to presenting them with information that challenges their beliefs. In the experiments by Cohen et al., affirmation had the potential to reduce partisan interpretations of a report critical of U.S. foreign policy, as well as make individuals more willing to make concessions in a deliberation regarding abortion. Similarly, Binning, Sherman, Cohen, and Heitland (2010) found that affirmations made partisan individuals less critical of opposing presidential candidates during and immediately after the 2008 election.

While the impact of the affirmation varies depending on situational cues surrounding the task, the idea of strengthening participants' self-concept prior to engaging in civic discourse seems to have potential. Recent research (e.g., Shnabel, Purdie-Vaughns, Cook, Garcia, & Cohen, 2013) with adolescents suggests that affirmation exercises can have a positive impact on academic achievement among groups that are negatively stereotyped and most susceptible to identity threat (e.g., blacks, Latinos, and academic achievement; female students and math/science achievement), but no studies were located that tested the impact of affirmation on secondary students engaged in civic discourse characterized by opposing views. The promise of affirmation lies in its simplicity. If schools can develop habits of self-affirmation in students prior to entering ego-threatening situations, it is possible that students may approach civic discourse with more open mindsets.

One common practice to be avoided prior to a deliberative exercise is to tell students to be open-minded and willing to compromise. For students with strongly held beliefs, such admonitions tend to activate ego defense mechanisms and make them more inflexible. Research suggests that it is preferable to remind all students prior to discussion that they have a right to their own opinions. This tends to reduce partisans' perception that they may be in a threatening situation (Cohen et al., 2007).

Community Building

As Haidt (2012) noted, often it is not the argument that is problematic for individuals, but rather the person making the argument. Having individuals who are perceived as strangers or, worse, as opponents challenge one's arguments or beliefs is a different experience than having a friend or colleague challenge them. Put differently, people are more willing to trust information when they trust the source of the information.

To what degree can teachers build strong classroom communities where students trust one another enough to express their opinions and give honest consideration to opposing views? Trust in the context of discussion can best be built through establishing an open classroom climate. Teacher practices that tend to facilitate a more open classroom climate include:

- regularly discussing controversial issues and current events
- encouraging students to express their views and develop their own conclusions on controversial issues

- inviting students to disagree with the teacher's viewpoints on issues
- demonstrating respect for students' opinions by giving their views careful consideration
- actively seeking and valuing a range of viewpoints during discussions
- being intentional about bringing multiple perspectives to bear on issues [2]

Naturally, an open classroom climate does not simply arise but rather requires teachers to intentionally establish and enforce the norms of good discussion (Parker, 2010). With practice, however, students will be able to internalize the norms and, hopefully, establish a trusting discussion environment.

Strategic Grouping

When students are allowed to choose their own groups, their preference for homophily will likely lead them to work with friends, most of whom will share their general beliefs and opinions. As a consequence, they are not likely to challenge one another's ideas, nor will they be exposed to different perspectives. Equally important, in like-minded groups, they are likely to become more extreme in their opinions following deliberation (Schkade et al., 2007). Groups that contain a balance of divergent viewpoints, however, are less likely to polarize (Martin, Hewstone, Martin, & Gardikiotis, 2008).

In a study conducted by Goldberg (2013), 12th-grade Ashkenazi and Mizrahi Israeli Jews reviewed evidence related to a historical controversy relevant to their ethnic identities.[3] They were taught how to evaluate evidence, after which they were placed in either ethnically homogeneous or heterogeneous groups and told to discuss their opinions of the policy's impact. They were then to jointly write an essay identifying their areas of agreement and disagreement. Although students' ethnic identity influenced their use and evaluation of the evidence, the effect was significantly stronger in the homogeneous groups, suggesting that the practice of working in heterogeneous groups and employing disciplinary practices broadens students' perspectives.

Although gathering data on students' viewpoints prior to discussion and subsequently assigning discussion groups to achieve balance may be possible for major discussion lessons, it is not practical on a regular basis. Rather than leaving students to their own devices, however, random assignment of groups will more likely result in students working with peers whose perspectives and experiences differ from their own.

Speaking to Values

While many of the above strategies work well in the classroom, it may be difficult to imagine their impacts carrying into the world beyond school walls. Indeed, when individuals encounter discussions of controversial issues later in life, it is unlikely they will have had time to build community among the discussants or that they will be strategically grouped for maximum exposure to diverse viewpoints. Though affirmation tends to make people more open to diverse viewpoints, it is easy to see how these techniques can be forgotten in the face of a discussion around contentious issues. In short, is there anything in the psychological literature that will help students engage in discussions when there is no teacher around to enforce the rules?

One approach is to focus on persuasive skills. Typically, persuasion is taught in strictly logical fashion with the assumption that the most compelling argument will emerge victorious. In a polarized political landscape, however, individuals may dismiss arguments for reasons that have little to do with empirical veracity.

Haidt (2012) noted, for example, that liberals and conservatives often seem to be speaking past one another. He attributed the problem to each group having different sets of fundamental values. Moral foundations theory lays out six axes commonly used to assess arguments: care/harm, fairness/cheating, loyalty/betrayal, authority/subversion, sanctity/degradation, and liberty/oppression. One of the chief hallmarks of recent political discourse seems to be that liberal messages only consistently appeal to three of the foundations (care/harm, fairness/cheating, liberty/oppression), whereas conservatives tend to appeal to all six.

Recent research suggests that careful attention to moral framings can make arguments more persuasive. Feinberg and Willer (2015) presented participants with arguments in opposition to their position on a contentious issue (e.g., universal health care, military spending). When the arguments were framed so that they aligned with participants' dominant moral values, however, they were more likely to be viewed as compelling. Feinberg and Willer also found that participants tended to generate arguments within their own moral frameworks (i.e., liberals tended to generate arguments appealing to liberal moral foundations).

These results suggest a need to expand what it means to take another's perspective. As improved perspective taking is a common goal of many social studies teachers, there is an opportunity for teachers to teach persuasion as both an empirical and moral matter. There is also a need for educational researchers to examine the problem of getting students to better speak to each other's values.

Caveats

We have described selected concepts and theories that may be relevant to the discussion of controversial issues in social studies classrooms. Introducing separate terms for various elements of cognition, however, may mislead readers into viewing them as independent and not overlapping. Most of these processes will often occur concurrently and even in conflict with other processes. Further, while it is helpful to have descriptions of psychological factors that influence discussion, it also creates the temptation to view these mental processes independent of context. The processes described in this chapter represent tendencies that may or may not be activated in an individual based on that person's personal experiences, beliefs, or social context.

Gaps in the literature may limit the applicability of the psychological research on discussions to school settings. Although there is enough overlap in the cognitive processes of adults and school-age children to warrant attention to the psychology of civic discussions, it is important to recognize that developmental differences between the two groups may mean certain processes function differently in children or are impacted by other confounding elements not found in adults. Further research is needed on student populations to more precisely determine how these psychological processes manifest in classrooms.

The focus of our psychological treatment of controversial issues' discussions has been largely on discussion participants and the processes that impact their judgments. It is important to note, however, that these factors also apply to the adult teachers in the classroom. We are all susceptible to motivated reasoning, biased assimilation, confirmation bias, homophily, and the like. However, because of teachers' power to shape classroom environments and set the agenda for classroom discussion, they must be extra conscious and critical of their own thinking when approaching controversial issues (e.g., selection of issues, the evidence we provide, listening to opposing views).

CONCLUSION: CIVIC IDEALS AND REALITIES

In a deliberative democracy, informed citizens come together to discuss the controversial issues of the day. They express their views, learn from one another, and attempt to achieve consensus, or failing that, actionable compromise. In practice, breakdowns can occur at any stage of the deliberative process.

Political polarization or homophily can preclude individuals from interacting meaningfully with one another. Emotional reactions generated by hearing opposing views can cause individuals to be unreceptive to ideas other than their own. Instead of expanding their ideas, students may become more entrenched in their own ways of thinking. Attempts at consensus or compromise may be hindered by conflicts among groups.

We have attempted to shed light on psychological processes that can drive these breakdowns in discussion. Though not often utilized in civic education, the psychological lens has the potential to enhance our understanding of the barriers to controversial issues discussion. Moreover, it serves to reframe some of the difficulties of discussion as natural by-products of positive psychological needs such as belonging and positive self-regard. We believe that multiple lenses are essential to understand the nature of complex discussions, and that the psychological lens is an important addition to the already robust research base in social studies education.

NOTES

1. Youth can and do reflect the characteristics of authoritarianism, and students with this tendency are likely to react differently to some curricular messages. In a study of the impact of a curriculum designed to promote political tolerance among adolescents, Avery, Bird, Johnstone, Sullivan, and Thalhammer (1992) found that while most students showed slightly more tolerance (or less intolerance), a small group of students (10 percent) who scored high in right-wing authoritarianism reacted against the message embedded in the curriculum and demonstrated more intolerance after participation in the unit. The researchers reasoned that the students perceived the curriculum as a threat to their beliefs.
2. These suggestions are based on items in the open classroom climate scale (Torney-Purta et al., 2001).
3. The historical controversy in question was the Melting Pot policy pursued at the time of Israel's founding.

REFERENCES

Abramowitz, A. I. (2010). *The disappearing center: Engaged citizens, polarization, and American democracy*. New Haven, CT: Yale University Press.

Avery, P. G., Bird, K., Johnstone, S., Sullivan, J. L., & Thalhammer, K. (1992). Exploring political tolerance with adolescents. *Theory & Research in Social Education, 20*, 386–420.

Avery, P. G., Levy, S. A., & Simmons, A. M. M. (2014). Deliberating controversial public issues as part of civic education. *Social Studies, 104*, 105–114.

Barr, D. J., Boulay, B., Selman, R. L., McCormick, R., Lowenstein, E., Garnse, B., . . . Leonard, B. (2015). A randomized controlled trial of professional development for interdisciplinary civic education: Impacts on humanities teachers and their students. *Teachers College Record, 117*, 1–52.

Baumeister, R. F. (1996). Self-regulation and ego threat: Motivated cognition, self-deception, and destructive goal setting. In P. M Gollwitzer & J. A. Bargh (Eds.), *The psychology of action: Linking cognition and motivation to behavior* (pp. 27–47). New York: Guilford Press.

Beck, T. A. (2013). Identity, discourse, and safety in a high school discussion of same-sex marriage. *Theory & Research in Social Education, 41*, 1–32.

Binning, K. R., Sherman, D. K., Cohen, G. L., & Heitland, K. (2010). Seeing the other side: Reducing political partisanship via self-affirmation in the 2008 presidential election. *Analyses of Social Issues and Public Policy, 10*, 276–292.

Campaign for the Civic Mission of Schools. (2011). *Guardians of democracy: The civic mission of schools*. Silver Spring, MD: Campaign for the Civic Mission of Schools. Retrieved from www.civicmissionofschools.org.

Center for Information and Research on Civic Learning and Engagement (CIRCLE). (2014, November 12). *Top 8 takeaways about young voters and the 2014 election* [Blog]. Retrieved from http://www.civicyouth.org/top-8-takeaways-about-young-voters-and-the-2014-election/.
Chaiken, S., Giner-Sorolla, R., & Chen, S. (1996). Beyond accuracy: Defense and impression motives in heuristic and systemic information processing. In P. M Gollwitzer & J. A. Bargh (Eds.), *The psychology of action: Linking cognition and motivation to behavior* (pp 553–578). New York: Guilford Press.
Cohen, G. L., Sherman, D. K., Bastardi, A., Hsu, L., McGoey, M., & Ross, L. (2007). Bridging the partisan divide: Self-affirmation reduces ideological closed-mindedness and inflexibility in negotiation. *Journal of Personality and Social Psychology, 93*, 415–430.
Commission on Youth Voting and Civic Knowledge. (2013). *All together now: Collaboration and innovation for youth engagement: The report of the Commission on Youth Voting and Civic Knowledge.* Medford, MA: Center for Information & Research on Civic Learning and Engagement. Retrieved from http://www.civicyouth.org/wp-content/uploads/2013/09/CIRCLE-youthvoting-individualPages.pdf.
Davies, P. G., Steele, C. M., & Markus, H. R. (2008). A nation challenged: The impact of foreign threat on America's tolerance for diversity. *Interpersonal Relations and Group Processes, 95*, 308–318.
Epstein, T. (2009). *Interpreting national history: Race, identity, and pedagogy in classrooms and communities.* New York: Routledge.
Feinberg, M., & Willer, R. (2015). From gulf to bridge: When do moral arguments facilitate political influence? *Personality and Social Psychology Bulletin, 41*(12), 1665–1681.
Fraser-Burgess, S. (2012). Group identity, deliberative democracy, and diversity in education. *Education Philosophy and Theory, 44*, 480–499.
Goldberg, T. (2013). "It's in my veins": Identity and disciplinary practice in students' discussions of a historical issue. *Theory & Research in Social Education, 41*, 33–64.
Greenwald, A. G. (1997). Self-knowledge and self-deception: Further consideration. In M. S. Myslobodsky (Ed.), *The mythomanias: An inquiry into the nature of deception and self-deception* (pp. 51–71). Mahwah, NJ: Erlbaum.
Groenendyk, E. (2013). *Competing motive in the partisan mind: How loyalty and responsiveness shape party identification and democracy.* New York: Oxford University Press
Hahn, C. L. (2002). Implications of September 11 for political socialization research. *Theory & Research in Social Education, 30*, 158–162.
Haidt, J. (2012). *The righteous mind: Why good people are divided by politics and religion.* New York: Vintage Books.
Hess, D. E. (2009). *Controversy in the classroom: The democratic power of discussion.* New York: Routledge.
Hess, D. E., & McAvoy, P. (2015). *The political classroom: Evidence and ethics in democratic education.* New York, NY: Routledge.
Hess, D. E., & Posselt, J. R. (2002). How students experience and learn from the discussion of controversial public issues in secondary social studies. *Journal of Curriculum and Supervision, 17*, 283–314.
Hetherington, M. J., & Weiler, J. D. (2009). *Authoritarianism & polarization in American politics.* New York: Cambridge University Press.
Huddy, L., & Feldman, S. (2011). Americans respond politically to 9/11: Understanding the impact of the terrorist attacks and their aftermath. *American Psychologist, 66*, 455–467.
Iyengar, S., & Hahn, K. S. (2009). Red media, blue media: Evidence of ideological selectivity in media use. *Journal of Communication, 59*, 19–39.
Iyengar, S., Sood, G., & Lelkes, Y. (2012). Affect, not ideology: A social identity perspective on polarization. *Public Opinion Quarterly, 76*, 405–431.
Iyengar, S., & Westwood, S. J. (2014). Fear and loathing across party lines: New evidence on group polarization. *American Journal of Political Science, 59*, 690–707.
James, J. H. (2010). "Democracy is the devil's snare": Theological certainty in teacher education. *Theory & Research in Social Education, 38*, 618–639.
Jost, J. T., Glaser, J., Kruglanski, A. W., & Sulloway, F. (2003). Political conservatism as motivated social cognition. *Psychological Bulletin, 129*, 339–375.
Journell, W. (2011). Teachers' controversial issues decisions related to race, gender, and religion during the 2008 presidential election. *Theory & Research in Social Education, 39*, 348–392.
Kahne, J., & Middaugh, E. (2008, February). *Democracy for some: The civic opportunity gap in high school* (CIRCLE Working Paper No. 59). Retrieved from http://www.civicyouth.org/PopUps/WorkingPapers/WP59Kahne.pdf.
Kardash, C. M., & Scholes, R. J. (1996). Effects of preexisting beliefs, epistemological beliefs, and need for cognition on interpretation of controversial issues. *Journal of Educational Psychology, 88*, 260–271.
Kawashima-Ginsberg, K., & Levine, P. (2014). Diversity in classrooms: The relationship between deliberative and associative opportunities in school and later electoral engagement. *Analyses of Social Issues and Public Policy, 14*, 394–414.
———. (2015). Challenges and opportunities for controversial issues discussion in racially pluralistic schools. *Social Education, 79*, 271–277.
Kelly-Woessner, A., & Woessner, M. (2008). Conflict in the classroom: Considering the effects of partisan difference on political education. *Journal of Political Science Education, 4*, 265–285.

Klaczynski, P. A. (2000). Motivated scientific reasoning biases, epistemological beliefs, and theory polarization: A two-process approach to adolescent cognition. *Child Development, 71*, 1347–1366.

Klaczynski, P. A., & Narasimham, G. (1998). Development of scientific reasoning biases: Cognitive versus ego-protective explanations. *Developmental Psychology, 34*, 175–187.

Lenz, G. (2012). *Follow the leader: How voters respond to politicians' policies and performance.* Chicago: Chicago University Press.

Levendusky, M. (2009). *The partisan sort: How liberals became Democrats and conservatives became Republicans.* Chicago: University of Chicago Press.

Lodge, M., & Taber, C. (2013). *The rationalizing voter.* New York: Cambridge University Press.

Lord, C. G., Ross, L., & Lepper, M. R. (1979). Biased assimilation and attitude polarization: The effects of prior theories on subsequently considered evidence. *Journal of Personality and Social Psychology, 37*, 2098–2109.

Martin, R., Hewstone, M., Martin, P. Y., & Gardikiotis, A. (2008). Persuasion from majority and minority groups. In W. D. Crano & R. Prislin (Eds.), *Attitudes and attitude change* (pp. 361–384). New York: Psychology Press.

McAvoy, P., & Hess, D. (2013). Classroom deliberation in an era of political polarization. *Curriculum Inquiry, 43*, 14–47.

Morris, J. P., Squires, N. K., Taber, C. S., & Lodge, M. (2003). Activation of political attitudes: A psychophysiological examination of the hot cognition hypothesis. *Political Psychology, 24*, 727–745.

Parker, W. C. (2010). Listening to strangers: Classroom discussion in democratic education. *Teachers College Record, 112*, 2815–2832.

Pew Research Center. (2014, June). *Political polarization in the American public: How increasing ideological uniformity and partisan antipathy affect politics, compromise, and everyday life.* Retrieved from http://www.pewresearch.org/.

Porat, D. A. (2004). It's not written here, but this is what happened: Students' cultural comprehension of textbook narratives on the Israeli-Arab conflict. *American Educational Research Journal, 41*, 963–996.

Pyszczynski, T., Solomon, S., & Greenberg, J. (2003). *In the wake of 9/11: The psychology of terror.* Washington, DC: American Psychological Association.

Schkade, D., Sunstein, C. R., & Hastie, R. (2007). What happened on Deliberation Day? *California Law Review, 95*, 915–941.

Shnabel, N., Purdie-Vaughns, V., Cook, J. E., Garcia, J., & Cohen, G. L. (2013). Demystifying values-affirmation interventions: Writing about social belonging is a key to buffering against identity threat. *Personality and Social Psychology Bulletin, 20*(10), 1–14.

Stoker, L., & Jennings, M. K. (2008). Of time and the development of partisan polarization. *American Journal of Political Science, 52*, 619–635.

Tajfel, H. (1981). *Human groups and social categories: Studies in social psychology.* New York: Cambridge University Press

Torney-Purta, J., Lehmann, R., Oswald, H., & Schulz, W. (2001). *Citizenship and education in twenty-eight countries: Civic knowledge and engagement at age fourteen.* Amsterdam, Netherlands: International Association for the Evaluation of Educational Achievement.

Afterword

Living in a Post-9/11 World

Ronald W. Evans

A day or two after the attacks of September 11, 2001, I attended a meeting of my Unitarian Universalist men's support group. There were six or seven men present, a mix of ages. We tell our stories. One of the men told of his brother's escape from the World Trade Center on the morning of 9/11. His brother was in his financial company's office on a midlevel floor of one of the Twin Towers and fortunate to get out before the tower collapsed. My friend was horrified at the heinous attack and thankful that his brother had broken out unharmed.

As discussion ensued, and we all shared some of our thoughts and feelings about the event, I asked what I thought was an important question: What has the United States been doing that some people want to attack us? My friend, horrified at the attack, and afraid for his brother, responded with anger, "I don't want to talk about that question."

Social studies in the United States suffers from a similar affliction. We don't want to talk about difficult questions, partly because it's too painful, it stirs up too many passions, too many feelings of guilt, envy, and fear. We tend to take it personally. Our education system as a whole suffers because of the lack of honest, straightforward, and compassionate study and discussion of the great issues of our time.

Instead, we focus on acquiring knowledge from courses in history and the social sciences with only a modest emphasis on active learning and discussion of persistent controversies and issues of the past and present. Why is this the case? Understanding why this remains the norm in the vast majority of classrooms is the focus of my brief commentary.

My thesis, a reflection of several years of study, is that the potential for excellent inquiry or issues oriented toward social studies teaching is being realized in only a limited number of classrooms. I suspect this remains true largely for two overarching reasons: curriculum politics and the "grammar" of schooling and social studies (Evans, 2011; Tyack & Cuban, 1995). The "grammar" refers to the intractability of low-level classroom practices, maintained by key facets of the educational context. The curriculum politics of social studies reflects the results of a long-term struggle over the social studies curriculum with multiple camps vying for influence.

Though there are several camps, I will simply define it here by characterizing them as traditional versus progressive. The traditionalists want emphasis on acquisition of knowledge and basic skills. They generally argue for a focus on American exceptionalism and are skeptical of multiculturalism and critical pedagogy. They tend to support traditional, teacher-centered approaches, emphasis on standards, discipline-based courses, coverage of broad amounts of content, use of a textbook as the backbone of a course, and a strong role for standardized testing.

On the other hand, progressives tend to focus on questioning American exceptionalism and are supportive of multiculturalism and more critical forms of pedagogy. They tend to support a more student-oriented approach featuring a range of hands-on, interactive, alternative approaches to teaching that will help students gain insight into the important issues and questions of the past and present.

Both camps have advocates and detractors. Though much of this discussion has taken place in rhetoric over schooling, it has had some influence on practice. Over the past century or so, through their rhetoric, writings, and active participation in debates over schooling, each side has had some influence on teaching and schools. Many teachers, most teacher educators, and many others support some variation of a more active approach to learning.

Partly due to misunderstanding and misapplication of progressive ideas, and partly due to disagreement over the purposes and function of schooling, we have witnessed protracted battles over the direction of the social studies curriculum that I have labeled the "social studies wars" (Evans, 2004). Building on the ideas of John Dewey and others, progressive education started out as an attempt to reform traditional teaching, to make schools more child-friendly and school subjects more interesting and relevant to the child's life.

As progressive ideas gained more traction in the rhetoric over schooling and began to have an influence on classroom practices, various critics argued against progressive ideas. This led to legendary battles and controversies over particular curricular reforms such as the Rugg social studies textbooks during the World War II years; over progressive education and schools writ large during the 1950s; over innovative projects of the 1960s such as Man: A Course of Study; and over a new wave progressivism of the 1970s epitomized by the mini-course explosion and a focus on relevance, social activism, and values clarification.

Since the conservative restoration and the 1983 publication of *A Nation at Risk*, traditionalists have gained the upper hand (National Commission on Excellence in Education, 1983). The movement for excellence, standards, and accountability reform placed traditionalist educators in positions of power and accelerated the trend toward centralized, top-down control. From the 1980s, neoconservatives such as Diane Ravitch, William E. Bennett, Chester E. Finn Jr., and E. D. Hirsch, in combination with government and business, have impacted school and social studies trends with strongly antiprogressive reforms that have had a troubling negative impact on the teaching of social studies in schools.

Business leaders, conservatives, and neoconservatives, motivated in part by the Powell Memo, fought back against liberal groups, unions, and educators (Powell, 1971). The rhetoric and reforms they supported gave us No Child Left Behind (NCLB); a Teaching American History grants program that was explicitly "anti-social studies"; and a host of other neoconservative and neoliberal initiatives.

Passage of NCLB, the most extreme phase of schooling for social efficiency, occurred partly as a response to the 9/11 attacks, as the nation's leaders looked to create a symbol of national unity (Evans, 2015). According to one recent estimate, the average student takes 113 standardized tests during their K–12 school career (Hart et al., 2015; Rizga, 2015). Systemic reform created schools in which testing and test prep are the norm, through which teachers and teaching are scrutinized like never before, and in which academic freedom and discussion of important and persistent social issues are at low ebb.

In recent decades, reform has been driven by the scapegoating of schools and teachers as a key problem behind claims of a U.S. "decline" in international economic competition (Berliner & Glass, 2014). While graduation requirements in core subjects have increased, progressive social studies has largely been left behind in the increased emphasis on schooling for human capital (National Center for Education Statistics, 2011). The impact of NCLB was examined in study after study, which found that imposition of standards and testing led to more traditional teaching, textbooks, factual acquisition, and memorization.

Moreover, NCLB resulted in curriculum "narrowing," reducing time devoted to subjects that were not the main focus of testing. Social studies, history, geography, and the social sciences were marginalized by NCLB requirements. Further, teaching was more frequently focused on drill and practice in low-level skills most often measured by high-stakes tests (Evans, 2015; McMurrer, 2007).

In social studies, accountability reform generally led to greater emphasis on memorization, quizzes, and traditional forms of teacher-centered instruction. It severely limited assignment of essays, projects, discussion, and other thought-provoking and motivational activities. With variation from state to state and school to school, in the typical social studies classroom there was less attention to creating a deliberative process.

This push for accountability meant less discourse, more teaching to the test, more teaching from the textbook, more memorization, and more emphasis on traditional forms of teaching that had been the bulwark and seemingly unchangeable grammar of social studies for years: teacher talk, textbooks, commercial instructional programs, and lecture. Emphasis on "scientific" research meant a de-emphasis on the qualitative, historical, and philosophical discourse needed for teachers to reflect on their aims and purposes and develop meaningful ways of implementing theory into practice.

The new watchword, it seemed, centered on what "works," promoting basic teaching truisms and social efficiency–driven practices exemplified by "effective schools" research focused on the benefits of traditional, teacher-centered approaches (U.S. Department of Education, 1986). This generally served to reify traditional teaching methods that focused on imparting content and did little to promote either disciplined inquiry or issues-centered study.

In the majority of social studies classrooms, students receive an education that is focused on content acquisition, with little inclusion of issues, decision making, or critical thinking. At this juncture, in about half the states, that traditional approach is supported and reified by some form of accountability testing in social studies (Stoddard & Hess, this volume).

In looking toward a future in which the gulf between the wealthy and rest of us is increasingly large, we face the likelihood of an unending War on Terror, the existence of a perpetual security state, and a continuing focus on systemic reform. While I would like to be hopeful and forecast a new era of authentic progressive school reform, unfortunately we are likely to see more of the same.

This is not to say that there are not some hopeful trends. The *Common Core State Standards* (Common Core State Standards Initiative, 2010) and the *College Career, and Civic Life (C3) Framework for Social Studies State Standards* (National Council for the Social Studies, 2013), which could be seen as a new consensus, offer an approach that places renewed emphasis on inquiry and deliberation. Moreover, some charter schools focus on progressive teaching practices such as project-based learning.

However, the *Common Core* and *C3* are policy documents, not a reflection of actual classroom practice. In most schools and classrooms, the gulf between rhetoric and reality remains. Teaching in social studies reflects the continued dominance of history and the continuation in most classrooms of a traditional, textbook-focused approach. As was true in the

1920s, the 1950s, and the 1990s, teachers know the buzzwords of "democratic" education, but still have a difficult time implementing it effectively. There remains a general lack of attention to issues, inquiry, and deliberation.

In short, social studies classroom practice is a weak reflection of what is possible, through a glass, darkly. As anthropologist Jules Henry (1963) wrote more than half a century ago, schools continue the business of "drilling children in cultural orientations" (pp. 283–284). To counteract this reality, we need to educate a cadre of iconic teachers with a strong sense of purpose, a relentless focus on issues and inquiry, the strength to withstand systemic directives that may run counter to their beliefs, and the courage to teach in ways we know can best interest and enlighten students.

REFERENCES

Berliner, D., & Glass, E. (2014). *50 myths and lies that threaten America's public schools: The real crisis in education*. New York: Teachers College Press.

Common Core State Standards Initiative. (2010). *Common core state standards for English language arts and literacy in history/social studies, science, and technical subjects*. Retrieved from http://corestandards.org.

Evans, R. W. (2004). *The social studies wars: What should we teach the children?* New York: Teachers College Press.

———. (2011). *The tragedy of American school reform: How curriculum politics and entrenched dilemmas have diverted us from democracy*. New York: Palgrave Macmillan.

———. (2015). *Schooling corporate citizens: How accountability reform has damaged civic education and undermined democracy*. New York: Routledge.

Hart, R., Casserly, M., Uzzell, R., Palacios, M., Corcoran, A., & Spurgeon, L. (2015). *Student testing in America's great city schools: An inventory and preliminary analysis*. Washington, DC: Council of the Great City Schools.

Henry, J. (1963). *Culture against man*. New York: Random House.

McMurrer, J. (2007). *Choices, changes, and challenges*. Washington, DC: Center on Education Policy.

National Center for Education Statistics. (2011). *Digest of education statistics*, Tables and Figures, 2011, "Table 159, Average Number of Carnegie Units Earned by Public High School Graduates in Subfields, 2009 High School Transcript Study. Retrieved from http://nces.ed.gov/programs/digest/d11/tables/d+11_159.asp.

National Commission on Excellence in Education. (1983). *A nation at risk: The imperative for educational reform*. Washington, DC: U.S. Department of Education.

National Council for the Social Studies. (2013). *The college, career and civic life (C3) framework for social studies state standards: Guidance for enhancing the rigor of K–12 civics, economics, geography, and history*. Silver Spring, MD: National Council for the Social Studies.

Powell, L. F. (1971). Lewis F. Powell to Eugene B. Snydor, "Confidential memorandum: Attack on American free enterprise system," August 23, 1971, Lewis F. Powell, Jr., Papers, Washington and Lee University School of Law, Lexington, VA.

Rizga, K. (2015, August 24). "Sorry, I'm not taking this test," *Mother Jones*. Retrieved from http://www.motherjones.com/politics/2015/08/opt-out-standardized-testing-overload.

Tyack, D., & Cuban, L. (1995). *Tinkering toward utopia: A century of public school reform*. Cambridge, MA: Harvard University Press.

U.S. Department of Education. (1986). *What works: Research about teaching and learning*. Washington, DC: U.S. Department of Education.

About the Contributors

ABOUT THE EDITOR

Wayne Journell is associate professor of secondary social studies education and coordinator of the secondary teacher education program at the University of North Carolina at Greensboro. A former high school social studies teacher, his research focuses on the teaching of politics and political processes in secondary education. He has published over fifty peer-reviewed publications, including articles in leading journals such as *Teachers College Record*, *Theory & Research in Social Education*, *Educational Studies*, *Phi Delta Kappan*, *Educational Leadership*, and *Social Education*. He currently serves as the editor for *Theory & Research in Social Education*, which is the premier research journal in the field of social studies education. In 2014, he received the Exemplary Research in Social Studies Award from the National Council for the Social Studies and the Early Career Award from the College and University Faculty Assembly of the National Council for the Social Studies.

ABOUT THE CONTRIBUTORS

Patricia G. Avery is professor of social studies education at the University of Minnesota in the Twin Cities. She has published extensively in the areas of civic engagement, political tolerance, and democratic education. She served as editor of *Theory & Research in Social Education* (2008–2013).

Keith C. Barton is associate dean of teacher education, professor of curriculum and instruction, and adjunct professor of history at Indiana University. He prepares history and social studies teachers and educational researchers, and he has conducted research on the teaching and learning of history in the United States, Northern Ireland, New Zealand, and Singapore. He is coauthor, with Linda S. Levstik, of *Doing History: Investigating with Children in Elementary and Middle Schools*, *Teaching History for the Common Good*, and *Researching History Education: Theory, Method, and Context*.

Elizabeth Bellows is an assistant professor in the Department of Curriculum and Instruction at Appalachian State University where she teaches elementary and secondary social studies methods courses. Her research involves intersections of critical social studies and teacher education, historical research as it relates to social studies education, and international inquiry about social studies education in Japan and Romania. Her articles have been published in *Contemporary Issues in Technology and Teacher Education*, *Social Studies and the Young Learner*, *The Social Educator*, *American Educational History Journal*, *Journal of International Social Studies*, *Social Studies Research and Practice*, and *Social Education*.

Ilene R. Berson is a professor of early childhood at the University of South Florida and coordinates the early childhood doctoral program in the Department of Teaching and Learning. Ilene teaches courses on integrated social studies, humanities, and arts in the early childhood classroom; ICT in the early years; visual research methods; and early childhood advocacy and leadership. She leads international studies on integrating social justice and child advocacy into early childhood teacher preparation and is engaged in collaborative, participatory research in Jamaica and Ghana to foster capacity building of educators of young children to promote civic engagement through multiple literacies.

Moreover, Ilene studies the intersection of technology and the pedagogy of inquiry in the early years with a focus on children's affordances of digital innovations. She has extensively published books, chapters, and journal articles and has presented her research worldwide. Ilene has been the principal investigator on numerous funded grants, collaborating with national and international organizations. She embodies the characteristics of an engaged scholar who works closely in reciprocal relationships with practitioners and policymakers to develop innovative solutions for emerging and long-term issues to promote young children's well-being.

Michael J. Berson is a professor of social science education at the University of South Florida and a senior fellow in the Florida Joint Center for Citizenship. He coordinates the USF College of Education doctoral program in curriculum and instruction with a concentration in social science education. Michael instructs courses in social studies methods, technology innovation in the social studies, elementary school social studies, visual research methods in education, and teaching the Holocaust.

Among his leadership positions, he was elected chair of the College and University Faculty Assembly of the National Council for the Social Studies, vice president of the Society for Information Technology & Teacher Education, a member of the board of directors for the Social Science Education Consortium, and a member of the advisory board for the International Society for the Social Studies. His numerous books, chapters, and journal articles have made substantive contributions to the field of social studies education.

He was named the Association of Educational Publishers Distinguished Achievement Award Winner in the Learned Article category. He has been the principal investigator, co-principal investigator, or primary partner on grants from the U.S. Department of Education, Florida Department of Education, the Spencer Foundation, and other funders. His research on child advocacy and technology in social studies education has achieved global recognition.

Christopher H. Clark is a doctoral student in social studies education with a minor in political psychology at the University of Minnesota in the Twin Cities. His research interests include controversial issues discussions, civic engagement, and political psychology.

Margaret Smith Crocco is professor and chairperson of the Department of Teacher Education at Michigan State University. She previously served on the faculties of the University of

Iowa and Teachers College, Columbia University. Her research interests include issues related to gender, diversity, and sustainability within the context of social studies education.

Ron Evans is a leading authority on social studies and curriculum history. His book *The Social Studies Wars* was named an Outstanding Academic Title for 2004 by *Choice* magazine. His biography of controversial progressive educator Harold O. Rugg, *This Happened in America*, won the 2008 Exemplary Research Award from the National Council for the Social Studies (NCSS). His book *The Hope for American School Reform*, on the origins and development of the new social studies of the 1960s, also won the Exemplary Research Award from NCSS in 2011. His most recent book, *Schooling Corporate Citizens* (2015), examines the origins and development of accountability reform. He was named recipient of the 2015 Jean Dresden Grambs Distinguished Career Research in Social Studies Award from NCSS. He founded the Issues Centered Education Community of NCSS in 1988 and serves on the group's steering committee. Currently, he is a professor in the School of Teacher Education at San Diego State University.

Lisa Gilbert is a doctoral student in social studies education at Saint Louis University. A former museum professional, her research interests include the use of critical theories related to race, gender, and class to explore ways in which individuals relate to historical narratives. She holds a master's degree in religious studies from McGill University, has worked as a bilingual French/English educator at the McCord Museum of Canadian History, and spent the year following 9/11 studying French-to-English translation at the Université de Rennes II–Haute Bretagne, where conversations with French classmates planted the seeds that eventually led to the chapter included in this volume.

Diana Hess is dean of the School of Education at the University of Wisconsin–Madison. Prior to that appointment, she was senior vice president of the Spencer Foundation and a professor of curriculum and instruction at the University of Wisconsin–Madison. Formerly, she was a high school teacher, teachers' union president, and the associate executive director of the Constitutional Rights Foundation Chicago. She earned a PhD from the University of Washington in Seattle, advised by Professor Walter Parker. Since 1997, she has been researching how teachers engage their students in discussions of highly controversial political and constitutional issues and what impact this approach to civic education has on what young people learn. Her first book on this topic, *Controversy in the Classroom: The Democratic Power of Discussion*, won the National Council for the Social Studies Exemplary Research Award in 2009. Her second book, coauthored with Paula McAvoy, *The Political Classroom: Evidence and Ethics in Democratic Education*, about controversial issues and civic education, was published in fall 2014.

Mark T. Kissling is an assistant professor in the Department of Curriculum and Instruction at Penn State University, where he teaches middle-level social studies teacher education courses and place-based education graduate courses. He previously taught social studies in Framingham, Massachusetts. He studies ecological citizenship, justice, patriotism, place, and sustainability in education.

Jane C. Lo is assistant professor of social science education in the School of Teacher Education at Florida State University. Her research focuses on the political engagement of youth, social studies curriculum development, and simulations. She currently studies simulations and role-play as civic educational practices in American high schools.

Stephen S. Masyada is currently director of the Florida Joint Center for Citizenship (http://floridacitizen.org/), which provides K–12 social studies teachers with professional development and resources relating to civic education. He is a recent graduate of the University of Florida, completing his PhD in curriculum and instruction in 2013. Steve worked as a middle and high school social studies teacher for ten years before taking a position as a K–12 social studies consultant with the North Carolina Department of Public Instruction. He joined the Florida Joint Center for Citizenship in 2014, and his research interests and work focus on the *C3 Framework*, civic education, and improving civic learning outcomes for students in K–12 schools.

Walter C. Parker is professor of education and political science at the University of Washington in Seattle. He studies the depth-breadth problem in curriculum development and civic education in schools. He is a fellow of the American Educational Research Association, and his books include *Educating the Democratic Mind*, *Teaching Democracy*, *Social Studies Today*, and *Social Studies in Elementary Education*.

E. Wayne Ross is professor in the Department of Curriculum and Pedagogy and co-director of the Institute for Critical Education Studies at the University of British Columbia in Vancouver, Canada. Prior to joining the UBC faculty in 2004, he was the distinguished university scholar at the University of Louisville. He has also taught social studies education and curriculum studies at the State University of New York and was a secondary social studies and day care teacher in North Carolina and Georgia. His most recent books are *Working for Social Justice Inside and Outside the Classroom: A Community of Students, Teachers, Researchers, and Activists* (with Nancye McCrary); *The Social Studies Curriculum: Purposes, Problems and Possibilities* (4th edition); and *Critical Theories, Radical Pedagogies, and Social Education* (with Abraham DeLeon). Find him on the web at ewayneross.net and follow him on Twitter @ewayneross.

Jeremy Stoddard is an associate professor in the School of Education at the College of William & Mary and associated faculty member in the Film and Media Studies Program. His work focuses on authentic pedagogy and assessment in democratic education with a particular focus on the role of media in teaching and learning history, politics, and citizenship. His research has appeared in journals such as *Teachers College Record*, *Theory & Research in Social Education*, and *Curriculum Inquiry*. He is also coauthor of two books: *Teaching History with Film* and *Teaching History with Museums* (Routledge).

Elizabeth Yeager Washington is professor and coordinator of social studies education at the University of Florida in Gainesville, a senior fellow of the Florida Joint Center for Citizenship, and a knight fellow at the Bob Graham Center for Public Service. She earned her PhD in curriculum and instruction from the University of Texas at Austin, previously served as editor of *Theory & Research in Social Education* (2001–2007), and currently coordinates the masters/certification program in social studies education at UF, where she teaches secondary social studies methods, civics and government methods, and global studies methods courses. Her research interests include civic education in the middle school, teacher professional development in civic education, and the teaching and learning of history.

www.ingramcontent.com/pod-product-compliance
Lightning Source LLC
Chambersburg PA
CBHW080541300426
44111CB00017B/2820